The Ghosts of Cape May

BOOK 1

3rd Edition

Craig McManus

The Ghosts of Cape May Book 1 (Third Edition)

Craig McManus

Photography by Maciek Nabrdalik

Story Editors: Kathy DeLuccia, Willy Kare & Gail Matarazzo

Printed in Hong Kong

Teams Printing Company, Ltd
4/F Prince Industrial Bldg
5 Sun Kip Street
Chai Wan, Hong Kong

Published by ChannelCraig, Inc.
P.O. Box 651
Ho-Ho-Kus, NJ 07423
craig@craigmcmanus.com

Third Edition: June 2012
ISBN 978-0-9785444-6-1

Opposite: The late Dr. Emlen Physick with one of his furry friends.

(Courtesy of The Mid-Atlantic Center for the Arts and Humanities, MAC)

This work is dedicated to the Ghosts of Cape May— who gave their lives to make this book possible.

Contents

Introduction

N this third edition of *The Ghosts of Cape May Book 1*, I will take you back to twenty haunts that I have spent, in some cases, years researching. I have updated each story, where possible and have included any new ghost activity or experiences. In a few cases, the hauntings have been scarce or even dormant and there is nothing new to report. Ghosts move around in Cape May and a house is only haunted — if the ghost is at home.

For hundreds of years people have traveled to the sandy shores of the southern tip of New Jersey known as Cape May. First, it was the Native Americans in search of fish during the summer months. Next, the whalers and their families arrived from New England and Long Island following the herds of whales. Finally, it was the resort seekers. Cape May's cool breezes and beaches of firm white sand offered a respite for those weary of the sultry summer city life. All of these former citizens of the peninsula have not only left historical legacies, but some have left us with something even more enduring — their ghosts.

Putting together the history of Cape May's ghosts and their families is like assembling a jigsaw puzzle. Each year I find new haunts and add them to the mix. Looking at the entire map of hauntings in Cape May, a pattern emerges. In the area's 300+ year history, many of the original settlers intermarried over and over again. In almost 90% of the hauntings I have investigated in Cape May, some or all of the ghosts are related to other ghosts in town. This fact is remarkable and should be noted. Did a few ghosts, hundreds of years ago, start a trend to stay behind in Cape May? The beautiful setting of Cape May has always been a strong draw for the living — and the dead. How often have you heard someone say, "I wish I could stay on vacation forever?" In Cape May, many have and continue to do so!

With the exception of America's battlegrounds, Cape May seems to have few rivals when it comes to ghosts per square mile. There have been several theories put forth by others and myself about Cape May. Some think the area sits on a convergence of metaphysical ley lines. These are alleged lines of magnetic energy that some people believe can affect geographical regions of the earth. Ley line theories originated in England in the 1920s, and these lines are thought to be the unseen connection between many of England's old medieval sites like Stonehenge. The existence of ley lines has yet to be proven. I do believe certain places have stronger energy than others do.

Another theory is based on two observations. First, Cape May is surrounded by water on three sides, two sides by the Atlantic Ocean and one by the Delaware Bay. Salt water, because of its mineral content, has amplified conductivity—the ghosts may take advantage of this available energy. Second, the Cape May Point beaches are strewn with large quantities of tiny pieces of weathered quartzite called *Cape May diamonds*. Energy workers often use quartz crystals to focus or filter energy. Some mediums use crystals for this purpose as well. Could the large quartz deposits have something to do with Cape May's high paranormal activity? If ghosts are fields of energy trying to exist between this plane and the next, is it not possible that these two conditions conduct and perhaps even magnify ghost energy? As a psychic medium, I am already operating outside of the boundaries of known science. The questions about life, death and what might happen in between are difficult, if not impossible, to test in a laboratory setting. While we are exploring possible explanations for ghosts and hauntings, I think it is important to stay open-minded. As a friend of mine often says, it's OK to be skeptical when investigating the paranormal, just don't be cynical. Being cynical closes the door to learning and understanding new things.

What makes this book different from many other contemporary works on ghost and hauntings is that it is written by a medium who is also a paranormal investigator. Many of my colleagues in the paranormal field have worked *with* psychics and mediums, but possess little or no ability themselves. I think being a paranormal investigator and a psychic medium is a valuable combination for ghost research. My psychic ability allows me to sense energies and view things that have happened. As a medium, I am able to communicate with energies that have a consciousness. Some of these energies reside on a higher plane and are referred to as spirits, while other energies I communicate with are closer to our level of existence, a place I refer to as the *Ghost Plane*.

I believe that ghosts and spirits are one in the same, they are just souls at different points in their evolution. The soul is almost ageless and goes through many transformations in its learning and growth process. Reincarnation is a way the soul can return to the Earth, revitalize its energy, and learn lessons that would be impossible in an all-knowing setting like the Other Side. In other words, if we have access to great amounts of knowledge when we cross over, it does not seem plausible that we would have much interest in trying to solve mundane problems like dealing with a difficult boss or learning to get our car serviced on a regular basis. On this plane of existence, what I call the Earth Plane, we do not have complete access to our higher intelligence, and so we need to solve problems and learn lessons by whatever intellect we possess here.

Death signals the end of another learning cycle. It is very much like graduating from school. Even tragic deaths are a learning process for souls and for those whose lives that death affects. When we die, our soul automatically begins another journey. Guided by friends and loved ones returning from the Other Side, we make the trip back home. Occasionally, we might get lost in the shuffle, due to a strong attachment to material things here or an emotional bond to loved ones. These attachments can overpower a soul's greater needs. I used to believe that it was only by accident that souls became stuck and entities became ghosts. Then I met Cape May.

My investigations in West Cape May, in preparation for my ghost trolley tour called, *Ghosts of the Lighthouse*, yielded several of Cape May's oldest ghostly inhabitants still haunting their homes from hundreds of years ago. A few of these ghosts were the great great grandparents of some of Cape May's more modern phantoms. I find this fascinating, and wonder, do they know each other? Is there still a family bond? These ghosts are products of all kinds of life-ending traumas, some physical, and some emotional. Does the haunting head of the family entice newer generations to stay put?

With so many generations of deceased Cape May residents, how do I decide what my focus will be? I investigate a place reputed to be haunted if I hear from more than one unique source about a haunting. I try to avoid "creating" a ghost, that is, uncovering one that has never been experienced by anyone else, unless the encounter is of such a strong or repetitive nature that it must be investigated further and reported. I will not disqualify myself as an initial witness in those cases. When I have done a walk-through or stayed overnight at a location presumed to have a ghost or ghosts, I try to collect as much background history on the haunting as possible. After I have completed my investigation psychically, I ask the owners of the property to tell me what they have experienced. I do not want to prejudice my feelings by hearing about their personal ghost encounters beforehand. Some paranormal investigators want to know everything about a site, its history and hauntings, prior to this investigation. I do not. It is actually a greater challenge for a psychic to read at a location where there has been a long and widely known tradition of ghost activity. The tales are often misleading and the information incorrect as you will see in the stories that follow. For those who wish to accuse psychic and mediums of scouting out the history of a venue prior to an investigation, I say, why would anyone want to waste time and effort investigating a house that they already know everything about? It would be like reading a book backwards and knowing the ending first. I personally have better things to do, and discovery during a haunting is what the thrill of an investigation is all about!

Think of my *Ghosts of Cape May* books as general works on ghosts and hauntings, using Cape May as a template. Here you can find every possible type of ghost. Some ghosts are more outgoing while some prefer isolation. Some are angry, or even aggressive. Luckily, very few of the latter type of ghosts have been found in Cape May. I have also attempted through photographs and documentation in this book to preserve some of the rich, local history for generations to come.

Before you start on this journey into the unknown, remember you must return to the Earth Plane when you are done reading! Sometimes a good ghost story, or a good ghost, has a tendency to carry us into the world of the imagination. I wish you well in your travels in the shadowy world of the paranormal. Watch your step — and keep the light lit — there could be a few *bumps* in the night ahead!

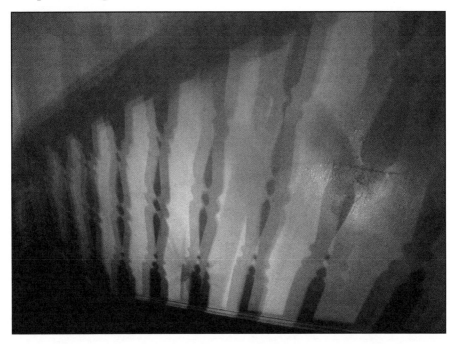

The Sea Holly

AN ENCHANTED COTTAGE BY THE SEA

815 Stockton Avenue - Whole-House Rental

C APE MAY is in the process of changing the way it does business as a resort community. At the time of this writing some of the wonderful old B&Bs have been converted to private residences or whole-house rentals. If a new generation of innkeepers does not come along and replenish the retiring innkeepers of Cape May—the B&Bs that have made Cape May famous since the 1970s may become a thing of the past. Yes, there are a handful of enthusiastic, young innkeepers in Cape May, but not enough I am afraid to save some of my favorite old inns from becoming private residences.

The Sea Holly, a longtime B&B, has now been beautifully renovated as a house rental, and continues to be one of my favorite homes in town. This majestic old cottage by the sea still graces the view of all who pass by with her landmark sea-green clapboards and fancy gingerbread trim. The house has been beautifully restored, and I am sure everyone involved with the Sea Holly is proud to have her back to her original grandeur—even her ghosts.

Our paranormal journey begins on Stockton Avenue. John Christian Bullitt (1829-1902) a highly successful corporate lawyer originally from Philadelphia who vacationed during the summers in Cape May, built many of the homes here in the 1870s. Bullitt was a regular land baron in Cape May and this property was listed under his name on the 1877 Swain's Map. Number 815 Stockton Avenue was built as a summer getaway to be used during the hot summer months. Not as large as some of its fellow haunts in town, this quaint Victorian "cottage" is impressive none-the-less.

The original deed for 815 Stockton Street, as with most of Bullitt's properties in Cape May, forbids any gambling, livestock or even bowling alleys to be on the property. Luckily, Bullitt forgot to include ghosts in that list. John C. Bullitt was heavily involved in finance in his day and most likely saw the potential for Cape May to return as a major seaside resort. After sliding in popularity after the Civil War, many of the wealthy southern businessmen abandoned the Cape. While south of the Mason-Dixon Line, Cape May was still in former "Yankee territory." Bullitt invested a lot of time, effort, and apparently money into Cape May. He built cottages and hotels throughout the city. If only John Bullitt were alive today to see what his and other's efforts had created. On the other hand, you don't have to be alive in Cape May to get things done — maybe Mr. Bullitt is still with us in some capacity!

The Sea Holly, an aquamarine sentinel standing watch over the ocean via the narrow parking lot of the Stockton Motor Inn, was built around 1876. One of the more charming houses in Cape May, the Sea Holly is a place where you can make yourself right at home for a day, a week or *a century*.

I was first introduced to the Sea Holly while taking the former Haunted Cape May walking ghost tour. I was immediately struck by the feeling that the Sea Holly was quite aware of our presence. Not that the house had a consciousness, but its unseen occupants did. I sensed a woman named "Rose," and a faint impression of a man in either military or fireman's dress with brass buttons and a pipe. I got the name "John Claire," who I later found out was a resident of Cape May in the late 1800s, although I have yet to find a link between him and the Sea Holly property. In addition, according to the 1876 Cape May Street Map, John C. Bullitt is listed as owning this house. Could Bullitt be the "John" I was picking up? He certainly was an influential and powerful man in Cape May's Victorian era.

On a cold and crisp February evening a few years back, I began what became a long love affair with this enchanting cottage. This was my first experience meeting the Sea Holly's then new owner, Walt Melnick. We came under the guise of "checking out summer rentals," as I do not like to alert people to a ghost investigation until after it is done. This keeps the investigation focused without any outside interference. Although after the popularity of my *Exit Zero* Ghost Writer columns, my ghost tours, lectures and books, my anonymity has now come to an end in Cape May!

Winter is the optimal time to conduct a ghost investigation here, when Cape May is truly a ghost town. At the time of my first visit, the sun had already set on that chilly February evening, and Stockton Street looked all but deserted. Most of the B&Bs were closed, and the summer rentals were locked up and dark for the season. I can remember glancing down the long, desolate street while waiting for someone to answer the door at the Sea Holly. The gaslights were about the only signs of life, except for the sound of the pounding winter surf a block away. I could sense something paranormal nearby.

Opening the front door, Walt definitely had on a "tough guy" face, although we later became good friends. When he answered the door that night, he gave us a once over and shook his head and said, "One, two, three, you must be the guests." In reality, Walt saw three guys and only worried that we would "wreck the furniture." For the record, all furniture remained intact.

Walt admitted his house had "energy", but he referred to the Sea Holly as "enchanted" instead of haunted. He just didn't believe in such things. He also did not go up to the third floor after 9 PM! Luckily, this psychic medium did, and here is what happened.

As I mentioned in the introduction, the psychic side of me picks up various energies and impressions in a location. The medium part of me gets in touch with any of those energies that

Philadelphia lawyer and Cape May land baron
John Christian Bullitt (1829-1902)
(Author's Collection)

have a personality or consciousness. Energy in a haunted setting that can be communicated with is usually referred to as a *ghost*. An energy that has no consciousness and cannot interact with the medium is called an *impression* or *residual haunting*. This is not a ghost at all, just a tape loop if you will, playing repeatedly.

In the paranormal world, we may encounter both types of hauntings, as we do at the Sea Holly. Residual haunting refers to left over emotions from one or more living people or events. The living generate the original imprint, but have nothing to do with the reruns. Only those people who are intuitive or psychic will sense residual energies like this. Some people live in a haunted house for years and experience nothing, while others experience things immediately. Hauntings are a *very* personal experience.

The Sea Holly has *both* types of energy. Let's talk about the first. Mediums can use a *trance state* of consciousness to connect with ghosts. I started my *trance channeling* after Walt had turned in for the night, and the house was quiet and empty.

Channeling is what a medium does to connect with ghosts or spirits. To refresh, I will refer to souls stuck in the *Ghost Plane* as ghosts and *higher guides* who come to communicate and help us as spirits. Spirit guides and Angels are higher forms of beings that exist on a different plane than ghosts. This book deals with ghosts.

The idea of contacting the dead has been around for ages. In the mid -1800s, during the rise of *Spiritualism*, a movement that dealt with contacting the dead and survival after death, channeling was the rage. There were *séances* or *home circles* conducted everywhere. The word *séance* comes from the Old French word, *seoir,* meaning *to sit*. People all over the world were jumping at the chance to contact their dearly departed by sitting around in circles with mediums.

Channeling made a comeback again in the 1920s after World War I and again in the 1970s. It is still popular today in various forms. When I work with clients in person or over the phone, I put myself in an awake-state channeling mode. I do not go into trance. My spirit guides and the spirits of loved ones come forward to help me connect them with their loved ones here. These spirits are of a higher energy and intelligence and *want* to talk to me. Ghosts, on the other hand, do not usually want to be bothered at all.

Ghosts are rarely chatty and typically do not seek me out. Ghosts of children tend to want to communicate more, but the adult ghosts generally want to be left to their own world. To get the story of why a ghost is still here, I need to do a little *psychic eaves-dropping*. I believe ghosts, and spirits for that matter, communicate through a form of energy that is more intense and more pure than our own physical methods of communication.

When I communicate with a ghost or spirit, I do not hear them in the sense that I may hear a human voice. I "get" the messages somehow delivered directly to my brain in a form I believe is pure intelligence which ghosts can use to a limited degree and spirits can use easily. A medium has the ability to receive this form of communication, interpret it, and relay it to the intended recipients.

Ghosts communicate mind-to-mind. Words and feelings are thought, not spoken. It's not like a phone call. I do not hear them with my ears, I hear them with my mind. Sometimes, a stronger method of communication is needed because of this. This method is called *trance channeling*.

When I trance channel I allow myself to relax and get in touch with the energies around me. I mentally remove myself from the here and now. I put myself in a different state of consciousness, a place where my mind can meet up with the minds of the ghosts. This method is often quite draining, as you will see in later chapters.

As I started my meditation to trance channel, I could feel the Sea Holly's energies. The water pipes for the heating system let out a rattling sound in all directions. A coincidence? Had my energy somehow agitated the resting water in the pipes? Water can conduct energy. We know that much. The movement of water was quite audible. The old house seemed to let out a groan because I was snooping around her eaves psychically.

The temperature in the room began to drop, sometimes a sign of ghost activity. We made a note that the temperature fell nine degrees in ten minutes. The heat was still running and the windows and doors were closed. A filmy mist, hanging from the stairwell, appeared to my two assistants. Ghosts are very rarely seen except in the form of a mist or shadowy blur caught out of the corner of one's vision. As my eyes were shut, I only witnessed this when the mist returned later that night. I could feel a presence start to move down the stairs and over toward us. For a medium, this kind of energy movement is like a heaviness in the atmosphere or a *density* in a space, unseen by the human eye.

When I am in a trance state, I can help the ghosts communicate through me by absorbing their thoughts and sometimes letting them use my vocal chords to speak. The presence made itself known to me as "Rose," a former servant who had died some years before. Rose told us her story, through my own vocal chords, in quite some detail. This direct process allows more specific information to come through, unlike the fragments that a medium can usually pick from a ghost's mind. I was surprised by this clear ghostly communication that night, as it was one of the strongest I had encountered in Cape May.

There had been a scandal. Rose had gotten pregnant by the widowed sea captain who lived in the house with his family. She was ordered to stay in the house during her pregnancy and not to emerge until after the child was born. This she faithfully did. She told us of her loneliness while the captain was away on business and of the coal boy coming by and smiling at her through the window of the house. She talked about her daughter, Katie, whom she raised in their third floor servants quarters. She talked about dying at a young age from disease. She may have originally been living elsewhere.

The "Captain's" energy also came through that night. He mentioned a few ships by name, kept talking of "Emerald Pearl" (later found out to have been the Cape May tax collector, Emery Pearl, in the 1920s.) The Captain spoke of ruling over the house, and then vanished abruptly.

Both entities were ghosts, but the Captain was much weaker in spirit, faded, almost weathered by time. I asked Rose why she would not move on.

"Obligation," was the answer. She still looked up to the Captain as a mentor to her. Rose, along with her daughter Katie, stayed behind to take care of the Captain, it seems, forever.

The Captain has been experienced over the last few years by several of the Sea Holly's guests. One of the guests claimed to see the Captain in all of his regalia, standing on the second floor front porch smoking his pipe. Others have often smelled cherry pipe tobacco in the house, which did not allow smoking in the rooms.

While the former owners of the Sea Holly Inn would mention seeing a woman in a wedding dress and having encounters in the back hallway with a former servant's ghost, I think the ghost of Rose, like the Captain, is also fading away.

I am not sure why some ghosts come and go or fade in and fade out. Perhaps they are simply tired, and their energy levels cannot be maintained, so they fall from our radar. While Rose and the Captain may have been on hiatus from haunting the Sea Holly, their daughter Katie was in full swing.

The types of haunting phenomena that were transpiring at the Sea Holly made me think a child's ghost was behind the bumps in the night. As we sat in our rooms the first night of investigating, we heard Walt come up from downstairs, walk past our doors and go to the third floor. We assumed he was turning off the lights, but they were still lit in the morning. We also never heard him come back down, but he could have used a back staircase.

In the morning, we were surprised to learn that when Walt went to bed at 10 PM the night before, he closed and locked the owner's quarters door and stayed in back until morning. The next night we again heard the footsteps at 12:06 AM.

Was the Captain checking the house to make sure all was locked up tight? Was it Rose, being a proper proprietress now and seeing that all was safe? Why were they both hanging out on the third floor? It was apparent and easy to surmise that a servant would have lived on the third floor in the old days in the "servant's quarters."

On the next visit, Walt inquired of a couple staying with us, "Did the bed shake last night?" I thought this a rather probing and rude question for a

B&B owner to ask, but as I later found out he was referring to the bed on the third floor.

Many guests had experienced the shaking bed at the Sea Holly over a period of years. The shaking bed has been experienced in several of the third floor rooms. I followed this phenomenon over the course of about four years. The event always happened when a woman stayed in one of the rooms. If the husband or boyfriend were asleep, the woman would be awakened, but not the man. It was a gentle, persistent shaking, as if to wake the woman up.

Walt assumed it was Rose or "Elizabeth," as the previous owner of the Sea Holly had named the ghost.

"No," I told Walt, "this is being done by a child, Katie." Katie may have been the illegitimate child of the Captain and Rose. Since they were not married, it would be a scandal to show off a pregnant maid in public. I believe Rose had the baby, who was kept in the house most of her early years. Could Katie be thinking the women in the beds were her mother? She might have awakened her mom in her lifetime to take her out in the yard or to the beach. Is she simply repeating past behavior? Ghosts can be very repetitive in nature.

Several guests had tried to take the bed apart to see just what it was that was shaking the bed. Some even accused Walt of having a device installed to shake the bed. I assure you, there is no physical explanation for the shaking bed.

We made the Sea Holly Inn our summer vacation spot for several seasons. It was on one early August morning that I first encountered Katie in full force. I was awakened by something on the end of my bed in the suite on the second floor. Thinking it was a cat, I started to lift up my head when I heard a child giggle in my ear. I then felt this same child jump from the bed and vanish. I never saw anything. However, I clearly heard a laugh in my ear, a sound so soft that only I would be the recipient.

Some people are gifted with *clairaudience* or the ability to hear things that others cannot. I do believe that ghosts can tap in on various electrical circuits going to our brains and add some extrasensory messages like smell, sight, and even sound. Katie had made herself present visually later that season to an older woman, the mother of a young couple staying with Walt. The mother was Italian and spoke little English, but tried to tell everyone in broken English at breakfast that she had seen a "little angel with a white dress and wings," sitting on her bed and dancing around the room. Katie again? Possibly. Was Katie putting her image into the woman's mind? Were the wings actually energy around her?

The former Room 7 on the third floor of the Sea Holly.
The mysterious shaking bed is gone — but are the ghosts?

Katie came to me again on another morning the same way. It was almost 5 AM, and I was still asleep. I felt a nudge and started to wake to hear the words, "Mister upstairs." At this point in one's career of dealing with the dead, the fear factor is a little more subdued, especially with the ghosts of children. I rolled over and *psychically* spoke to her, "I need to go back to sleep." She must have vanished up to the third floor to shake a few beds, because shortly after that the guests above me in the "shaking bed" room jumped from their bed and started walking around.

I had heard from Walt on several occasions of people checking out in the middle of the night. Many times, hysteria will lead over active minds into creating a ghost in a haunted place. In one case, I think the ghost was enjoying creating the hysteria!

Walt told me a story about a couple who had checked into the downstairs suite. These rooms were originally the parlor and dining room of the house where the fireplace was. During the first night's stay, the husband and wife were annoyed late at night by piano music coming from the back of the house and by the guests on the second floor making a racket. Walt assured them that they were the only guests and the Sea Holly did not have a piano, at least not in his tenure as owner.

During the second night, someone running up and down the stairs again awakened the couple. There was a knock at the suite door, and the husband got up to find no one there. Now a bit peeved, the husband decided it must be a child running up and down the stairs, playing a joke on them, so he waited by the door until just the right moment, when he heard someone run to the door again. He flung open the door to reveal — nothing, just an empty living room. No child, no piano, not a living soul present — just the Sea Holly at its finest. A dark, empty room staring him right in the face.

Walt told me the couple had checked in with the intention of being frightened. They arrived on a Monday and by Thursday had enough. They checked out early having satisfied their curiosity!

Katie, like many other children's ghosts in Cape May, simply wants to be a child and play and seems to enjoy the company of others, even if they are not particularly fond of enjoying hers!

In a related incident, the teenage son of a family renting several rooms at the Sea Holly went into his parents' unoccupied suite on the second floor to use the bathroom. As he glanced in the mirror above the sink, he was startled to see a young girl staring at him from behind. He quickly turned to find nothing. Glancing back, the mirror was now also empty!

Fast forward to the present. As I stated at the beginning of this chapter, the Sea Holly is now a whole house rental. I had the opportunity to meet Nancy, the Sea Holly's newest owner, at another home the family owns in town. Nancy has a love for history, and I truly enjoyed talking with her about the Sea Holly. Recently she had Mike Conley of *House Tales* complete the history of 815 Stockton Avenue, and she was kind enough to share it with me. We never really knew much about the Sea Holly except what I have already told you. Nancy was able to put many of the pieces of the puzzle together through her research, and Mike's research.

The house was built about 1876 for a man named Albert Luther Haynes. Haynes and his wife Orrilla settled in Cape May where Haynes ran a successful business selling stoves, tinware and home furnishings. He also was big in Cape May real estate owning twenty-five homes in Cape May including the Sea Holly. He owned many homes near Lafayette Street in a section once called "Haynes Alley." He was connected with many businesses in town, and involved in the local government with the city of Cape May. A strong life/place connection like this can tend to sidetrack a soul from leaving to Heaven. However, the Sea Holly was only one of his many properties in town.

Here is part of Albert Haynes' obituary from the *Cape May Wave* dated March 19, 1904:

"Albert L. Haynes, one of Cape May's largest real estate owners, prominent in business circles and identified in a large number of undertakings that tended towards the advancement of the city, died at his home in this place, early Monday morning from Bright's disease, after an illness of three months. He was sixty-nine years of age.

Mr. Haynes was born in Deposit, Delaware County, New York, March 2, 1835. After obtaining an academic education he came to Cape May City, and for a number of years was principal of the public schools. Later he entered the mercantile world and conducted a stove and tinware store on Mansion street. He served as a member of City Council in 1887, 1888, and 1889, and was a member of the County Board of Freeholders from 1891 until 1897. He was a charter member of the Cape May Building and Loan Association, and a director of the First National Bank."

Haynes is the only person to have a lifelike bust above his grave in Cold Spring Cemetery (opposite page). Mrs. Haynes died shortly after her husband in 1904. The problem with trying to fit them in as the ghosts of the house is they did not live at the Sea Holly. They lived on Mansion Street, and died there. The Sea Holly passed to Haynes' daughter Alletta and her husband George Mackenzie in 1909. It stayed in the family until they sold it in 1921. At one point during the Great Depression, the home was taken over by the Merchants National Bank.

As I looked through the chain of ownership there was one thing that stood out. Nowhere did it mention a captain or a Rose. Of course, the deeds only mention the principle owners of a property, not their families or people who worked for them. The Sea Holly was always used as a summer cottage. It is possible that it was rented to outsiders, as is done today.

Armed with this new information, I recently stayed at the Sea Holly while I was hosting one of my weekend events in Cape May. I sat quietly in the living room and asked the ghosts questions while I ran a recording on my laptop. I asked if any of the Haynes family were present, who was haunting the house, and if they would tell me anything that would shed some light on the mysterious spirits who have been sensed by people over the years. Not a peep. Nothing on the recording that would indicate any ghost activity. Had the renovation pushed them out the door for good?

About 3:30 AM the following morning, something jostled me awake from a sound sleep. I sat up in bed and inspected the room. All seemed quiet, nothing was disturbed. I fell back asleep and, soon after, had a very vivid dream of finding a child's red rubber ball in my bed. I had the strongest sense that some unseen child had put it under my back as a joke. The dream was so real I thought I actually *did* find a ball in my bed, and I sat up and yelled! Of course there was no ball, but why was I dreaming of a child in the room?

Everyone else in the house woke up around the same time. This was before I had the dream and yelled. Was something moving around the house that woke us all from a sound sleep? A coincidence? Katie?

The most amusing thing that happened on that trip was arriving to hear a beeping sound coming from the kitchen. There had been a power failure on Stockton Street a few days earlier and the stove had not reset itself properly. It was flashing an error code, and beeping non-stop. We finally reset the

Albert L. Haynes' bust at Cold Spring Cemetery —watching over the graves.

breaker and silenced it—about the same time we found the old advertisement in a scrap book of Nancy's showing that Haynes' was a *stove* dealer. Albert Haynes? The Captain? Rose? A coincidence, again? Maybe.

People tend to haunt where they lived, not where they died. If Haynes and his wife lived and died in their home on Mansion Street, behind what is today the Washington Street Mall, it would be highly unlikely for them to be haunting on Stockton Street. Haynes' children all married and moved away. I would have to make an educated guess on the identity of the ghost(s) of the Sea Holly. I think they were either tenants or they are transient ghosts from a nearby dwelling. Perhaps ghosts get to pick their haunts.

Someday I hope to solve the mystery of the Sea Holly. In the meantime, I highly suggest it as a summer rental. Tell the Captain, Craig sent you.

The John F. Craig House

LAYERS OF CAPE MAY HISTORY—AND GHOSTS PACKED INTO ONE B&B

Bed & Breakfast — 609 Columbia Avenue

HE beautiful Bed and Breakfast, known today as the John F. Craig House, has been rumored to be haunted for many years. The main house was built on Columbia Avenue, the original "Beach Avenue" in Cape May in 1866. What makes the Craig House unique, from a paranormal point of view at least, is that there are actually two houses. The rear of the Craig house was originally a small home built earlier in the 1800s and moved to its current location from elsewhere in Cape May. During that time in Cape May, manpower was cheaper than lumber and many old homes were moved and salvaged. The Craig House's "new" front addition was added in 1866 after Columbia Avenue was laid out and developed. The 1866 house was also built by developer John C. Bullitt, the wealthy lawyer and land developer from Philadelphia mentioned in the Sea Holly chapter.

The house Bullitt built, at what is now 609 Columbia Avenue, was originally sold to George Richardson, president of the Cape May & Schellinger's Landing Railroad, until he lost it in an 1870s sheriff's sale. Richardson later drowned in the sea during an 1891 storm. Benton Knott Jamison of Philadelphia, owner of B. K. Jamison & Co. Bankers, bought the house next. Jamison was known for throwing wild parties and entertaining the wealthy at his seaside home. In 1891, Jamison sold the house to fellow Philadelphian John Fullerton Craig. The Craig family reigned at 609 Columbia until the 1950s. Some are still reigning.

I had the opportunity in 2003 to meet the Craig House's newest owners, Chip and Barbara Masemore, during one of the Mid-Atlantic Center for the Arts' historic house tours. Getting inside the Craig House gave me a completely new feel for the place. I could sense two energies. Not people or ghosts, but distinct energy patterns representing different time periods.

When I psychically read a location, I pick up many different feelings and images. Usually, one "energy" will dominate. That energy or "piece of time" will contain a ghost or in some cases simply a lot of residual imprints. As I mentioned previously, residual imprints (residual hauntings) are just that, leftover images trapped in the "ether" that sensitive people can tap into. These imprints have no ghostly consciousness or interaction ability. They are just random ideas that play repeatedly like a tape loop. They are like an eternal drive-in theatre that shows the same picture forever. They should really not even be called a "residual haunting," because no ghost is present.

I try to sort out what energies are residual imprints as quickly as possible, note them, and then ignore them to get to the real ghost activity. Ghosts can and may interact with me and others who can sense them, and this interaction can be a great source of information about what is going on in a haunted place.

I first want to reexamine the words *haunted* and *haunt* as used in ghost investigations. I feel I have to throw some support and sympathy to the ghosts, the souls that are stuck in the shadowy world, somewhere between the Earth Plane and the Other Side.

The word haunting is really a pejorative descriptor for a ghost. It is a bum rap. Most ghosts are only trying to do one thing, coexist. They do not want to scare, terrify or trick anyone, for the most part. Many hauntings are benevolent. So why don't we call hauntings something like "ghostly visitations" or a term more apropos? Because we *like* the word haunt and all the chain rattling, howling, moaning and Halloween-like activity that goes with it! Going with the popular vote, I will continue to use the word *haunt*, but with reservations.

I am often asked just what a ghost sees. Do they see what was? What is? What they want to see? The answer is "yes" to all of these depending on just who the ghost was and what type of person he was when he lived. A living person will see his surroundings, but what if the person has some form of mental illness that distorts his reality? If you died suddenly, and did not realize or accept the fact that you were dead, how would you feel? Perhaps you might experience a mental breakdown. Every ghost is different. Every person is different. Some of us handle and cope with trauma more easily. Some of us know how to adapt. The personalities of ghosts are the same as the personalities they held in life, these personalities are soul deep. This is why every haunting is different.

One of the more active rooms in the "old" section of the house.

Wandering through the beautifully decorated Craig House is like stepping back in time. One has to keep checking out the window to remember it is the 21st century! While I love the B&B, the ghost stories told about the house had always bothered me. Let's just say they just did not sit well with me psychically. There were reports about the ghost of a former servant, called Lucy Johnson who, legend has it, seemed to have a penchant for sewing on lost buttons. I had heard and read the stories, but just didn't feel the ghost was indeed a woman named Lucy Johnson.

From the outside of the house, as in many haunts, it is difficult for me to psychically read with any accuracy just what is rumbling about inside. In some houses, it is easier to pierce the veil, but others, like the John F. Craig House, seem to keep their ghostly business private and behind closed doors.

As I mentioned, there are two Craig houses that have been coupled for the last hundred and thirty-eight or so years. They are like two different tenants in the same living space, each with his own unique energies. With this kind of setting, I need to get up close and personal to read the ghosts.

Head (Ghost) of the House — Emma Craig
(Courtesy of Barbara and Chip Masemore)

When I made my way to the older part of the house, I experienced a group of ghosts moving up and down the old, narrow staircase. They were more interested in talking to each other about fishing victories. They were laughing and carrying on like a group of guys just returning from a party boat, after a day of fishing and drinking on the water. I moved into the room named for an old servant of the Craig family, Lucy Johnson.

I spent some time meditating in what was thought to have been Lucy's room. The room did have the most energy of the three upstairs rooms in the older section of the house. I could not tell if Lucy was still there, as there was too much racket from the group of ghost "pals" romping around the house. There was a psychic "feeling" of a caretaker's presence, however. This ghost asked me to tell the "lady of the house" to "restore the oil lamps that had been stolen from the rooms." Barbara mentioned to me that they did not like to put anything flammable in guest rooms for fear of fire. I suggested taking the wicks out, that this servant would be happy with just having lamps back.

Apparently, the ghosts do not like to have doors kept closed either. The former owners told Barbara that they thought the ghost of a former male servant kept opening up doors on the second floor of the old house. I could imagine with all the ruckus, comings, and goings of these sailors and anglers, doors did not have much of a chance of standing still!

Questioning Barbara about her experiences as the newest owner of the Craig House, she mentioned she too had heard "the crowd on the back stairs." In fact, since taking over the house with her husband Chip in October of 2002, Barbara had experienced the noises several times. In a few instances, she would get up and turn off her television set to listen. Barbara also has had several guests report a cat ghost, but that's another chapter all together!

As I moved into the "newer" section of the house, I asked Barbara who the "Emma" was that I was sensing following us around?

"Emma Craig," she responded, "the wife of John Craig, the owner." It seemed Emma Craig was quite interested and aware of who I was and what I was doing there. She was an imposing presence, definitely in charge of the house. She seemed to come and go from the front of the house to the older section in the rear.

Entering the living room, I "spotted" the ghost of a white-haired man, smoking a pipe on the porch. He acknowledged me by nodding and continued puffing away. This man was not your typical aloof spirit — in fact, he seemed quite fascinated that I could sense him at all. He told me he was annoyed by progress. That he used to be able to see the ocean while smoking his pipe on his front porch. He told me that Columbia Avenue (named for the old Columbia House hotel) used to be "Beach Avenue" and that all the land between his house and the Ocean was marsh and swamp. Barbara Masemore confirmed the clear view to the ocean once existed for the Craig family. Several, old-time Cape May residents later validated the fact that Columbia Avenue was once called Beach Avenue.

The stairway going up to the 1866 section of the house's second floor is lined with old pictures. I spotted a small picture of the house from years ago and asked Barbara who two of the people in it were, as they were the ones I saw now. As it turned out, they were John F. and Emma C. Craig. I rather assumed this, but since there had been several generations of Craigs, it was good to be able to validate just which Craigs I was contacting.

John Craig's ghost told me that the old part of the house was *not* from 1850, but earlier, from the mid 1830s, 1834 to be exact. He also wanted me to tell Barbara and Chip it had been moved from Lafayette Street to the current site. Barbara told me that the Fairthorne's cottage behind them had come from Lafayette Street, but was not aware theirs had.

According to Cape May history, in 1866 John C. Bullitt and a partner bought The Columbia Hotel and the vast property to the east of the hotel grounds. Bullitt then subdivided the area and created Beach Street (which later was renamed Columbia Avenue after the hotel of the same name) and Gurney Street. Once the streets were laid out, the houses were erected along the north side of Columbia and west side of Gurney.

Speaking with Barbara during one of my visits to Cape May in late March of 2007, as I was preparing the second edition of Book 1, she mentioned she had come across a piece of literature about the history of the house that specifically mentioned the back addition. A printout given to her by the realtor when they bought the house mentioned the back edition was built before 1850 and was part of the "vast Bennett Plantation." Where was that — I thought? There were several Bennetts in town in the 1800s, but I had not remembered anyone mentioning a plantation. The only plantation I knew of was the old Corgie Plantation over in the area by where the The Southern Mansion was built.

I checked with Jim Campbell, Walt Campbell and Harry Bellangy (whose grandmother was a Bennett,) but none of them could remember hearing of a Bennett Plantation in Cape May. Old maps also turned up nothing. The closest thing I could find was a W. Bennett living near the edge of town on Lafayette Street and an A. Bennett living near Lafayette and Ocean Street on the 1850 Numan Map. No mention of any Bennett Plantation.

The old Numan Map Inset from 1850 also shows empty land where the Craig House would later be built, with the exception of a small dwelling owned by an "S. Shields." The closest link could be the two properties labeled "S. Shields" on that map. One small house sits next to the W. Bennett property on the Numan map, while the other sits on Ocean Street near where The Craig House stands today. Could Shields have moved a house from his neighbors the Bennett's property on Lafayette to be nearer the ocean? People did move houses in the old days, and the rear section of The John F. Craig House came from somewhere.

It was not until late one evening, as I was wearily proofreading and updating this second edition for the umpteenth time, that I happened to open up a scan I had made of one of Walt Campbell's old newspaper clippings. The article from *The Cape May Star and Wave* was talking about the house I had investigated for Book 2, now called The John Hand House, at 1129 Washing-

Now you see 'em — Dining with the Craig Family circa 1900
(Courtesy of Barbara & Chip Masemore)

ton Street. It is probably one of the oldest houses in Cape May. In the brief article the house was said to be "the original house on the Aaron Bennett Plantation." I could not believe my tired eyes. The information was right under my nose all that time. At this point in my research, I have found that the Bennetts owned much of the acreage from near what is now Schellinger's Landing (by the Lobster House) down into Cape May along Lafayette Street and stretching to the ocean. Lafayette and Jackson were in the early days one old and crooked road called, "Cape Island Road."

Aaron Bennett, like many of the early Bennetts in Cape May, was a Delaware Bay Pilot. If this house was also owned by the Bennetts originally, perhaps this is the reason the ghosts in the older section of the Craig House were

John and Emma Craig in front of their summer home on Columbia Avenue.
The ghostly figure sitting on the porch behind them is actually
Salomé Carp, Emma Craig's mother who lived to be almost 100 years old.
(Courtesy of Barbara and Chip Masemore)

carrying on about fishing and boating. I think the connection to merchant Samuel Shields is the best guess as to how the house was moved from Lafayette to Ocean Street. Shields owned property at both locations and maybe, when Ocean Street was cut through in the mid 1800s, Shields and his wife Jane decided to move their home and children a little closer to the beach. On the 1850 Numan Map Inset of Cape Island (see page 37,) the "S. Shields" house appears almost exactly where The John F. Craig House property is today. I think Samuel Shields moved it there in the early 1800s and John C. Bullitt used its location to start his row of houses for the Columbia Avenue development. This is another great piece of early Cape May history that had been forgotten. Good thing we have ghosts around to remind us!

Many times ghosts will alert current owners or residents of impending trouble with a home. It is apparent that the Craigs still love the house. They were especially concerned that Chip look into a crack that had developed in the foundation. Outside the house, Chip, who I think is a bit more skeptical than Barbara, showed me the crack in the foundation that John Craig must have been talking about repairing. John is very happy that Chip is fixing up the old section of the house. Now if I can only get them to start speaking and listening to each other, it would be the ultimate renovation team!

I returned to the Craig House several times since my initial interviews. Emma Craig was definitely the strongest presence in the house. I remarked to Barbara that it was most certainly Emma, and not Lucy, who was roaming the halls with authority. But why would the lady of the house be hanging out in back in what would have been the servant's quarters?

Some Cape May ghost mysteries may never be solved, but to the Masemore's and my surprise, this one was. The next summer I received a call from a very excited Barbara Masemore. While she and Chip were out shopping, two strangers had arrived to pay the house a visit. I should specify, living visitors. The surprise guests were Carrie and Frank Heston, the Great Grandchildren of John F. Craig!

The Hestons left word with Barbara's guests that they were passing through the area, but could not stay. They did, however, leave their names and phone numbers to allow Barbara to contact them and "catch up" on some old family history. When I say the Hestons were grandchildren of John F. Craig, you will notice I did not mention Emma's name. As it turns out, Emma was not John Craig's original wife. His first wife was Susan Kerbaugh Bird, born in Camden, New Jersey and died in Philadelphia in 1882 at 36.

The real story of the Craigs is that a widowed John Fullerton Craig, born in Glenarm, Ballymena, Northern Ireland on February 12, 1840, died on March 3, 1926, purchased the home on Columbia Avenue as a summer retreat for him and his children in 1891. They would travel to Cape May each summer with their *housekeeper* — Emma Camp. According to the Great Grandchildren, Emma was a very strict housekeeper who also watched over the children. She apparently terrified the children of the house.

Eventually Emma and John got married, which, according to the family, was a great scandal at the time. The children, it is said, were never allowed to go into the servants' quarters before Emma and John got married. Hmm. It seems that Emma was never really accepted as the new matriarch of the family, and there was possibly a falling out between parents and children. In 1922, four years before John Fullerton Craig died, he changed his will leaving everything to Emma including, a pension of $8000 a year, monies he made as a wealthy sugar merchant in Philadelphia.

While the male heirs to the Craig sugar fortune seem to have lost out, the daughters inherited the house and what was left after Emma Craig died. Emma's mother also lived in the house until she was almost 100 years of age. No wonder the place is so active! John's daughter Susan Heston finally sold the house in 1950, and it has changed hands several times since.

A few years ago, I started doing séance weekends at the Craig House. The guests and I gather on Saturday night in the parlor of the house. The lights are extinguished, with the exception of a lone candle and the fireplace. As I slipped into trance states, I could feel ghostly presences moving in around me. It took me quite by surprise when I first realized that these ghosts were not just from the Craig House, or its history, they were from the surrounding inns and B&Bs in the area! It seems there is quite a concentration of ghosts in that immediate neighborhood, and they can see my psychic light. Ghosts are transient, and in the case of most of my séances, they came in numbers!

The Craig House has wonderful energy. You can imagine why so many people love to stay there—some for centuries. This house is a perfect paranormal example of ghosts from different times coexisting peacefully and really not paying much attention to each other. Sailors frolicking in back, Emma Craig checking up on them—living guests frolicking on the sun porch, a typical Cape May experience!

This Bed & Breakfast is one of the best places to stay in town. Barbara and Chip Masemore are wonderful innkeepers, and Barbara is a delight to chat with at breakfast and tea. The house will afford the psychic and paranormally inspired to take a trip back to several of Cape May's most exciting early periods in history, in addition to allowing one to enjoy everything that *this* century has to offer.

Next time you walk by the Craig House on Columbia Avenue and want to get a "sense" of what it was like in old Cape May, stop for a moment and look out towards the ocean. Perhaps the current buildings will disappear in your mind's eye, and a certain pipe-smoking ghost named John may take a few minutes out of his busy schedule to reminisce with you about the days before "progress" blocked his view, and men were ghosts.

Opposite page: Inset from The 1850 Numan Map of Cape Island

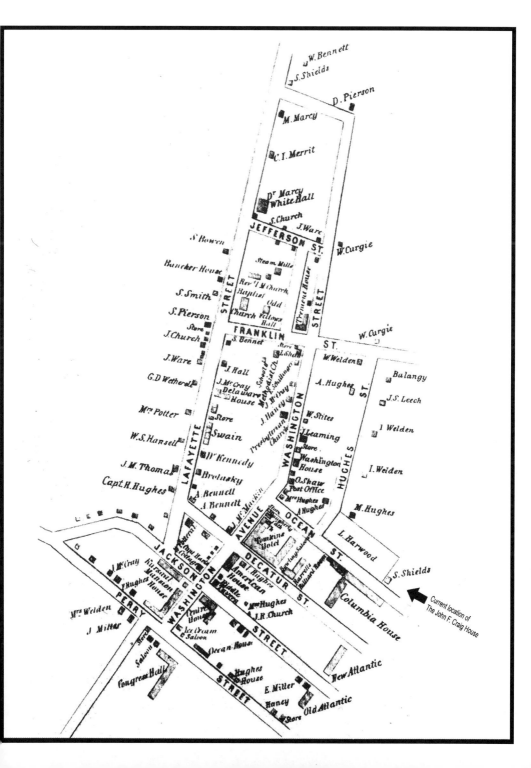

J.W.Bennett

S.Shields

D.Pierson

M.Marcy

C.I.Merrit

Dr Marcy
White Hall

S.Church   J.Ware

S.Bowen

Bancker House

S.Smith

S.Pierson

J.Church

J.Ware

G.D Wetherel

Mrs Potter

W.S.Hansel

J.M.Thomas

Capt.H.Hughes

JEFFERSON ST.

STREET

W.Curgie

W.Curgie

Steam Mills

Rev'd M.Church,
Baptist   Odd
Church Fellows
Hall

FRANKLIN ST.

S.Bennet   Store
L.Shaw
W.Welden

J.Hall

J.McCray
Delaware
House

Store

Swain

Wm Kennedy

Brotasky

A.Bennett

A.Bennett

LAFAYETTE STREET

School
Methodist Ch.
Schillinger

J.Haney

A.Hughes

W.Stites

J.Leaming

Store

Washington
House

O.Shaw
Post Office
Mrs Hughes

A.Hughes

J.McMakin

AVENUE

OCEAN

WASHINGTON

Presbyterian
Church

Balangy

J.S.Leech

1 Welden

I.Welden

M.Hughes

HUGHES ST.

L.Harwood

S.Shields

→ Current location of
The John F. Craig House

Tomkins
Hotel

DECATUR ST.

T.Hughes
American
House
Boule
Russel

Spring Saloon

Bardill's
Billiard Room

Columbia House

JACKSON

Doct Hand's
Cottage

Hansell
Mansion House

J.McCray

T.Hughes

Mrs Welden

J.Miller

PERRY

WASHINGTON

Andrew
House

Ice Cream
& Saloon

Ocean House

Store
Saloon

Congress Hall

Mrs Hughes

A.J.R.Church

STREET

Hughes
House

E.Miller

Haney

Store

STREET

New Atlantic

Old Atlantic

The Windward & Saltwood

THE LOVE AFFAIR THAT LIVED FOREVER

24 & 28 Jackson Street — Bed & Breakfasts

BEFORE I take you into the next haunt, the Edwardian seaside cottage on Jackson Street called Windward House, I want to talk about a few more aspects of ghosts and hauntings. As I said in the introduction, this book is a primer for anyone wanting to learn about the paranormal. I am using Cape May as a template to illustrate the many different aspects of haunted places. Many haunts in Cape May have an interesting history. It is important to understand just what kind of haunting is occurring — and why — before you get swept up in the imagery and romance of the setting.

On my last visit to England, I was amazed at how comfortable everyone was with the idea of hauntings and ghosts roaming about the countryside. It seemed almost everyone had a story, if not a ghost of his or her own! The most impressive thing was just how long many of the hauntings had been going on, some over periods of hundreds of years. I quickly concluded that we Americans have nothing on the old world when it comes to a history of ghosts.

The ghosts I most often encounter in Cape May have been around for 100 years on average. Their British counterparts would probably consider them fleeting hallucinations, rather than full-fledged apparitions. What about those old ghosts in the dark corridors of dank and dusty castles and manor houses? Do they have any idea of how long they have been dead? Don't they get bored? The answer to both questions is no. Ghosts do *not* wear watches.

Ghosts seem to remember their ghostly lives in bits and pieces. Memory is an imperfect experience in the best of conditions. When you think about a ghost's actual age, it's a wonder they can remember anything! They no longer have physical bodies to experience and remember sensations from the five senses. All of their *soul mind* records are fragments of experiences, interactions, events and emotions. The problem is where to store this information. Ghosts have no physical brain in which to store memories, so all that data must go somewhere. My theory is that ghosts, thought to be fields of energy, can store thoughts around them in the form of energy.

In the age of cellphones, sending information through the air to communicate is nothing out of the ordinary. As a psychic medium, I like to think of myself as a sort of human cellphone. The only difference is that I can send and receive messages without the help of any technology. We know information can be sent through the ethers via radios, televisions, pagers and cell phones — we just do not yet know how people like me do it.

It is logical to assume, then, that if one can pick up information from a ghost and communicate with a ghost in a limited fashion, ghosts must be able to store themselves and their "minds" somewhere that is no longer in our physical plane. If ghosts can pierce the veil to haunt a place, they must be able to come and go between planes at will. We usually cannot see them, but we can hear them, feel them and sometimes communicate with them. So where are they?

As a psychic medium, I am able to use my mind to meet the ghost in some middle ground between here and the Ghost Plane, where they seem to remain stuck. Stubborn and sedentary as most of them are, they usually have no desire to leave their homes or haunts. I think it is a bit like trying to stand firm in the tide. The motion of the surf constantly erodes our footing and knocks us off our feet, to be carried away into the vast ocean, or throws us back on to the physical beach. The Ghost Plane seems to be a lot like the surf, its inhabitants constantly battling an energy tide that tries to move them over to the Other Side or sends them slamming back into our physical Earth Plane.

While souls exist in the Ghost Plane, they seem to be focused on, or even obsessed with, some internal struggle, or unfinished business. Whether it is guilt, fear or a broken heart, these ghosts appear to be rather lonely sometimes. Perhaps they do not cross over to heaven because they do not want to admit they are wrong, or perhaps they simply like it with no one telling them what to do.

A ghost will continue its own internal drama forever, if need be. Only they can decide to move on. It is often much easier to bask in their own drama, to be the kings or queens of their own small realm. When you put ghosts' lives in this perspective, you will start to see just why they only occasionally interact with the living. They simply do not need us.

If you have ever been in an actively haunted place and experienced a ghost first hand, you will learn quickly that we can occasionally get in their way, and that is when they will let us know who is in charge! They just want

Jackson Street around 1904 looking north toward Washington Street.
The Red Cottage is on the left, followed by Windward House and Saltwood
House. Look carefully and you can see Charles T. Campbell standing on his
front steps at The Saltwood. (Walt Campbell Collection)

to coexist peacefully with us, not to be told to go away. Only they will decide when to move on. You can suggest for them to go. You can suggest, but that is about as far as you will get!

Jackson Street, reputedly one of the most haunted streets in the country, is home to many ghosts who will simply not be told to take a hike. Now dismiss, right away, the image of witches and goblins flying all over the street and headless coachmen checking people in at the old Virginia Hotel—it just does not happen. That is pure Hollywood!

When I say a street is haunted, it means that many folks have decided to stay after they should have left, because they like the place. Wouldn't you stay an extra week in Cape May if your vacation schedule allowed? I sure would. Ghosts would also, and they do. Think of them as permanently retired. They each have reasons for not crossing over. The challenge is learning their story, and figuring out why they are still earthbound.

The heart motif, cut into the shutters and woodwork, throughout the Windward House and The Saltwood House may be the only signs left of a long-faded romantic tryst between neighbors—now long departed.

Number 24 Jackson Street is a lovely Edwardian seaside home, now called the Windward House. George Baum built the house in 1905 for his wife and family. Several other buildings have stood on this same site, including three different hotels, all victims of Cape May's infamous fires.

Baum, a wealthy businessman from Philadelphia, built the house as a summer getaway with an added amenity, a mistress. Rumor has it that Baum had a house built next door (now the Saltwood) for a certain woman friend. This early love tryst survives today in the form of heart-shaped cutouts on the shutters and interior railing of both the Windward House and the Saltwood House.

Was it Baum or one of the following owners of the house who was leading a double life? The answer has been lost in history. What this medium was able to ascertain, however, was that the love interest in this early Edwardian plot is still very much a part of these two houses. It is the ghost of this woman, who some call Katherine, that seems to walk between the two houses.

Windward House was one of the first of the new B&Bs that slowly started to replace Cape May's perennial boarding houses in the 1970s. Tom and Sue Carroll, who went on to restore the stately Mainstay Inn, began refurbishing the old private residence at 24 Jackson Street in 1972. In 1976, the house was sold to Owen and Sandy Miller. Sandy, a former elementary school teacher from outside of Philadelphia, runs the B&B today with her son Owen and daughter-in-law Vicky.

Sandy is truly the *Grande Dame* of Cape May's B&Bs. Many innkeepers could take a few lessons from her on how to run a B&B properly—with style and grace. Sandy's warm and friendly personality is what first attracted me to stay at Windward House, although the ghosts also had something to do with it. I have been enjoying her hospitality and friendship ever since.

It was during the first summer the Millers had opened their B&B when they knew something was different about the house.

"We had three, maybe five, different people come down to breakfast that summer and report experiencing something. Most of the reports came from the third floor in what is now called the Wicker Room," Sandy told me. "In those first years the Wicker Room had no fans or air conditioning and got really hot in the summer. We had a young man stay there in July and expected never to hear from him again!"

The man, as it turned out, was taking a course in parapsychology (the study of ghosts and hauntings) and called Sandy back a few months later, requesting the same room.

"It seems he had experienced something that July and, when he came back, he was writing a paper for the class on ghosts. He told us he felt a feminine presence in the room on both occasions. We asked him to send us a copy of the final paper, but he never did," Sandy added.

That summer, the Millers received various reports from guests about a ghostly woman moving about the third floor. A friend of Sandy's, who was into the paranormal, witnessed a woman wearing a shimmering gold fabric. In many instances, guests would mistake the ghostly woman for Sandy and assume they had walked in on her cleaning their room.

"One woman came rushing down the stairs and stopped when she saw me in the parlor. She asked how I got downstairs so fast, as she had just seen me cleaning her third floor bedroom. I told her I had not yet been up to the third floor."

For many years there have been stories about an Irish servant named Bridget, who hangs out in the Wicker Room on the third floor of the Windward House. Well, Bridget must have been back in Ireland visiting her dead relatives when I stayed in the Wicker Room, because the room had no paranormal energy that I could sense. The stories also have twisted the look of the ghost to a young Irish servant girl. However, from the reports I have heard from Sandy, the woman seemed to have a different appearance altogether. I have yet to meet a dead Victorian Irish servant wearing gold lamé!

I do not doubt there may be a leftover Irish servant floating around the etherial eaves of the Windward, but I have never encountered her in the Wicker Room. If there was a young servant girl hanging around the third floor, she is now gone — or at least she has not surfaced in recent years or in my investigations. There *is* activity on the third floor, just not a dead Irish girl.

One of my favorite places to stay is in the Cottage Room, on the second floor in the front of the house. I, along with many guests apparently, have heard the footsteps moving back and forth up on the third floor and the banging and noise out on the third floor deck late at night, when the living are only dreaming of making a ruckus.

Who is this ghost who loves to walk out on the deck in the moonlit starry nights for which Cape May is famous? During a recent stay at Windward House, and I *highly* recommend one, I decided to find out what owner Owen Miller experienced on the second floor, when he was vacuuming and felt something, "go right through him."

I sensed strong activity in and around the second floor middle bedrooms. It was a quiet night — the other guests had gone and I had free run of the house. I sensed the ghost of a middle-aged woman coming up the stairs. She moved past me in the hallway and went into one of the bedrooms. I tried to make contact with her, but she ignored me and vanished. A few hours later, she was back, this time giving me a sense that she was now head of the house — it was hers, at last.

Katherine, as I will refer to her, directed my attention to the Saltwood House next door, using images I picked from her thoughts. (Telepathic eavesdropping on ghosts is sometimes the only way to get *any* valid information from them.) She gave me a feeling that she once lived next door, was the lover of the man who lived here, and when he died, continued to love him. After the man's wife died and sold the house, the woman had intended to buy it, but she died before that could happen. Therefore, she did the next best thing. She moved her spirit into the house to claim her trophy.

I spoke to Don Schweikert, proprietor of Saltwood House, after sensing ghostly activity next door in his B&B. I pitched the idea to Don about Katherine moving between the houses. Don told me the old timers in Cape May remember talk about a mistress and an affair. When he moved into the Saltwood House in 1992, the former owner of the Puffin next door informed him that he was living in the "mistress's house." The Saltwood was built between 1905 and 1906 after The Windward House, so perhaps Katherine moved in after the Baums.

Don told me his haunting activity was also concentrated on the third floor, making him believe it might be the ghost of a former servant. It does seem that many hauntings in Cape May take place on the upper floors of homes and hotels. Is it possible that many former servants have stayed behind? Or could it be that the ghosts simply want to get away from us? I think the latter makes more sense.

One of Don's friends, who had been staying in the third floor bedroom when Don had first bought the place, experienced the ghost of a woman at the foot of her bed. She told Don that the ghost gave her the name "Katherine."

A few years later, when Don's neighbor at The Puffin was researching the history of his own home, he looked up the history of his neighbor's homes as well. Don told me a Katherine Campbell was listed as living in the house in the 1910 census. Could it be the same Katherine whose ghost was seen by his friend that night?

According to deed research of the property done by Tom and Sue Carroll and passed on to the Millers, James and Catherine Mooney owned much of the property on that side of Jackson Street in the late 1800s. Catherine seems to have outlived James. James Mooney was one of the many wealthy Philadelphians, like Baum, who invested in Cape May after the great fire of 1878. He had erected The New Columbia Hotel on the west side of Jackson Street, just above where the Seven Sisters houses sit today, a sprawling high Victorian, Queen Anne-styled behemoth that stretched down most of Jackson Street between the ocean and Carpenter's Lane. This beautiful new hotel was short lived and burned to the ground in 1889. Could this be the Catherine in the house? Did a love tryst develop between herself and Mr.

THE NEW COLUMBIA HOTEL
BETWEEN PERRY STREET & JACKSON STREET, CAPE MAY
BUILT BY JAMES MOONEY 1879 - BURNED SEPT. 25TH 1889
STOOD ON THE GROUNDS NOW OCCUPIED BY WINDWARD HOUSE, SALTWOOD HOUSE & THE PUFFIN

The New Columbia Hotel stretched from Perry Street to Jackson Street
(Picture courtesy of the Cape May County Historical Society)

Baum after Baum bought property from them? Unfortunately, history is not completely clear on the matter.

With Don's lead, I was able to find the Campbells in the 1910 census of Cape May. The only problem was that she was also listed as living at 28 Jackson Street with her *husband* Charles and *two young children*, Katherine and Elizabeth. According to the census, the Campbells must have just been married when they bought the summer home on Jackson Street. The glove here does not really seem to fit. How would a newlywed with two young children have the time (or inclination) to have an affair? The Campbells later moved to Ocean Street by 1930. I asked local historian Jim Campbell about them, but unfortunately, he is of no relation. Charles Campbell was listed as a real estate agent, which Jim also confirmed. Jim told me to contact a friend of his from North Cape May named Walt Campbell. Jim felt there was some relation to Walt and the Campbells of Jackson Street and he was right. After meeting Walt Campbell he, like namesake Jim Campbell, had become a good friend and an invaluable source of Cape May history. Born in West Cape May and raised in Cape May, Walt seems to have known everyone in town at one point or another! Sadly, Walt passed in December of 2010.

Katherine Loftus Campbell was the wife of Walt's Great Uncle Charles. Not only did I finally make the connection, but Walt was able to supply me with a picture of his Great Aunt! (Right)

The old stories about a mistress came from somewhere. One thing is for sure. Either Katherine Campbell or Catherine Mooney seems to have survived fires, scandal and death. As Don told me, things like affairs were not written about in those days, so even though the story

Katherine Loftus Campbell
1873 – 1964
(Walt Campbell Collection)

may have survived, the evidence has not. The heart motifs, thought to be original to both houses, are the only surviving hint that something amorous and clandestine may have been going on. Katherine's energy is also much stronger at The Saltwood House. I felt her presence several times on the wonderfully spacious third floor. I decided it would be a good thing to return her image to her old abode and framed a copy of the picture for Don. Katherine now hangs proudly on the living room wall at The Saltwood House for all guests to see.

This is definitely a ghost on the move—and ghosts do indeed move from place to place just like the living will travel around.

"Katherine seems to have a habit of moving little things around," Vicki Miller once told me, a few years back when she worked at the house, "but she doesn't mess with me." Vicki simply accepted, as we all should, the existence of a ghost as "just another person hanging around the house." Katherine, after all, pays as little attention to us as she does to the time, day or year. Her "life" is all that matters to her. The rest of us are simply pieces of ethereal furniture — out of her view, but still around her.

One of the more interesting stories that Sandy Miller tells of her ghost is the "powder room incident." A few years ago, the staff became frantic that someone had passed out or died in the powder room downstairs as the door was locked from the inside, and no one would answer. The door had a simple hook latch on the frame that could only be placed into the ring on the door from the inside.

After finding someone to climb up a ladder on the side of the house, break the screen and pry open the window, Sandy and her staff were (somewhat) relieved to find that no one was in the powder room. Baffled, but chalking it up to a freak accident, they forgot about the matter until it happened again several weeks later. This time a young man helped them take the door frame apart to unhook the latch, finding once again no one in the powder room. Perhaps ghosts, too, have to answer the call of nature.

I had my own vivid encounter with the spirits of Windward House one summer a few years ago. I had invited several friends to join us for a few days one Memorial Day weekend. My friends, Danny and Gail Matarazzo, and their teenage son, Chris, had decided to brave the Wicker Room.

It was about 3:30 AM when something woke me up. As I lifted my head to listen, I heard footsteps going back and forth throughout the Wicker Room. I assumed my friends were making a few late night trips to the bathroom. That's what I thought, until I heard the SCREAM! It came from everywhere in the house, downstairs in the parlor, upstairs on the third floor, down the dark hallway on the second floor. Someone or something had been frightened and the terrible gasp echoed throughout the old house. I quietly rose from my bed and gently nudged my bedroom door open, inching my head out into the hallway. The house was quiet — not a creature was stirring, not even a ghost.

The next morning, the entire breakfast table gathered around to relate what they had experienced the night before. My friend Gail said her son Chris was choking in the middle of the night, and she woke up and reached over to shake him awake. Neither Gail, Danny nor Chris had left their beds during the night.

A guest from the second floor also heard the scream, as did a couple from the third floor. One of the guests described it as if a ghost in the middle of the night had startled someone. Or did someone startle the ghost?

Ghostly footsteps, screams in the night—just another day in Cape May's oldest and most haunted street!

While reworking these chapters for the third edition of this book, I could not help but get emotional reading this chapter and thinking of the loss of my dear friend Walt Campbell. I did not realize that, as my own father was dying in hospice in December 2010, Walt was also gravelly ill in a hospital in Cape May. Walt

Walter Homans Campbell
1931-2010
My late, great buddy & historian

passed on December 28, just a few days before my dad. I received an email from his daughter shortly after he died, but I was in the middle of dealing with my own father's final days, and could not make it to the funeral.

Walt was one of those guys who would do anything for you. If I had a Cape May history question, or especially a question regarding anything to do with West Cape May, Walt could usually answer it with flowing conversation, and pictures to back it up. He was an avid history buff, and being a native of Cape May, he had lived through a good chunk of Cape May's modern history. I was very fortunate to get to know him and to be able to call him a friend.

As for Katherine Campbell, her late great grand nephew Walt told me she died June 9, 1964 at the age of 91, in her house at 206 Ocean Street. That house, demolished during urban renewal in the 1960s, sat on Ocean Street near Hughes Street on the same side as the Queen Victoria.

Luckily for Katherine, she had lived at several other addresses in town in her life, so she would be able to have a "permanent residence" in the afterlife at one of her former abodes—if she is indeed the one doing the haunting.

I wonder if Walt has ever come back to pay her a visit. I can see him smiling at the thought of it now being possible. Maybe he can solve the mystery!

Congress Hall

THE MYSTERY OF NUMBER 23

251 Beach Avenue, Cape May

CONGRESS HALL is one of the last surviving great hotels of the Victorian era in Cape May. It has stood on the site in one form or another since 1816, and even that building is said to have replaced an earlier hotel on the "road to the water." It should be inevitable that the old place would have a ghost or two lingering about the L-shaped behemoth with its long corridors and dark cellars and, indeed, it does.

There is a particular summer vacation memory that I can recall from my early days visiting Cape May's many beaches. We had been strolling around the newly enclosed pedestrian mall, then called "Victorian Village." At the end of the mall was Congress Hall. There was something imposing about the

old place to a young child. Walking around the building with my parents and uncle, past the giant columns and tall windows, I remember asking my uncle if the place was haunted. I do not remember his answer, but I can recall somehow sensing ghosts, even at that early age. I remember peering into the windows. Possibly we even walked through the lobby. I can remember the vastness of the place and those old, massive, stretched mirrors in the lobby that seemed to reflect more of the past than the present.

Those memories are almost 40 years old now and have faded with time. The ghosts of Congress Hall, however, may well remember my childhood visit as if it were last Tuesday, for that is how ghosts' minds work. Time is meaningless to them.

In the spring of 2000, while the building and grounds were undergoing a major renovation, transforming them back to their earlier and grander state, Congress Hall's general manager, Patrick Logue, was kind enough to let me do a psychic walkthrough. For anyone interested in ghosts, this was a dream come true. The setting was perfect for a ghost investigation. The place was free of noisy humans and was undergoing a major renovation, which is a given for stirring up ghost activity!

My partner Willy followed with a tape recorder so we would be able to document all of what I picked up psychically. We began on the ground floor in the vast area that has served as the hotel's lobby since 1879, when the last incarnation of Congress Hall was rebuilt after the great fire of 1878.

In the lobby, I was picking up psychic images of water flooding the place. Patrick mentioned I was standing right in the spot under a pipe in the ceiling that had burst on him the previous winter and flooded part of the lobby. I also could sense palms, a black wrought iron fence and a big canopy, all things Patrick confirmed had existed at one point in time in the lobby, but were now gone.

It was at this point I began picking up the number 23. I am not into numerology, so I do not actively seek out number meanings everywhere I encounter them, but this number was psychically repeating in my head. There was no room 23, but there were several rooms that ended in 23. On later visits, I continued to hear this number. Could it be that the ghosts, and there are indeed more than one, are trying to tell me there are 23 of them in the building?

One would think that if this were the case, lamps would be flying through the air, beds levitating and apparitions roaming around like guests on a holiday! This is not the case, though, and is a common misconception with multiple hauntings. Ghosts want nothing to do with us. If we encounter them, we have usually found them, not the reverse. With the exception of children's ghosts, who are looking desperately for companionship or some parental energy, most ghosts will hardly ever make themselves known, except, that is, if they detect a person to be intuitive or psychically open to their energy. Then, well, read on.

My first encounter with anyone or anything I could call a ghost was in the section of the first floor where the shops are now located. The name she gave to me was Liddie, short for Lydia, I assumed. She was very concerned about fire from gas lamps, which obviously means she has been there many years.

I had heard stories from people who worked at the shops in the late 1990s when the hotel was closed, with only the shops open. One of the ladies who had worked in the lingerie shop at the time told me that on some nights, she would be the last person in the entire place when closing up the shop. Eerie, disembodied footsteps and shadowy figures became a nightly occurrence in her tenure at the hotel.

Is Liddie the one who followed shop workers during those dark and lonely nights? We cannot be sure. She was the most active of all the energies I could sense on the first floor. Liddie also mentioned a name like Thiel and a daughter named Emma, and kept referencing the name Cake, which Patrick identified as one of the proprietors of Congress Hall (although not a Lydia Cake.) She went on to mention the name of someone who worked there at the time named Field and friends of hers who were staying at the hotel named Monroe and Whitmore. The hotel has been in business since 1816, and more than a few guests have checked in and out, so it becomes a futile task to search all of the names.

I made a very interesting discovery about Lydia in 2007 while researching Congress Hall for the second edition of this book. When I had done my initial walk-through of the hotel with Willy and Patrick Logue, the name Lydia was unfamiliar to anyone. A few years later, Jack Wright arrived in Cape May and began his major historical work on the hotel, *Tommy's Folly*. I had been emailing Jack to ask him some questions about the hotel and he asked me, "Don't you have a copy of my book?" Digging through various boxes and bookcases I did manage to uncover his book, that he had given me a few years earlier. As I read through the early history to correctly ascertain how many hotels there were with the name Congress Hall, I hit a paragraph that read that in 1826, Thomas Hughes and his wife Leydia sold the hotel to Samuel Richards. Lydia was Leydia Hughes! She is still at the hotel, even after she and her husband sold the property 181 years ago. Now *that's* dedication!

I emailed my friend Jim Campbell on "Leydia Hughes." Jim emailed back that the correct name was actually *Lydia* Paige Hughes and she was born on May 13, 1767 and died on May 3, 1828 in Cape May. So Lydia "Liddie" Hughes it is. One ghost down, 22 more to go.

The lobby area certainly has activity, at least from my point of view. During a visit to Congress Hall a few years after my initial walk-through, I was questioning the front desk staff late one evening about their ghosts and getting a rather indifferent response.

I was with a few friends, and we were all sitting in the wicker chairs by the elevators. Within a few moments the room temperature dropped substantially which, we thought, was due to the air conditioning coming on. There was no one else with us in the lobby sitting area, but we all had the feeling of someone or something moving around us — as if circling and giving us a once-over. Suddenly the elevator door opened without any prompting, revealing an empty car and releasing an icy blast of air . When the elevator door finally closed (and the car started moving up) the temperature returned to normal. Was it one of the ghosts heading back to his room? The elevator, by the way, went to the fourth floor. Why not — the view is great!

As I have mentioned, there are different types of hauntings. Let us refresh. A ghost is an active, interacting energy that has a consciousness. When we die, we pass on or cross over to the Other Side — Heaven, if you will. A higher plane of existence. If we choose to come back, hang out and help those on the Earth, we are called spirits. If we die and get stuck between this plane and the next or decide to stay anchored here, we are referred to as ghosts. A ghost is a person who has chosen to stay after death — for some reason. If you see an actual ghost, it is called an apparition. Ghosts are sometimes seen, more often not.

The other, non-ghost, type of haunting is called a residual haunting or an imprint. Like a tape loop, this energy has no consciousness, cannot interact with you and replays the same thing repeatedly. It is like watching a movie. You can understand the story, identify with the characters, but you cannot become part of the story. You are only a viewer. My psychic impressions of water flowing, wrought iron and a canopy that I mentioned at the beginning of this chapter are types of residual energies. Furthermore, one is only able to be a viewer if one possesses some degree of natural psychic intuitiveness and is open to the energy. Many people do have this innate ability and either choose not to recognize it or are afraid to believe it is for real.

If someone saw a residual image of a canopy or a wrought iron fence for a split second, it is doubtful if he or she would classify it in his or her mind as any kind of haunting. However, if the residual imprint is one of a living person and the imprint is showing some kind of activity like walking up a staircase, then that would most definitely be considered by many as some form of ghost or haunting. In the field of parapsychology, which includes the study of ghosts, this is what is known as a residual haunting.

There is a lot of residual energy in Congress Hall, as there is in any old building that has seen so many people pass through its doors. The interesting thing about this hotel is that it is now in its forth incarnation and the exact location of the buildings has changed several times since it was first built in 1816. Four hotels on the same spot equals lots of residual energy!

Without going into great historical detail — you may find that information in Jack Wright's book on the long history of Congress Hall called, *Tommy's Folly* — it is important to at least know that while a physical building can change over time, the ghosts will stay the same. Some ghosts will come and some will go. They will relocate to the newer structure in most cases.

Here is a very abridged history. In 1812, Jonas Miller built a small hotel near the water's edge two blocks south of Jackson Street. A larger building replaced that early version in 1816. This building was sold to Thomas Hughes, son of Ellis Hughes. The 1816 structure burned in 1818 and was again rebuilt in 1819. In 1826 Hughes and his wife (Lydia) sold the building to Samuel Richards who in turn sold it back to Jonas Miller. Miller then turned over ownership to his son, Waters Burrows Miller. It was the younger Miller who greatly expanded what was then named Congress Hall (named in 1828 in honor of former Congressman and owner Thomas Hurst Hughes.) Waters B. Miller added an immense wing in 1854 creating the L shape that the current incarnation mimics today. This version of Congress Hall was the largest and stretched back along South Lafayette Street and down Perry almost to the ocean with the two wings shadowing the great lawn in front of the hotel facing the ocean. Still with me? There will be a quiz at the end of this chapter.

In November of 1878, a mysterious fire broke out across Perry Street at The Ocean House shortly after its proprietor, Samuel R. Ludlam, had closed up for the season. As that hotel went up in a blaze, embers drifted across to the Perry Street wing of Congress Hall and set that property on fire. As the great hotel burned, so did 35 more acres of prime downtown, beachfront real estate. Many great hotels and buildings were lost. A year later, Cape May had been rebuilt in the Victorian style of the day and Congress Hall had returned as a smaller and safer (all brick instead of wood) structure to welcome back the next season's guests.

Congress Hall was a very popular structure in all previous incarnations and certainly is one of the draws of Cape May today. Four presidents stayed at the old Congress Hall in the 1800s as did tens of thousands of others. The exact spots of all of the incarnations of Congress Hall overlap only on Perry Street, from what I can determine from old maps. The ghosts seem to have followed the real estate. I think ghosts will relocate if there is a fire, just as living people would do.

Today's Congress Hall also has a fourth floor, which the 1854 version did not have. The fourth floor is where some of the strongest energy is experienced. Again, I feel ghosts go to the highest level to get away from living humans and Congress Hall is no exception.

With so long a history, it is no wonder a place like Congress Hall has so much residual energy floating about. Some of what I encountered back in 2000 when the hotel was closed and under renovation, was residual imprints, while other energies were stronger and changing, bearing the mark of a ghost.

I am repeating my encounters with the residual energies, as well as with the ghosts, for the sake of showing you how a psychic medium like myself works during an investigation.

As we made our way to the higher floors, I was able to pick up several more distinct energies. On the second floor, I sensed an older man in his sixties, a kind of General Burnside-looking man in 1800s garb, with a name like Ammerman or Ammermore. I noted on the tape that I thought he might be residual, since he did not interact with me. A little further down the hallway, I encountered a frail-looking older woman named Minnie Haskell—again, no interaction. Maybe she was a shy ghost or was she just residual energy? With time, a psychic can determine what kind of haunting a specific place is experiencing. I have since returned to Congress Hall many times, but, unfortunately, it was never quite as quiet and empty as it was that first day. Perhaps I should have taken a room for the night!

On the second floor, near the elevators, was another point in the original walkthrough where I kept getting the number 23. It would interrupt the rest of the investigation. SOMEONE wanted me to know the number for some reason. Each floor had a 23—223, 323, 423. Was that it? Were there really 23 ghosts in the place? I would only be conjecturing at this point. Nevertheless, the idea of it did intrigue me!

Moving along the second floor, I picked up a person with the name of Edmund Morris and then a woman named Miss Abbie or Miss Abigail. A little further down I sensed a man with the name of Harold Tucker, who, I was told, lived in Philadelphia. There was also something about a boy dying of cholera. The Abigail name came back even stronger and now was associated with Hand, which I knew to be a big name in Cape May in the old days. Slowly moving into the oldest part of the hotel, last used as a hotel in 1993 and the original staff quarters, I picked up multiple energies and a strong name of Catie with a "C," not a "K," as if for Catherine. This older building had so much energy that I could barely sort out all the names and events, truly layers upon layers of residual energy. Or perhaps it was some kind of warp or rift in time? Could actual people and events be bleeding through

The aftermath of the August 31, 1869 fire in Cape May which burned two blocks
of the downtown business district. Congress Hall was spared until the
Great Fire of 1878 reduced the third incarnation of the hotel to ashes.
(Walt Campbell Collection)

from the past, WHILE they are happening back then? Some paranormal researchers believe warps do exist in haunted places. People who are sensitive to the energy may simply be picking up a transmission from another time, instead of ghosts in this time. Warps certainly would explain many of the symptoms of classic hauntings, but until science can help parapsychologists and psychics, we are going it alone.

As I mentioned the upper floors of Congress Hall seem to be the most active. We were also treated to a wonderful EVP caught on our tape, on the third floor. As we were talking with Patrick, a strange noise appeared on my cassette tape. In addition to the voices, the sound of horses whinnying, quite dramatically, was heard. I do not know WHAT a corral of horses would be doing on the third floor of Congress Hall, but they were there on the tape,

The old boiler plate from Congress Hall's massive former furnace, now tended only by the ghost of Jonas Miller, the hotel's original proprietor.

and they were upset about something! Maybe the ghosts were just horsing around.

Congress Hall is thought to have been built over the oldest building in town, which had been a stage stop, a hotel, a gambling house and a tavern in colonial times. It would have been one of the only taverns for people visiting the beach, giving even more credence to the idea of built up residual energy.

I began to get that dizzy and detached feeling I sometimes get when I have a close encounter with a ghost. I felt a stronger energy moving towards us. It was the ghost of an older man with receding gray hair. This was not a piece of the residual jigsaw puzzle in the ethers of the building — this was a presence so strong and active there was little doubt that this was a ghost! The man seemed to be near us, then below us, then all around us. It was the strangest feeling. It was as if he were moving around the building in more than one place at once, almost omnipresent.

The man identified himself as Jonas, and told me he was concerned about the boilers down below. He walked up to me and got in my face. I could feel him look directly into my eyes and, if that wasn't unnerving enough, he then walked right through my body! He kept giving me the mental image of a large boiler. I found it odd that the large hotel would have boilers in the side annex building, but thought perhaps that at one time this may have been the case. "This is over the boiler room, this building," said Patrick. "There is a coal furnace down there," he added.

As we made our way down through the former health club into the really dark (and dank) boiler room, I could sense the ghost of Jonas following us. The ancient laundry equipment and huge menacing old iron boiler reminded me of the movie, The Shining!

Descending deeper into the dark void under Congress Hall, Jonas kept uttering a name like Schmitty. Patrick had not known of anyone associated with the hotel named that, but Jonas kept mentioning it. "Please don't hurt Schmitty," was put into my head. Again, when I hear a ghost, I am not hearing in the sense that one would normally hear. In some way, ghosts and spirits can manipulate their thought energy through our neuro pathways that lead to the auditory part of our brain. It could be compared with a telephone repair person climbing up on a phone pole, tapping into a telephone line, and calling someone. Somehow, in an ethereal state, ghosts and spirits are able to communicate directly with the brains of the living. They can send thoughts, smells and even sounds.

Jonas was non-stop about the name Schmitty. A few minutes later, as we walked around the back side of the boiler, I glanced down at the imposing old iron boiler door. Clearly shining in our flashlight beam were the words, "Schmidt Boiler Company — Pittsburgh, PA" on the boilerplate. Schmitty was the boiler!

I mentioned to Patrick that if they wanted to appease the ghosts of the place, they had better take care of his Schmitty. Patrick told me that the room was being turned into a nightclub, and the boiler would be cut up and used to decorate the walls. You may see the boilerplate yourself at the bottom of the stairs leading to the nightclub by the entrance. This spot in the cellar is another hot spot for ghost activity. The rest rooms are located down here, and on more than one occasion I have been visited by ghostly residents in there! The most memorable experience I had was a late evening visit to the men's room. As I walked in, I heard someone whistling in the stall. I used the stall next to it. I could see the shadow of a man against the floor moving around. As I left my stall, I noticed the shadow was gone and the whistling had stopped. I hesitated a moment and glanced briefly at the floor under the stall door, realizing there was no one in the stall at all! No one had opened the door or left the room. The shadows moving on the floor were definitely that of a person.

Another night, one of the hotel's many ghostly inhabitants (who have a penchant, I guess, for cleanliness) must have been caught off guard by me. As I entered the bathroom, I heard the sink water turn on. When I entered, it was running, and I decided to leave it that way! The water soon turned itself off, and I heard the door open and close. I was otherwise occupied and could not get a good view of the event, but again, no one was there to turn the water off and then leave.

In 2003, after the grand opening of the new Congress Hall, while having dinner at the Blue Pig Tavern, I noticed Patrick Logue at the next table, talking to a few gentlemen from Scotland about hotel advertising. Upon finishing dinner, I stopped by the table and jokingly whispered to Patrick not to forget his ghosts in the advertising campaign.

Enjoying a cocktail in the lobby, we had the chance to talk to one of the gentlemen, David Gray, who was writing for *Exit Zero*. David was fascinated with the idea of channeling and spirit communication and asked if I would channel for him and his girlfriend. Maciek Nabrdalik, who would eventually become *Exit Zero's* photographer and also this book's brilliant photographer, joined us. I gave them a fast channeling session and, I think, made believers out of all of them.

David mentioned Jack Wright's book about the hotel, *Tommy's Folly*. I was able to find a copy in the lobby and quickly thumbed through it. Being optimistic his research would uncover one or more of the mysterious names I had picked up three years earlier, I turned a page and focused on a familiar face, a picture of one of Congress Hall's original owners, Jonas Miller. The mystery was solved. After reading the book, I realized that the original building that Thomas Hughes built was on the spot of the annex building in which I first encountered Jonas.

On one dark and very stormy night, with thunder crashing overhead, lights flickering and lightning crackling over the ocean, Jack and I decided to take ourselves and a camera and see if anything was up and about the old place.

The third incarnation of Congress Hall, that burned in the Great Fire of 1878, ran along South Lafayette Street and Perry. *(Walt Campbell Collection)*

Lightning seems to add just the right amount of static ions to the air to help ghosts manifest themselves. There is a reason many stories of ghosts and hauntings of old are set during lightning storms. Some believe ghosts are based on fields of negative ions and that lightning adds more negative ions to the air and almost recharges a ghost. If anything, it was a good night to roam the halls — it was late, the hotel was quiet and most of the folks were either asleep or dead.

As I started down the third floor hallway, I glanced down and had a feeling of something moving, almost zigzagging back and forth in the hallway. There were no visible apparitions, just a density to the space that I sense with ghost activity. I moved slowly down the corridor, quietly extending my arms to better sense the energies using my hands and arms as antennas. (It works for me.)

It was not one, but two small ghosts — children. I watched them in my mind's eye as they moved from door to door, trying each doorknob to see which room was open. Now they probably could pass right through the doors, but some ghosts respect our physical boundaries, or they may be simply respecting the physical boundaries that they knew as living children. I felt they were brother and sister. The sister was older, maybe around seven or eight . The brother was only about five or six years old. They were holding hands and dressed in what looked like old-fashioned nightclothes or bathing wear.

The girl tried turning the knob with one, then both hands for strength. When it would not turn, she backed away to go to another door, and the little brother gave it a turn by pushing both hands on the door. They were very persistent. Were they looking for their parents? I asked them what they were doing and their only response was, "The waves ate us." I realized they had drowned. It seemed like they had lost their lives directly on the beach in front of the hotel. Perhaps their family was staying at Congress Hall at the time. There are several ghosts in Cape May of people who drowned and are still trying to get back to where they were staying.

Jack was able to confirm the story for me. While researching *Tommy's Folly*, he had spent a lot of time going through old newspaper archives to find anything to do with Congress Hall. He said he did remember reading about a young boy and girl drowning on "the lawn" of Congress Hall, the "lawn" being the beach in front of the hotel. I think this must have happened in the late 1800s by the look of their clothes. Jack also felt the story appeared sometime in the 1800s.

I was to meet these two children twice more, once again roaming the halls of the hotel and another time on the beach near the hotel. My sighting on the beach was much more disturbing as I saw the girl laughing and gagging up chunks of seaweed and spitting out an endless supply. It was grotesque and made me think they were near the spot where they had drowned and were simply having fun with me by showing me what happened to them. When you remove the scare factor from this scene, you can see this is something living kids might do to freak out their parents. Ghosts of children are no different. They love to play, and they love to play jokes!

The Cape May Star and Wave contacted me several summers ago about an incident reported by one of the guests. A family from England was staying in the hotel, and the mother was taking a shower with the bathroom door locked. After she cleared the soap from her eyes, there were apparently a child's handprints in the condensation on the shower door. She also reported a red hand print on her thigh. All the hand prints appeared to be those of a child. Were the children simply having fun with the woman?

Some day I hope to be able to find the article Jack mentioned, and perhaps when I know their names, I can try to get these two kids to cross over to the Other Side. In the meantime, remember; when it comes to ghosts of children, kids will be kids and ghosts of kids will be kids, so watch out! I put in a late night call to Congress Hall's auditor, Dennis Zaicevs, before finalizing the Congress Hall story. Dennis has worked for the hotel for over three years and told me he has spent many nights alone and has never heard or seen any-

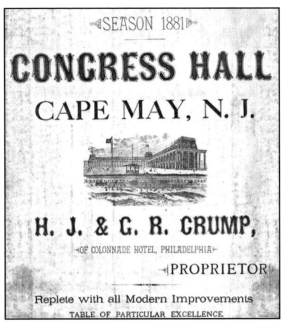

Vintage advertising poster from Congress Hall's 1881 Summer Season. Congress Hall has been a star attraction in Cape May for almost 200 years. So many summers—So many ghosts!

(Walt Campbell Collection)

thing out of the ordinary. He chalks it all up to people's imagination. Indeed, an over-active imagination can turn any home into a haunted house in one night!

In an interesting aside to this story, one of the things I do as a psychic medium is past life readings. I try not to let clients get too caught up in their past lives because one needs to live in the here and now. This is the time that is most important to all of us. When I first met Jack, I knew he was an old Cape May soul who had simply chosen to return and enjoy life on the Cape one more time. One night, while sitting in Congress Hall and doing a little channeling in the lobby, my spirit guides gave me a very important piece of information for Jack. The message stated, "Jack Wright was Thomas

Hughes." Jack had unknowingly written his own past life's story when he wrote *Tommy's Folly* — the book named for Thomas Hughes' original hotel, as it was known before it became Congress Hall. Stranger things have happened. When we fall in love with a place after seeing it for the first time, our soul has probably seen it before — our current incarnation simply does not recognize it. In every life, we always have some memories of our past lives, but we just cannot place them.

In the Congress Hall's famous Brown Room lounge, there is a large group picture of the staff of Congress Hall in front of the hotel, taken in 1928. I often stare at this large gathering and wonder just how many of them are still tending to their duties around the hotel. I have always had a strong feeling many of the "long term residents" of the hotel were once employed there. Next time you stop by the Brown Room for a drink, take a look and raise a glass to the old crew. They have not told me who among them has yet to retire — maybe they will tell you!

In the last two years Congress Hall's star paranormal attraction has been the two ghosts of the young boy and older girl, the same couple I detected checking the doors that stormy night a few years ago. One visit to MAC's Museum Shop on the promenade level will yield you volumes of first hand ghost experiences, should you happen to speak with Iris or Dorothy, the shop's two Managers. Toys and dolls are left neatly packed on the shelves at night, the alarm (with motion sensors) is activated at closing and the doors locked. Upon arriving the next morning, staff members will sometimes find those same dolls and toys *on the floor*, having been played with during the night! Ghosts do not set off motion sensors that are looking for a combination of movement and heat. They are usually movement and *cold*.

When I have been in the shop I had occasionally detected ghost activity. I believe the phantom duo works at night and probably, knowing the huge number of children's ghosts in Cape May, do not work alone. When I have inquired to a few of the other shops on the first level about ghosts, the shop keepers have given me a reaction somewhere between bothered and constipated. They *just* do not get the whole paranormal thing. Too bad for them.

The similarity of age and the characteristics of these two ghostly children have made me think, on more than one occasion, that they may be the same two ghosts that haunt the Lace Silhouettes/Cotton Company store. Ghosts do travel and that store is only a few blocks away.

I have also received various emails about activity on the fourth floor. One woman even said she and her husband heard cow bells in the middle of the night coming from the hallway. Well, I guess if I can hear horses, others are allowed to hear cows. What will be next—ghost roosters crowing at 5 AM calling guests to breakfast?

In all seriousness, several people have reported to me that they have experienced a few bumps in the night on the fourth floor. Ghost bumps. One visitor to Congress Hall was staying on the fourth floor and told me she did not believe in ghosts at all, but she heard the sounds of footsteps walking around her bed at 3 AM followed by those same footsteps heading for the bathroom. Then something jarred open the bathroom door just a few inches. Interesting isn't it that ghosts refuse to go in one sense but may have to "go" in another.

When I can occasionally corner one of the housecleaning staff to ask them about their ghostly occupants, they will admit things like; hearing people in a room that should have checked out, only to discover upon entering that room, that it is empty. Like many places in Cape May—when the people check out, the ghosts check in. Remember, ghosts do not want to bother or be bothered by us. It's that simple. The top floor has the best view and is the farthest floor away from the bars and restaurant downstairs.

The Congress Hall ghosts are usually quiet and respectful of the living guests, so you need not worry about losing any sleep. I imagine Cape May's grand old hotel will be standing, in one form or another, for the next 200+ years. Some day in the distant future, you or I might be vacationing there in ghostly form, before crossing over ourselves! Hey, there has to be some reason why Cape May is so darn haunted. Maybe the ghosts, like the rest of us, just love the vacation spot!

Congress Hall has now returned to its original grandeur, and I would highly recommend a stay there. My favorite room, probably my favorite in all of Cape May, and one said to have some activity, is the last room at the end of the fourth floor hallway facing west toward the lighthouse. If I were a ghost and going to move into a place, I surely would pick a beautiful spot like this! The long corridors with their shuttered doors, airy rooms and ocean views harken back to a quieter time where one can imagine the sounds of John Phillip Sousa's band playing on the lawn once again.

The Hotel Macomber

WHERE "VACANCY" DEPENDS ON YOUR POINT OF VIEW

727 Beach Avenue, Cape May

ONE of the most famous ghostly haunts in town is the old Hotel Macomber, which stands on the corner of Beach and Howard Street. Sara S. Davis, wife of Sussex Davis, was the first to build on the vast Stockton Hotel property in 1918, after the massive 1869 structure was torn down in 1910. I am sure the Stockton Hotel, which stretched from Beach Drive back to Columbia Avenue, and took up most of the space between Gurney Street and Howard Street, was, in its own day, haunted. I have, on more than one occasion, picked up residual energies in the aforementioned area. Silverware clinking, dishes clanking and people walking up a great staircase are a few of the residual imprints leftover from the old Stockton. The ghosts, however, left the hotel and moved elsewhere.

When a building is demolished, ghosts, like people, are not going to be silly enough to ride to the ground with the wrecking ball. They move out, and they simply find new quarters close by. It would be easy to surmise that when Davis constructed her new small single frame hotel on the corner of the great lot, a few of the Stockton's old resident ghosts decided to check in!

An *S. S. Davis* is listed as living at Howard and Beach in the 1918 telephone directory of Cape May with a phone number of 3-28. Originally I had heard that the hotel was completed by 1921, but I now think some form of dwelling was on the site in 1918. Davis also appears in the 1932 city directory as Mrs. Sussex Davis and is still listed as residing at Howard and Beach.

The New Stockton Villa, as Davis named the place was eventually sold to New Yorker Henry W. Macomber and renamed, The Hotel Macomber. Macomber was already managing properties just east of The New Stockton Villa. Long-time resident Bob Fite told me Ed Smith was the builder of the Macomber, the same man who built his current home on Howard Street.

As the hotel passed through the tumultuous years of the 20th century, new owners came and went. The ghosts came also and kept coming. Some left, most did not. When one has such an active group in so small a space, the best way for a psychic medium to communicate with them is through a trance channeling, the same method that I used to reach the ghosts of the Sea Holly Inn.

Many people ask me what the difference is between a psychic and a psychic medium. There are many psychics out there, but only a small percentage are also mediums. A medium is just that, someone in the middle — in this case, in the middle of a communication between the living (us) and the dead (them.) A medium is very much like a telephone operator who keeps the connection live, until both parties have communicated what needs to be said. The medium also has the important role in helping the person for whom they are reading to interpret the messages coming through from the Other Side. A medium *channels* the information from the Other Side to this plane. This is why mediums are also known as channels. It is true that we all have the ability to open up to psychic energy and tap into a form of spirit communication. As with any ability, there are those who are great artistic painters, those who finger paint, those who master the piano to the concert level and those who get as far as the classic, *Chop Sticks*.

People often comment on the quality of my channeling. From the positive feedback I have received over the last 20 years, I know that the information that comes through for me will be generally accurate. No psychic or medium is 100% accurate, though some of us have much higher accuracy rates than others. Until the day when college degrees are given out for psychics and mediums, feedback and accuracy is all we have to gauge our performance.

I have been channeling professionally for many years now, and I have been an avid fan of ghosts and hauntings since long before that. It was not until I started doing psychic readings, in the form of tarot cards, that I realized I was tapping into much more than just feelings about people's lives and love interests, I was actually sensing and communicating with entities on the Other Side and entities on the Ghost Plane.

I remember vividly, in those early days of being a psychic, sitting on the floor of a client's apartment reading tarot cards. I kept getting distracted from the deck by the feeling of someone watching me from the other side of the room. In my mind, I could see an image of an older man and heard a name — George. I relayed the information to the woman for whom I was reading, and discovered that George was her landlady's late husband who had passed a year prior. He had looked as he appeared in my mind.

This was my first *professional* encounter with a ghost. It was also the point in my career where I realized that I did not need tarot cards any longer to contact the Other Side or to investigate a haunting. *I was my own equipment.* It is this internal equipment that has allowed me to contact and research ghosts and hauntings for many years. It is a type of ghost investigation that can uncover much more than the normal parapsychologists' meters and gauges. It also makes for more interesting reading!

We checked into the Macomber in the late winter when the hotel was still quiet. There is nothing worse for a ghost investigation than having a bunch of living people running around, making noise, and slamming doors. We ate dinner at the fabulous Union Park restaurant in the Macomber, and retired afterward to the Macomber's lobby for a glass of wine and some spirits.

Before the channeling session, we encountered Lenka Adamcova, the Macomber's night manager. It seems that the ghosts regularly make themselves known to Lenka at night when it is late and quiet in the hotel. Lenka told us about a time last winter when she was the only one in the hotel. The front doorbell would ring at 2 AM. However, when Lenka would look into the surveillance camera on the porch, no one could be seen. This went on for a few hours until finally, I presume, both Lenka and the ghosts went to bed!

Union Park restaurant's former manager, Maya, also told us that several years ago on New Year's Eve it was not only the living customers who were having a good time. As all of the guests dined in the restaurant, Maya and another patron could hear what sounded like furniture being moved around upstairs, yet no one living was on the upper floors. This kind of sound is a very common occurrence in many hauntings. Now it seemed everyone had a ghostly tale to tell, and we would soon find out.

I will refresh a little about channeling at this point. Channeling can be done via three methods: awake state, light trance and trance channeling. When I read or channel for a client over the phone or in person, I work in an awake state, meaning that I am awake and fully aware of what I am doing. If I am working on a more serious problem for someone, I may relax and go into a light trance, where I am somewhere in consciousness between this plane and my own higher consciousness or existence. The third type of channeling is much more intense and requires someone to be with me to work with the entities that come through me vocally.

In trance channeling, I allow these discarnate entities, usually spirit guides from the Other Side, to use my vocal chords to speak. I am still in control of my body, but they will sort of drop in and communicate. In the old days of Spiritualism, these entities were called drop-in communicators. Now do not be alarmed. Everything I do has prayer of protection as part of the preparation. The spirits do not possess me! I have spirit guides who monitor just who comes through and instructs them to leave when I get tired. Spirit guides are sort of like guardian Angels who watch over us during our lifetime on this planet. I keep mine on call 24/7, I think!

That evening at the Macomber, I asked the spirit guides to allow the ghosts to come forth and converse with us, and they did. The first personality to come through called herself "Pinky," a nickname she used apparently, as she was reluctant to give us any more details. One thing about channeling that always amazes me is when someone records my work, and I get to hear myself later on. This is not done often, as I would rather pass on the information to whomever is listening and forget it. After listening to an audio recording of the evening, the thing that really got me was Pinky's voice. It was so distinctive and unlike my own, or anything I think I can generate, that you would swear, listening to the tape, that I was having a conversation with a total stranger in the room!

My partner Willy, who was with us that night, asked Pinky about the woman in Room 10. This woman, according to owner Crystal Hardin, was a frequent guest of the hotel in the 1940s and 1950s. She came each year with her husband and children. After her husband died, the woman's children convinced her to continue her annual trek to Cape May. She returned each summer with all of her trunks and stayed in the same room as always, Room 10.

Room 10 is on the second floor of the hotel in the rear of the building facing Howard Street. It has seen its share of haunting phenomena over the years. Dresser doors open and close at night by themselves, the bathroom door will slam shut and the doorknobs will turn. Crystal recalled a story of the first years she and her family had taken over the Macomber, and a woman staying in room 10 complained that the housekeepers kept doing their laundry every night at ten past twelve. The washing machine would begin on spin cycle each night and awaken her, only there was no laundry in the machine and no housekeeper in the hotel at that hour!

So who is the "trunk lady" who frequently returns to Room 10 for a good night's haunt and a little R & R? Pinky would only say that, when she is active, the woman calls for Pinky to bring her clean glasses and linens. It seems the woman took a lot of medication in life and continues to think she does in death. What *would* today's HMOs do with her?

In March of 2007, while preparing the final draft of this second edition, I was finally able to hook up with Jerry Reeves. Jerry's family had owned the Macomber for ten years. However, their tenure was from 1967 to 1977. Jerry remembered this about the Macomber:

"My parents bought the hotel in 1967 from Mr. and Mrs. Robert Fuller. I was 12 years old at the time, and my first job was bellhop and doorman. The Fullers had owned it since the late 1940s, I think it was 1947. When we bought it in 1967, it was a fully functioning Hotel and Dining room. We ran it on the same basis until we sold it in 1977. The customers rented rooms for one price which included a full course breakfast and dinner for no extra charge, (American plan style). We sold it to a man named Peterson, a realtor from Washington. He let his son, (aged approximately 22) run the property for about 8 - 10 years. They rented out the dining room operation for two years as a separate operation, but the tenant died in 1979 and they did not find a replacement tenant. They stopped running the property as a hotel their second year, and started renting rooms for the season to local summer workers. They sold most of the furnishings and the property deteriorated badly. The Cordes group bought it in the late 1980s and started some renovations. They sold it after 2 or three years to a group including a fellow named Donaldson. His brother had worked as a waiter at the business when we owned it. The Donaldson group did some more repair work but only kept it for two or three years. In the early 1990s they sold it to the Hardin family... They reopened the dining room for the first time since 1979."

I took the opportunity to ask Jerry about the "trunk lady" who stayed in Room 10. It always baffled me why no one knew her name. Even in the channeling I could not make direct contact with her, although she may not have been on the premises at the time. Ghosts will come and go. Jerry had the information I was looking for!

"A nice old girl named Miss Wright stayed in Room 10 each season for many years. She seemed to have no family and would stay until we closed for the season. She traveled extensively the rest of the year and often took cruises or trips to Europe. She was an incessant talker and we would try

The most popular room in the house — Room 10.

to avoid contact with her if possible. She died in the late 1970s, but I never saw her ghost... Miss Wright bathed in perfume and we had to air out her room after she left... Miss Wright's name was Irene. She lived in Germantown, Pa.."

The "trunk lady" has a name — Irene Wright. However, from the "Miss" before her name, was she married with a family or not? Her long stays at the Macomber ended during the Reeves family's time. Jerry also mentioned she would always ask for certain supplies to be replenished every day, which may be what Pinky was talking about when she said, she had to bring her new linens each day. Old habits die hard. I posed the married/single question to Jerry and also told him about her nickname, the "trunk lady."

"I do not believe Miss Wright ever married. We are certain she had no children. She like many of our guests had been staying at the hotel for many seasons. When our dining room was closed for the season she would eat at the Washington Inn every night. She never drove and never owned a car, so the steamer trunk was a common piece of equipment for many of the old generation of the hotel trade. When we bought the hotel in 1967 many girls wore white gloves to dinner and no gentleman was admitted to the dining room without a jacket. The waiters wore starched white dinner jackets (and no air conditioning)," Jerry emailed me back.

There you have it. Trunk, yes, married with kids, no. Another ghost mystery in Cape May has been solved!

I will tell you I spent one of the most peaceful nights in Cape May, staying in Room 10. The room just has a good feeling about it. I would book it again, if someone or something were not already staying in it. I did not experience anything paranormal staying in Room 10. Across the hall, in room 15, it was a different story.

Two summers ago, we were staying in Room 15, a spacious room with two beds and a rear location. After taking a morning shower, I came out of the bathroom and caught a fast glimpse of two men in different military uniforms, like Army and Navy uniforms. They quickly vanished when I noticed them. Later I would learn that during World War II, the Army and Navy had taken over the Macomber to house the troops that operated the gun turrets at Cape May Point.

You will also notice, if you look at Room 10 from the outside of the building that the power lines come in right below that part of the structure. Could the excess electromagnetic fields back here be helping to manufacture a haunting? Do the ghosts of Miss Wright and the two servicemen feed off the excess EMF fields? Some parapsychologists think so.

Another, more stressed entity came through moaning about being trapped in some kind of vortex or warp of energy in the place. I think this was "the Growler," a ghost who makes growling noises, but is seldom seen. He occasionally appears on the lower level of the Macomber where the shops are now. He is quite tall with long straggly hair on the sides and balding on top. He is always seen wearing a long trench coat. He got his name from the growling sounds he apparently made at some of the people who have worked in the Macomber basement shops.

In death, as in life, human beings seem to live in emotional dramas of one sort or another. These dramas can often create a haunting because after people die, they may have such a strong need to clean up unfinished emotional business that they become mired and stuck in their own internal quests.

Sometime in the mid 1930s, Sara Davis died or retired and left the New Stockton Villa to her children. It is rumored that Davis committed suicide. This is, as of yet, unsubstantiated. Davis's children leased the property, with the option to buy, to Henry Macomber. Macomber had already been managing the properties further east along Beach Avenue. According to Crystal Hardin, Macomber met Harriet Murdock Storer, the wife of an old friend from seminary school in Binghamton, New York, at his friend's funeral. The story goes that even though Macomber had a wife and family, he moved Mrs.

Storer into the Macomber, and they ran it together for many years, while having a long-term relationship. I have yet to substantiate this as well.

I have "seen" the ghost of Sara Davis several times on the stairway of the Macomber over the past few years. She always seemed to be watching over the place carefully. The night of the channeling, she came through, as did Harriet Storer. I could not tell whether Mrs. Storer was a ghost or a spirit returning from the Other Side to help with my research, which she did. Harriet Storer told me there were seven ghosts, at present, inhabiting the Macomber. From what I have channeled, I would identify them as: Sara Davis; the two servicemen John and George; Arthur from the early days of Cape May; Pinky; Miss Wright in Room 10; possibly a waitress or even Harriet herself; and a man downstairs. The Growler, as the man is called, may have been a guest, not of the hotel, but of the *drunk tank* the military had set up under the front porch of the Macomber during World War II!

I also feel that the place has residual energies of ghosts that may have moved on or simply are not active at the moment. If my theory about ghosts coming over from the Stockton is correct, then these transient souls may have moved to yet another location in Cape May. I have a strong psychic feeling that Pinky had something to do with the old Stockton Hotel. Was she one of the staff who died there during her tenure? As with Congress Hall, I cannot see why hotel guests would be haunting a place, unless they died there. We usually haunt where we lived, not where we died. Vacation spots seem to be an exception! Most of the hauntings in old hotels in Cape May are attributed to former owners or staff members. Maybe they were so dedicated to their jobs, in death as in life, it is all they know how to do.

When I was researching the story of The Merry Widow for *The Ghosts of Cape May, Book 2,* I had the chance to interview Kevin Cordes, the man who had done much of the renovation there. While we were on the topic of ghosts, Kevin told me that his family had also purchased the Hotel Macomber back in the late 1980s and had done extensive renovation to that property as well.

As it turned out, it was Cordes who encountered the ghost of the woman in period clothing roaming through the downstairs section of the building. I was glad to have finally placed the source of this old encounter.

This was the only report of that ghost anyone can remember. The former pastry chef of the restaurant also reportedly felt "pushed" by an icy hand into the walk-in freezer. The restaurant and kitchen staff told me that they experienced nothing at all. My only experience in the dining room was several years ago. A group of us were sitting enjoying our meals when the chandelier

HOTEL MACOMBER · ANNEX · MACOMBER ANNEX
CAPE MAY, NEW JERSEY

The original Macomber trio — circa 1930s. The older Macomber Annex was demolished to make way for The Camelot. The Macomber and Annex (now called The Stockton Manor) survive today. (Author's Collection)

above us started flashing and pulsing for a good 10 minutes — no other lights in the room were affected. After I spoke with Kevin, I wondered whether that woman was Sara Davis. She would have been in 1930s dress, not Victorian period clothing, as some tell the story.

In the spring of 2006 I decided to spend the night, once again, in the enchanted Room 10. The rooms had been recently renovated and the famous slamming bathroom door (and bathroom for that matter) was in a different place altogether. Room 10 is one of the best deals in town. The room is spacious, has a great breeze coming off the ocean and once the miniature golf course closes for the night and the lights are turned out, Room 10 is very peaceful. The hotel was still not too busy as it was early spring and Cape May is generally more quiet then. We had been out for drinks at my all-time favorite nightspot in Cape May, the Virginia Hotel, and we arrived back to our room about midnight. The hotel was quiet with the exception of the night manager at the front desk.

As I drifted off to sleep and sounds of the street diminished to a whisper and mixed with the soothing repetitive crash of the ocean surf, I felt completely at peace. No wonder the trunk lady loved this room so. About fifteen minutes after we had turned the lights out, I had just fallen asleep when a thundering *knock* sounded on our room door. After composing myself and getting my adrenalin at bay, I called out to see who was bothering us so late. There was no reply. Maybe just another guest going to their room I thought, as I returned to catch up on my peaceful slumber.

KNOCK went the door again! This time sounding even more impatient. I jumped out of bed and flung open the door revealing — an empty hallway. Not a living creature was stirring. After the fourth knock, I thought it best that I clear my vintage Port clouded mind, leftover from a night's partying at the Virginia, and focus on my work for a few minutes. It's so hard to enjoy good spirits with dead Spirits barging in all the time!

I thought a cassette tape recorder was in order to attempt to capture some EVPs. Back then I only carried a camera and tape recorder to document the experiences. I placed a 60 minute tape in the portable machine and hid it in the hallway behind a vase, opposite my door. The next morning, when I retrieved it, I found various odd noises on the tape. Doors could be heard opening and closing, and the sound of a woman breathing heavily popped in at one point on the tape. When I inquired about other guests on my floor, the front desk person told me we were the only ones there that evening. Who was knocking at our door all night? Miss Wright? Had I locked her out? Or was it Dead Housekeeping?

Electrical malfunctions are also a common haunting phenomenon at the Hotel Macomber. The lights have flickered and dimmed when I have done trance channeling on more than one occasion. The most humourous instance however, did not involve ghosts (I think.) I had just taken the luggage out of the car at the beginning of one of my Macomber stays. Willy and I were walking along the side of the building to check in when there was a crackling explosion and a loud *BANG*. The lights in the entire building went dark. Above us, across the street, a kite had wrapped itself over and over around the wires, pulling them together and causing a major short. The Macomber was without power for hours. On seeing me walking in the door soon after the explosion, the front desk clerk exclaimed, "I knew it."

When I first started coming to Cape May, I stayed at the Macomber quite often. I sensed residual energies throughout different parts of the building on several occasions. The hauntings here don't seem to follow a particular pattern. Although the ghost of Irene Wright seems to surface each June and November in Room 10. This is a building that has seen a lot of history and a lot of action. Even a fire claimed the top floor in 1936 that was soon rebuilt. I have not heard any recent reports from the shops downstairs about the ghost once called the Growler. Sadly, Diane's Boo-tique is now gone and has been replaced by another shop. I will have to pay the new shop owners a visit this summer to see if they have had any paranormal experiences.

When a building has stood for this long, a lot of people have come and gone. For the Macomber, much mystery still surrounds the ghosts here. I have never been able to find out what really happed to the first owner, Sara S. Davis. We also know little about the ghostly waitress that shows up in the dining room and kitchen from time to time. Even the Growler's identity is a mystery. Was he a former serviceman stationed in Cape May who had his quarters in the Macomber during World War II? Is the ghost of Room 10 really Irene Wright, or is it just a case of mistaken identity?

The Hotel Macomber has been a favorite venue in town when it comes to ghost investigations. It seems to be one of the more active haunts. As for the Macomber itself, it continues to be one of my favorite places to stay in Cape May. The prices are reasonable and so are the ghosts. Just be careful, though. If you check into Room 10, your bed may be taken! At the least, don't forget to say — "Goodnight, Irene."

Cabanas & Martini Beach

RE-TELLING A POPULAR GHOST STORY
FROM THE GHOST'S POINT OF VIEW

429 Beach Avenue, Cape May

FREQUENT VISITORS to Cape May are usually quite familiar with Cabanas and Martini Beach, two of the town's most popular watering holes, which attract both local patrons and vacationers year round. The building, on Beach Avenue and Decatur Street, is also known to be one of the most haunted places in town. This does not seem to bother the patrons, for many people love to hang around there for a few drinks and some good company, living or dead. There is one woman though, who has never "hung" at Cabanas or Martini Beach—her name is Julia, and this is *her* story.

Contrary to popular local folklore, a waitress named Gloria never hung herself after a trolley killed her daughter in front of the building on Beach Drive where she worked. In fact, her name was not even Gloria. Her name was Julia, she had a son, not a daughter, and there was NO trolley involved in either of their demises.

Why then do people keep talking about the "hanging on the third floor of Cabanas" if it never happened? Simple, a good ghost story can be twisted around over the years like a game of *telephone*, in which each party adds his own special spin to the topic.

Welcome to Julia's place and the spectral world at Cabanas and Martini Beach, and the old building that was once called *Denizot's Ocean View House.*

I had heard all of the stories over the years. According to Charlie Walters, one of the current owners of the building, the rumors began a few years back when a person taking a photograph upstairs in the building snapped a shot of the front window on the third floor and captured on film what appeared to be the ghost of a young child, standing in front of the window. From here, it seems, the story grew. Not only was there a child, but now there was a ghostly mother, who just happened to be a prostitute. Both the mother and

the daughter have been called Gloria, depending on which version of the tale you hear. One day, after escaping from her mother's watch, little Gloria ran out of the building into the street and was hit by a trolley. In grief, the mother decided the only thing to do was to hang herself in the third floor staircase.

The folks at Cabanas admit the story has been passed down and mangled so much that it holds little truth any longer. So why should anyone care about it now? As a psychic medium, I try to have compassion for ghosts. Their situations can be hopeless, or at least, very lonely. I soon realized that someone was very upset by the story, and did care about what was being said and twisted around. It was the ghost herself who was concerned, and she made a strong case to me that I needed to let her living colleagues know the truth.

I first visited Cabanas and the upstairs bar called Martini Beach while on vacation in Cape May a few summers ago. One of the servers was kind enough to take me through the place. Victor Denizot had rebuilt the building after the great fire in 1878. Denizot, who went on to build the Hotel Lafayette next door, called his new hotel The Ocean View House, which operated as a small hotel and bar.

Today, Cabanas beach bar and restaurant occupies the first floor, and Martini Beach bar and restaurant sits above it on the second floor. The old hotel rooms on the third and fourth floors are now office space and storage —and haunted.

As we moved up to the third floor, above Martini Beach, I noticed that the stairwell, where Gloria's mother is said to have ended her life, was simply not a place where anyone could easily hang, as the ceiling was too low.

I immediately sensed the ghost of a woman. She was quick on the introduction and fast to get to the point. There was NO hanging. She had been working at the hotel and trading her domestic services for food, room and board. She had a baby out of wedlock, a boy, and he was the mischievous type. She needed to work during the day. When he got old enough to walk, she was not able to keep track of his movements, and she worried as any mother would. He managed several times to get out of the room and find his way down the steep stairs of the place. To stop him she would place a chair in front of the door to keep it from opening. This part of the story seems to be the only fact to have survived the last 100+ years of retelling.

Eventually, the son, who seemed to have some sort of disability, died at a young age. She would not elaborate because it was too painful for her. Ghosts have feelings too.

Julia, as she later referred to herself, felt his ghost still walked the halls of the old Ocean View Hotel. When she eventually passed in mid-life, mother and son must have been reunited. For a reason to be revealed to me at a later time, the decision was made for them to stay on this plane. This is a decision we can all make at death, although not the right one.

"Yes," called out Karin Rickard, Martini Beach and Cabanas' general manager, from her office, "that is the true story, I think! That's more like what we heard from the people who worked here." There was more, but I sensed another ghost on the next higher floor, lurking about and quietly watching our every move.

Climbing the stairs once more, we arrived at the top floor of the old building. Even though it was in the dead of summer, I felt a cold sensation in the back of the building and sensed something looking behind a padlocked door marked with an ancient "4." Entering the room I felt the presence of an older man, long dead, who seemed to be telling me that he lived here through summer and winter, with little in the way of amenities. He seems to have worked here also.

It was time to leave. The staff was busy and I did not want to overstay my welcome. The validation from the staff that Julia's version of the story was much more accurate gave me some sense of comfort. At least I knew my psychic meter was still in working order! But there were so many questions, and we did not have any more time to spend at the site.

Why does Julia still haunt? The thought ran through my head repeatedly. Several times when I would walk on the promenade at night and glance up at the third floor windows above Martini Beach, I felt that Julia was watching me; I could feel her and hear her talking to the others — spirits with the spirits, so to speak! Who were these people? I knew they had a story to tell and a purpose for sticking around and haunting this building.

It was not until I began to write my columns for *Exit Zero* that I decided to return with some friends to the site. As luck would have it, Martini Beach had just hired a new administrative assistant, Jimmy, who was very much into spirits (the ethereal kind.) I spoke with Jimmy later, and we struck up a friendship, both having similar interests. Jimmy told me the story of server Amy, who worked at the restaurant at Martini Beach. She had seen a chair in the hallway and moved it out of the way to get through. The chair was soon back in the hallway again. On moving the chair the second time, Jimmy told me Amy heard the chair slide back to where it came from! Obviously, Julia

is *still* worried about her child falling down the stairs, or she simply wanted to keep the hallway clear. Sometimes I think Julia has fun with people who start telling the hanging story by moving the chair around to scare them. Ghosts can also have a sense of humor.

I was renewed in my quest to unlock the secrets of the ghosts of the old Ocean View House. I took Jimmy on a psychic walk-through, as I had done the previous year. Once again, Julia denied the hanging. In fact, she was quite upset about people thinking she was a suicide. She told me about her life. She originally came to Cape May one hot summer, as a teenager, from Philadelphia. She fell in love with a man she met in town, who loved to swim and run on the beach. They had an affair, and she became pregnant. On hearing the news, her father told her not to come home, that she was a disgrace to the family. Therefore, she had no choice but to stay in Cape May and find work, which she did with Victor Denizot at his hotel. These details were pieced together from psychic imagery given to me by the ghost. It is impossible to get details 100%, but I think this is her basic story.

Jimmy and I chatted in the office as I channeled the spirit of Julia. Like some of the older ghosts I have encountered, she is quite aware of what is going on in Cabanas and Martini Beach — so aware that she seems almost to be running the place! Let me give you a few examples.

Jimmy had called me to ask if I would be able to meet with Charlie and Sharleen Walters, the building's current owners. The Walters were intrigued to hear my psychic impressions of the place. I offered to take the Walters and some of the staff members through the building and to try to get the ghosts to communicate with them. Julia was more than happy to talk. She relayed through me, that the "girls at the bar" should check the fruit garnishes for the drinks. It seems that she was quite annoyed at seeing patrons get a bruised lemon peel or dented cherry!

As we sat at the bar another day, enjoying some spirits of the liquid kind, Julia caught my attention and directed us to look at a women and her husband on the other side of the bar, way out of our direct site.

"Brown fruit," I heard her say, and instructed Jimmy that she also said, "It happened again, right here." Jimmy let the bartenders know and one of the women approached the couple and asked if she could inspect their drink. The patron was a little confused as to what was going on until her lemon peel in her drink was turned over to reveal it was brown on the underside. The bartender changed the piece of fruit and the woman was heard asking how

Opposite: The ghost-driven chair at the foot of the staircase above Martini Beach.

the bartender ever noticed that tiny detail. "The ghost told us," she replied to the woman, who was now a little more shaken than her martini.

Julia has also put in a few complaints about the kitchen staff who seem to "cuss" a little too much for this Victorian woman's ears. Even though they have denied experiencing her, she is apparently trying to get them to clean up their acts by banging the pots and pans.

Julia also seems to also be able to get up close and personal with a few of the employees. One of these workers appears to have irked Julia with some bad habits one time too many. Julia told us how the man "picks his nose." (In fairness to that employee, I have been told he has allergies, and it is scratching an itch, not picking that is going on.) Julia told us, on the mini ghost tour I did with the owners and staff, that it drives her nuts when this man picks his nose, and she yanks and tugs at his hair to make him stop.

"Oh my God!" several of the girls shouted, "He *does* constantly fix his hair back there!" Later that night, while the same employee was sitting at Martini Beach, I was told he scratched his nose, and an empty Martini shaker fell on the bar in front of him without anyone near it! Julia or allergies? Hmm.

It was on this last visit that I had started to get the spelling of a name like GIL or GIUL. I thought perhaps it was a correct version of Julia's name, perhaps Giulia? Then the energy got stronger while I was channeling with Jimmy on the dance floor of Martini Beach...it was Gil... Gilbert to be exact, and he showed me that he mixed drinks and did some general maintenance around the place. Both Julia and Gilbert mentioned Victor Denizot, the original owner of the building, who had it built in 1879. I had originally sensed a man, also upstairs, with a name like Manfred, but he has since faded.

Both Gilbert and Julia seem to have stayed after their lives ended back in Victorian times. I think they keep each other company, as many ghosts will do. Ghosts have been known to congregate with each other, and in many hauntings you will find more than one ghost present. I think this is the case in this site.

As they talked of the old days and kegs of beer being stored under the building in the summer, ladies coming in through a different entrance from the bar entry, and people and time gone by, I could not help but noticing just how interactive these ghosts were. One night, while working up in Martini Beach, bartender Kerilyn went to answer the ringing phone. The phone displays the origin of all in-house calls — except this call was coming from a dark and empty kitchen on the second floor, in view of Kerilyn! She raced down to tell Ray in the Cabanas kitchen, and he laughed it off as hysteria, when suddenly HIS phone began ringing. It was now the phone at Martini Beach calling the back kitchen! Kerilyn was the only one upstairs, and when she raced down the back stairs, she left the floor empty, or did she? Maybe Julia wanted to order some food. Julia has called out Ray's name in the kitchen. Megan, another server, has also been paged, along with others who worked at the bars.

Cabanas/Martini Beach is a locale where EVPs seem to be picked up on tape more easily. When I did my walk-through with the staff and owners, we stood on the third-floor landing, talking about Julia. You can hear in the quiet of the tape a woman's voice sweetly utter "Julia." It seems to have been a validation for me, in physical form, from Julia. I consider it a special gift. She does not appear to have left any other EVPs on that tape, although a cat's meow is heard at another point! Julia mentioned she had taken in a stray cat to keep her son company. The cat would claw the carpet and walls and did quite a bit of damage.

Julia told me that the cat's meowing is often mistaken for a baby crying. Many of the staff members told me they have heard the sound of a cat or baby, so at least that mystery seems to be solved. Cape May, by the way, has its share of ghost cats. I would not be surprised to find a spectral animal rescue group in my psychic travels.

Martini Beach is also a great place for me to trance channel. After dinner there, on more than one occasion, I have slipped easily into a trance and brought through many spirits with messages for my friends who had gathered to listen. It seems that the position of the old Denizot building and the sunken remnants of the old iron pier in the surf across the street somehow magnify psychic energy to allow the ghosts (and me) to communicate more easily.

During one of my channeling sessions at Martini Beach, I first encountered the ghost of Hester Hildreth, who belongs to the Winterwood Gift shop up in Rio Grande. Maybe the ghosts, like the rest of us, enjoy the atmosphere at Martini Beach.

Electrical malfunctions, sometimes a ghost's calling card, seem to indicate Julia wants the attention of the staff. The light in the hallway of Martini Beach will often go off like a strobe light for no apparent reason. The circuit has been checked to find nothing on this plane could be affecting the lights.

While some ghosts seem to be unattached to current reality and living in some past internal drama, Julia is much more in the here and now. My

investigations in Cape May have led me to believe that the Ghost Plane is simply another plane on which a soul can exist. It exists, so nature created it for some reason. The possibilities are endless and, with this book at least, I will not get into debates about string theories or quantum physics. For now, I will simply accept the idea that Julia has found a place she likes to be.

Julia is a benevolent ghost. So is Gilbert. They just want to coexist with the living peacefully. During one final revelation, Julia explained that she would not cross over to heaven because she knew her father was waiting for her there, and she was not ready to forgive him just yet.

Next time you go to Cabanas or Martini Beach, don't forget to say "hey" to Julia and Gilbert. Since the staff now knows the true story and the folklore has been dispelled, Karin and the others have told me Julia seems to have quieted down.

Denizot's Ocean View Hotel, now Cabanas and Martini Beach, is a fabulous source of *positive* energy in Cape May. This psychic medium likes the place a lot. Julia suggested to the owners and staff that the slogan should be "Always Good Spirits." I agree wholeheartedly. She told us that she along with the current owners are only the caretakers of a building. No one owns anything forever. Positive energy from all tenant owners, past and present, has created a wonderful vortex of good feelings for all current and future patrons to enjoy! One could say that all of the stories, including this one, are unsubstantiated, but I would put my money on Julia's version. I think first-hand experience is always the best source for a good ghost story.

When I was writing the first edition of this book, Cabanas was being completely gutted and renovated in time for spring 2005. Renovation is a big motivator for ghostly activity. Tearing down walls and changing a structure seems to release residual energies that have been pent up in a place for generations. So far, the paranormal feats here have not ceased with the new decor. From a place that is already so rich with paranormal activity more exhilarating proof keeps coming forth that life does not end with death— it just begins, at Cabanas and Martini Beach!

This building never disappoints when it comes to the paranormal. Julie has been keeping busy, keeping the staff busy, since my last writings. This is a great night spot, any time of the year. Remember Julia's slogan, "Always Good Spirits." Don't just take my word for it, go and see for yourself!

Opposite: A man's ghost lurks in a forgotten room on the top floor of the old Ocean View Hotel building high above Cabanas and Martini Beach.

Columbia House

THE GHOST BAKER AND HIS HAUNTED SUITES

Guest Suites — 26 Ocean Street, Cape May

A blank tape where there should have been over two hours of recorded interviews, digital camera batteries draining on two different cameras, files disappearing off a computer. It seemed like the ghosts at Cape May's Columbia House wanted to remain anonymous. Nevertheless, let's tell the story anyway, just for fun. My engagement with Columbia House actually had nothing at all to do with ghost hunting. I was looking into ideas for summer rentals and wanted to try something different. Searching the real estate web sites in Cape May, I stumbled across a listing for Columbia House. I thought to myself, Columbia House? It couldn't still be standing after being destroyed by the great fire of 1878.

No, it was not that Columbia House, but in fact, a newer namesake built in the early 1880s on the property of the great old hotel by a local baker named William Essen. So I packed my bags and brought along my partner Willy and my assistant Pierre for a two-day trial stay.

When I saw the pictures of this beautiful, large guest house, which had been converted to weekly rental suites, I had to stop and think for a few minutes about just where the house was located. I had walked all over Cape May and never remembered seeing this beautiful home. I was quite amazed when I found out from the realtor that the house stood at one of the busiest intersections in Cape May, on the corner of Ocean and Columbia, opposite the Queen Victoria and diagonally across from the House of Royals. "Ah!" I thought, "That's why I never saw it. Every time I cross that intersection, my eye is always drawn to the haunted House of Royals and the stories of her lady ghost!"

When we arrived at Columbia House I also noticed two large trees masking the view of the front of the house. What a beautiful house to hide behind trees. The minute I saw the place, I thought this is the type of house that I LOVE to stay in, a big old Queen Anne-styled Victorian beautifully painted in period colors, turret and all. I also wondered if there might be a ghost or two lurking around.

The charming Laura Zeitler, who, along with her husband Jim, purchased Columbia House the previous year, after giving up life as restaurateurs in Pennsylvania, greeted us at the door. The Zeitlers have totally renovated and redone the inside of the Columbia House, restoring it to 19th-century elegance.

We chose to stay on the second floor in what used to be the family's bedrooms, now converted into a large suite. I am not sure at what point I let

Laura know about my occupation. Perhaps she had been reading my column or perhaps I had mentioned it when making reservations. One thing she made certain to tell me was not to tell her if I sensed any ghosts!

Owners of homes are sometimes uncomfortable when first hearing from a psychic about their "other" occupants. My job is to try to bring both parties to a mutual understanding. Fear should not be a factor in a haunting. We should first realize it is the fear of the unknown that scares us. To lose our ability to control things that happen in our own homes can be a bit unnerving. We are, by nature, control freaks. With a haunting, you have to let go. We must realize that ghosts bridge the gap between our reality and the rest of existence. The big picture is not all about us. We are only part of the equation. We must eventually come to terms with the fact that there is more to existence than what we know. Most people only realize this upon death when loved ones reappear to help them cross over. I have been there to witness this transition in friends. It gives you a completely new outlook on life and death.

Laura took us on a tour of their newly refurbished home. It was indeed something to be proud of and I could see the amount of hard work and passion that had gone into the restoration. Stepping inside Columbia House is like stepping back to a grander time.

As we ascended the great staircase to the third floor, I could sense someone hanging about. Laura opened up the door to the magnificent third floor suite with its great ocean views, and I knew immediately there was someone else with us. A strong, but friendly sort of presence, an older man I thought. I wondered if Laura had experienced anything up there.

Our suite on the second floor was equally impressive, and we settled in for the afternoon. I usually try to reserve channeling for the evening. Sometimes I am just too tired after the three-hour ride down to Cape May, and sometimes I just want to enjoy the living for a while!

When we returned that night, I sat on the couch and started to feel very relaxed. So relaxed, in fact, I started to slip into a trance. I find in places with a high amount of ethereal energy (like haunted houses) I am able to slip into a trance more easily. Do the ghosts come to me and start the process or do I meet them halfway? It is hard to say. I do know that when I spontaneously go into trance, something is happening in the energy around me to cause it.

I rarely remember the details of a trance channeling. That is why I have friends around me on investigations with tape recorders all the time! This time, however, we were not anticipating a channeling session and the two people present, Willy and Pierre, were taken slightly off guard. In the trance, I talked about a bakery and a woman named Tryphene. I apparently rambled on in the deep and weary voice of an older man who claimed to own the house. The man identified himself as Essen. Lacking anything to take notes, Pierre rushed downstairs, where Laura was staying with her son while her husband tended to business back in Pennsylvania. Pierre asked Laura from the stairs for a pad and pen and inquired if she knew the name Tryphene. Even in a trance, I can hear someone scream! Laura did not know a Tryphene, but upon hearing I was channeling a ghost, became just a little freaked out. I advised Pierre not to burden her with any more information, as I do not like to frighten anyone who may have a fear of ghosts or hauntings. Therefore, I waited to tell Jim later. (Laura is now cool with the whole thing, by the way.)

The name Tryphene kept repeating. The man talked about his legs and indicated he might have been in a wheelchair. He seemed sad about what had happened to him or his family. He was a very strong presence and had made his permanent home at Columbia House.

Local historian and Essen family genealogist, Jim Campbell, could later substantiate much of what I had channeled. Jim had written several articles on the Essen family for the Cape May County Historical Society. Some names and events I had channeled were very specific, but too personal and uneventful to have been documented in history. Most of what I channeled, including William Essen's debilitating illness that left him with one leg and wheelchair bound in his final years, gave us a very good idea of just why a man would stay behind.

William G. Essen was the son of German baker, Gerhardt Wilhelm Essen, and his Scottish wife Caroline. The elder Essen built the bakery that still stands as *La Patisserie* on Washington Street in 1872. William G. took over the bakery in 1895 and ran it until 1918 when he sold it to Carl Kokes. The senior Essen held large amounts of real estate in Cape May. He built both the Columbia House and what is now the Celtic Inn next door. William G. and his bride Tryphene Crowell, from Cape May Point, eventually lived in the house at 26 Ocean Street.

As one of Cape May's only bakers and confectioners, William G. Essen made a small fortune keeping the local hotels in bread and ice cream during the summer months. The Essen family accumulated a lot of wealth and property in Cape May and held lavish parties that graced the social pages of the local papers.

According to Jim Campbell, his health began to deteriorate in his older years and he developed diabetes. Using up vast amounts of his fortune on medical care, he eventually lost his leg to diabetes and was confined to a wheelchair. Jim told me that on William Essen's 50th anniversary with the Free Masons, the installment was held at the Essen house instead of the lodge, due to Essen's immobility.

Jim Campbell met with the Zeitlers and myself one fall afternoon on the front porch of Columbia House. Armed with old family photographs that he had acquired from Essen descendants, Jim spoke of the life and death of Cape May's great confectioner and baker, William Essen.

William G. Essen
(1857–1938)

(Courtesy of Jim Campbell)

I told Jim Campbell I was sure Essen was still in the house. I was not sure just how far he would go in the belief of the paranormal, so I let him do most of the talking. As I listened to him talk about what a strong personality William Essen was, I could see Laura occasionally throwing me a glance and cringing just a bit.

Laura was at first reluctant to talk about her experiences with her ghost. She eventually confided in me that while she did experience something a few times in the house, they had now come to a mutual understanding and were peacefully coexisting. This, folks, is the key to living anywhere with a ghost — peacefully coexist. If you start telling ghosts to "get out" or "leave the house," you will probably just get them annoyed and may never find your car keys again!

I thought about my first encounter with Mr. Essen. After the initial channeling session on the couch, I thought I had heard the last from that ghost.

It was our last night at Columbia House, and as we arrived back in our suite, I sensed someone sitting in the kitchen area. The suite was dark except for the hall light, so I carefully moved into the living room (such a silly term for a room in a haunted house, isn't it?) and made my way to the kitchen table. I could feel a presence come over me. My arm started to tingle, and I knew from years of automatic writing it was time to get a pencil and paper.

Automatic writing is a way, like trance channeling, of obtaining communications from ghosts. A medium will slip into a semi-trance state and allow the entity to direct the writing instrument. Anything can come through automatic writing. Sometimes it is legible, and sometimes it is not.

My assistant, Pierre, grabbed a pen and paper and put it in my reach. I began drawing concentric circles and finally scribbling something that was illegible. I then heard a scraping sound like something being dragged across the kitchen floor. Pierre gasped and called out to Willy. According to what he saw, one of the kitchen chairs at the opposite end of the table *slowly started moving backward*, as if *something* was getting up from the table! I kept repeating the name Tryphene, over and over again until I felt the presence lift from the room and vanish.

Jim Zeitler told me later that if there was anywhere in the house where he tended to "feel" something, it was in the kitchen area on the second floor. This may have been the Essen's master bedroom, but no one is certain. William Essen was calling out for his wife. It is sad to think that she has moved on and left him behind.

According to Jim Campbell, when William G. Essen died in 1938, he left his dear wife Tryphene, living on the edge of poverty. The properties had already been sold to raise capital, with the agreement that Tryphene could stay until her death. She finally passed in 1946 in Philadelphia, but seems to have left without her husband. Was the physical distance in her passing a factor? I did not encounter Mrs. Essen as a ghost. If she was there, she was moving under my radar screen. I cannot think of why Mr. Essen would stay behind. Guilt, perhaps, for leaving his wife destitute? It remains a mystery.

As I slept that last night on our first visit to Columbia House, something stirred me awake early in the morning. I was still half-asleep and thought I was home in my own bed. I felt what I thought was my cat, Harry, walking around the bed. I could feel the purring as he got close to my face and the light impressions of his paws walking across my legs as he often does at

*Chairs in Cape May have a way of moving by themselves—
especially when something is sitting in them.*

night. Then I woke up. I was not at home. There were not supposed to be any cats in the place, and I still felt the cat purring by my side!

In one of those embarrassing moments for a weathered psychic, I called out to Willy and Pierre for help, exclaiming there was a "ghost kitty." Sigh. Okay, even we paranormal workers get scared in the middle of the night when we are awakened from a dead sleep! The ghost cat vanished, and Willy noted the time as exactly 3 AM. Many hauntings take place between 3 AM and 5 AM. The fact that everyone is quiet and asleep has a lot to do with it, but I also think it has something to do with the ghosts themselves. I don't think they sleep in the same way we do. Maybe they are all night owls, enjoying a people-free world! Maybe they don't sleep at all.

Laura later confirmed that the previous owners, Bob and Barbara Dagget, told them that several guests of theirs had encountered the cat ghost of Columbia House. The phantom feline is thought to be Alex, a house cat who belonged to the owners before the Daggets, but was cared for by the Daggets until he died. Alex was buried in the side yard until landscapers inadvertently may have disinterred and reburied his ashes. At least poor Alex was safe and dead inside the house when this travesty occurred.

Just another Cape May cat ghost experience, and Cape May has lots of them. The reason very few people experience cat ghosts is they create sounds and effects that simply come off as everyday house noises.

When summer finally arrived that year and I was greeted by a long awaited vacation at the beach, we arrived in Cape May to find Columbia House brimming with guests. My duties as The Ghost Writer for *Exit Zero* had kept me busy on every trip to Cape May during the year, but I was determined not to do any ghost or psychic work, at least for that week!

One warm afternoon, I left the book I was reading on the front porch and decided to take a walk to the beach. I stopped by Leith Hall to engage in a little historical chat with proprietor Elan Zingman-Leith. We had previously stayed at the lovely Leith Hall, and I was well acquainted with Elan. At some point Elan asked where I was staying, and I told him Columbia House.

"Oh, they are supposed to have a ghost... on the third floor, a man I think, and he can have a little bit of an attitude, at least that is what the previous owner used to tell me, but she said they came to a mutual understanding after a while."

It was gold to a ghost investigator's ears! Not only did I now have proof that there was a previous history of a haunting at the place, but it was a man with an attitude, our own Mr. Essen!

Laura was surprised to hear the news. She and Jim had thought they felt something in the house when they were first looking to buy it, but the previous owners had told them they really didn't think the house had a ghost. (Can you picture Mr. Essen in a corner of the room smiling and nodding his approval at the former owners as they were speaking?) Like many of Cape May's haunted businesses, people have a lot of money invested in a place that they feel may be jeopardized by talk of a ghost. This is not the case at all. If there is a ghost, people are usually more interested in hearing about it than not.

Now, I had my ghost. I returned to our downstairs suite and exclaimed into the house, "So you are a man with an attitude, aye?" Big mistake. I went to turn on my digital camera to take a few interior shots, and the batteries went dead, after I had just recharged them. Picture taking was out. I turned in for the night with a good book and eventually fell asleep.

Around 4 AM, I was awakened to the sound of something sliding around the room on the floor. I began to hear a beeping sound, sat up in bed, and saw the air conditioner temperature reading changing from 70 degrees up to 90 degrees! I grabbed the remote control for the unit next to my bed, turned the unit off, and back on again. I assumed it was a power failure. In a few minutes, it started beeping again. This time the temperature reading said 48 degrees! Just a wee bit chilly for sleeping indoors. I got out of bed to adjust the unit manually when it turned itself off completely. The minute I fell back to sleep, it came back on with about 20 beeps and started changing from high fan to low fan while flashing a temperature of 32 degrees, something I do not think room air conditioners normally do!

At this point in a haunting, a psychic medium needs to eat white crow. I yelled, "Okay, you are not a nasty old ghost with an attitude, I'm sorry!" I capitulated. Essen did not. He really knew where to get me, heat. I HATE the heat, and live in nice *cold* air conditioning in the summer, and it was hot that night. The air conditioner shut off for good. I unplugged it to make sure and fell back asleep. Luckily, it was our last night at Columbia House, and I could sneak out the next morning while Jim and Laura were cleaning the upstairs suite. I did leave them a detailed note, omitting the part about the ghost until after I got back my security deposit!

Months later when I recalled the story in the kitchen of the same suite with the Zeitlers, Jim Campbell and Sue Tischler and Stephanie Madsen from CapeMay.com, I noticed something strange happening behind Laura. The microwave time was changing from 11:30 to 40:80, then to all kinds of bizarre numbers. "I've never seen it do that before!" Laura exclaimed to the group. Ghosts do have a way with numbers. At least it was only the micro-wave this time and not the air conditioner!

As we moved the group to the front parlor of the Columbia House, Jim and Laura talked of how much they loved the house. You just have to take one look at the place to see what a magnificent job they did restoring it. I could sense Mr. Essen, wheeling himself through the bedroom to the open-ing of the doors to the parlor.

"He most likely lived his last few years on this floor, being confined to a wheelchair." Jim Campbell told us. "He also died here." I know Laura did not need to hear that, but it was inevitable someone was going to ask the ques-tion, and Jim answered it.

I could see Essen, laughing now, as if he were really enjoying the new "kids" who were running his place. I could sense he was content and maybe eventually would pass on and join Tryphene. Laura told me recently things have been quiet at the old Essen place. She also accused me of making her ghost out to be too wishy-washy! Her kids were apparently complaining that other people in town have better and scarier ghosts. I told her I was sorry. There were some scary ghosts in Cape May, but an ice cream store owner in a wheelchair - not a chance. Wait - I think I just heard my air conditioner beep.

Columbia House is one of my favorite spots to spend a summer vacation or a fall weekend in Cape May. While I had experienced stronger energies in the third floor Turret Suite, I had never actually stayed there until this past autumn. It was Halloween weekend and I was doing my *Ride with the Ghost Writer* trolley tours and the Columbia House was conveniently located near the trolley stop. After years of hearing about all the activity in the third floor suite, Willy and I finally decided to give it a try ourselves.

Folks, this guest suite is one of the hidden gems of Cape May! At pres-ent, it would have to rank #1 as my favorite room in Cape May. There are many great places in which to spend a night or two in town, but this third floor suite is both luxurious and charming at the same time. Did I mention haunted?

There must have been 50-mph winds the night we came down for Hal-loween weekend in 2006. Laura Zeitler checked us in to the Turret Suite and told me not to start trouble and stir up any ghosts. I asked her if she had a *Ouija Board*® that I could borrow (Just kidding.) The suite on the third floor spreads out over two bedrooms, a living room, kitchen and two baths. The part of the suite that drew my attention was the master bedroom that had a sitting area in the top of the turret with a small table and chairs.

I actually *did* comment to Laura what a great séance table it would make — she was not amused. I told her I was just kidding, but she knew better. As I sat at the séance table that night — wait we aren't there yet.

As I walked around the large bedroom and set my things down I could sense a presence come immediately into the room and move behind me. I thought, wow, that was fast, as the ghosts usually take a little time to warm up to people.

This was not the ghost of Mr. Essen. Instead, it was the ghost of *Mrs.* Essen, a spirit I had yet to encounter in the house. Tryphene Essen moved around the room with a welcoming energy. I laid down on the bed and closed my eyes to try to better communicate with her. Her message was brief, we were to be left alone and she would move to another part of the house to give us privacy. At first I thought this was a wonderful gesture, but then Willy and I began to feel as if we had pushed her out.

That night, as I sat with a tape recorder running at my nifty makeshift séance table in the turret, I asked the ghosts of the house if they would like to join us. The house was quiet. The wind was about all that could be felt or heard. Where were the Essens? After about 20 minutes, I sat back and opened up my psychic line to try to expand it trough the entire house. I send out this signal to ask the ghosts to come forward. They decide whether or not they feel like replying to my invitation. The Essens — were definitely out. Something else began to tug at my psychic line at that point. It was a younger boy in his late teens. I concentrated on the energy and made sure it was not malevolent (it was not) and then allowed the connection to happen.

The boy seemed to climb up the side of the house and come through the wall. He sat at my table. With the lights out I could see a dark shadowy figure in the chair across from me. The ghost told me he lived across the street, that his name was Joseph and he had died. He gave me the image of the house next to The Queen Victoria, what they call the Prince Albert Hall today.

I later figured out this boy was the ghost of Joseph Smith Higbee Gregory (1863-1879), Douglas Gregory's teenage son. He had been washed overboard while working on a pilot boat in his sixteenth year. His father had not yet built the Queen Victoria or Prince Albert houses, but the ghost of young Joseph Gregory must have been following the family and moved with them to the new house in 1882. He seems to roam the area in search of (living) friends. Just another ghost in a very haunted town.

The Ugly Mug

WHERE THE DRINKING AGE IS 21 TO 121

426 Washington Street (Mall), Cape May

I
T WAS a dark and stormy night... how many times have you heard THAT line in classic ghost stories? So what is it about storms and nighttime that has so many ghosts acting up? Thunderstorms are not just effective ambience for a haunting. Some in the field feel that excess humidity and static electricity from a thunderstorm may enhance hauntings. As I have said in previous chapters, when the air is filled with negative ions found in lightning, ghosts seem to be able to manifest much more easily.

It was indeed a dark, stormy, and cold night when I first visited The Ugly Mug, the perennial bar at the corner of Decatur and Washington Streets. A patron, who told me that the servers were afraid to go up stairs after 9 PM, had tipped me off about the ghostly activity. I decided to show up late one March evening when Cape May was (literally) a ghost town.

MaryAnn Riley, the night manager, and Mary Sexton, the server, greeted us. Both women were anxious to see what a psychic would pick up inside the building. You see, Mary would *not* go upstairs anymore, day or night. I first interviewed MaryAnn about what she had experienced. The Ugly Mug has been a bar for more than 60 years in Cape May and has seen its share of patrons come and "go." The activity I sensed was happening upstairs, on the higher floors. "Yes," stated Mary rather nervously, "that's where the ghost throws the boxes at me when I try to walk down the kitchen hallway." It seems some rather large bread and banana boxes have dislodged from their stacks every so often as the girls make their way back downstairs!

I climbed the old staircase up to the second floor, where I found a labyrinth of winding hallways, doors, equipment and just about everything else one would find in a restaurant and bar storeroom. We experience the image of a ghost with our minds, not our eyes. If one does spot a ghost, then called an apparition, one will see it with his or her mind's eye. The only thing we *might* see with our eyes is a shadowy image that quickly moves past us, or we may catch a glimpse of something out of the corner of our eyes. I pick up my visions of ghosts in my head. Ghosts are all about energy, and it is with

the energy that they can communicate with us. Their thoughts are broadcast on a frequency some mediums can tune into and understand. The broadcast that evening was not coming from the kitchen this time, but from a higher floor. As I reached the third floor, I was relieved to see the place was a completely renovated apartment. The clutter and disorienting passageways had been left behind on the lower floor. The third floor had a livable feel — even if the person there was not living at all. I tried channeling in the living room section of the apartment, but the energy was calling me to come down the long, dark hallway.

As we made our way down the dark hallway (there was only one light in a bathroom at the end of the hall), I noticed how cold and damp it was. The wind was howling outside, and it was starting to rain again. A middle bedroom, now used to house fishing equipment, gave off quite the opposite feeling to all of us. It was warm and comfortable, even though the heat on the upper floor was turned off!

The top floor of The Ugly Mug is a world of its own. The noisy kitchen and vast storage rooms below give the third floor the feeling of an isolated oasis. The floor had an eerie calmness about it. At one point this floor was living quarters, though the most recent tenant said he had experienced nothing while living there.

My assistant began to snap a series of pictures in the dark, using a flash. Almost all of the photos yielded orbs, the balls of light some associate with spirit energy. Orbs are usually just light refractions. In this case, I would have to agree with those orb folks, because the room had a feeling that made me suspect that we were far from being alone.

Psychically, in the dark and lonely room, I picked up a boy saying, "My name is Dan... Danny... Danny Boy" in a half serious, jovial kind of tone. He was young, maybe in his mid-teens, and he had died in some kind of accident. I could see in my mind that he had two broken legs. It seems he was working on a building, and he slipped, fell, and perhaps even died.

Danny came across to me as a kind soul. He talked about "living" in the room we were standing in, or in whatever room used to be there. He mentioned working nearby. He also spoke quite slyly about secretly watching the "girls change their tops!" Now for a ghost, remember time has no meaning. These "girls" he is referring to may now be ladies, senior citizens or dust. However, I had a feeling we were more in the contemporary with this young man.

Upon my telling the story of the boy's ghost to MaryAnn and Mary, poor Mary gasped with horror. It seemed that *she* and the other girls often changed into their uniforms in the third floor bathroom at night! Obviously,

Danny keeps a keen eye on the goings on at the Mug, and has noticed the girls more than once. I chose not to reveal the fact that Danny mentioned one of the girls had an interesting birthmark or tattoo on her side, for fear of all of them suddenly quitting!

Danny admitted to throwing the boxes "once" and having "fun" with the girls, but said he had some help. Maybe some of the kitchen staff was also playing ghostly tricks on their living counterparts.

You must understand, from this ghost's point of view, he is a lonely teenager who thinks and acts like a teenager, even if he is probably now over 100 years of age!

I tried to get Danny to tell me something about where and, most importantly, when he lived. Ghosts seem to avoid the question of *when* the most. Perhaps it upsets them to think of being stuck for such a long time. Just how long WAS Danny hanging about the eves in The Ugly Mug? I would later find out.

"Pharmacy—I work in the pharmacy—for Mecray" (at least that is what it sounded like in my mind.) He told me "Mr. Sawyer just had an accident there—died—right on the sofa by the counter, then again in the toilet." I was not sure just which Sawyer he was talking about, because I was under the impression that Henry Sawyer (of the Chalfonte) had died and was thought to be haunting his home across town. "Lots of wagons and flowers, I had to deliver lots of flowers, got paid ten cents." If I could determine who the Sawyer was, then I could date the event and hopefully Danny's life.

Danny also complained to me about the "noisy men" at the bar down below. It seems two patrons were making a racket every night after closing and sat at the far corner of the bar all night. He told me they keep him awake. He also told me, "I think they are dead!"

Here is an interesting paradox I have only encountered once before (at the former Inn at Journey's End on Columbia Avenue) in Cape May, a ghost complaining a place has ghosts! It is commonly thought that ghosts can see each other and many times socially interact. There are those, however, who think that ghosts cannot see each other and do not interact at all. I agree with the former group.

I soon made my way out of the room with my partner Willy and *Exit Zero* publisher, Jack Wright. As we moved up the hall toward the bathroom with the light, we heard a loud crash. We quickly returned to "Danny's room" and saw one of Ugly Mug owner Bob Ransom's heavy deep-sea fishing rods lying in the middle of the room.

The fishing rods had heavy reels on them, which kept them weighted against the wall. One of the rods had flung itself, against gravity, out into the middle of the room!

"This is just incredible... but people will think it sounds so hokey when you tell them," Jack quipped as we decided to head down to the bar, rather quickly.

Gathered around the bar, MaryAnn offered us a round of drinks and poised herself to hear "the ghost story." I told her about the two ghosts at the bar. I also told her they were present at that moment and pointed to where I felt their "energy" or presence at the end corner of the bar. "One is named Junior, and he is talking to a Phil," I told them.

"Oh my God!" exclaimed MaryAnn, "there WAS a Junior, and I think his brother was PHIL!"

I think I now had everyone's attention. The wind started howling again, and suddenly there was a loud banging on the outside window. One of the awning poles had suddenly pulled apart, and the pipe was ramming the window with enough force to smash it. Jack went to secure it as best he could as I continued my "chat" with Junior and Phil.

According to the owners at the time, Bob and Lisa Ransom, Junior and Phil were senior customers, living at Victorian Towers in the 1970s. They both passed in the early '80s. They were regulars who sat exactly where I saw them sitting almost every night on the far corner of the bar by the front door.

At this point, I told Jack that his Scottish grandfather was coming through from the Other Side and wanted to buy him a drink. (He was a spirit who crossed over and came back, not a ghost who was stuck.) He suggested Campari and soda with only THREE ice cubes. Jack said it tasted disgusting and the three cubes referred to the fact that in Scotland drinks are served with very little ice. As Jack sipped his drink, the silence of the room was suddenly shattered by the bar's jukebox turning itself on and playing "I Drink Alone." The jukebox had been silent the hour or so we were there.

"That's song number 6507," noticed Jack surveying the machine. "I was born in July of 1965!" Cosmic mail from his grandfather?

Suddenly, Mary screamed at the top of her lungs from the dining area that adjoins the bar. A chair at one of the tables, far away from where she was cleaning, threw itself backwards on to the floor with a crashing thunder. Did Danny decide to join us for a bite to eat? Junior and Phil had absolutely nothing to say to me but a nod, as if to say, "Hello." So, I decided to let things rest, as it seemed I had stirred up all three ghosts of the Ugly Mug and was

Opposite: The Ugly Mug on Decatur and Washington (left) across the street from the former Marcy & Mecray's Pharmacy (right.)

now attracting MORE from the street. Ghosts can sense my energy. I am like the flame, and they are the moths. I quickly extinguished the flame. The Ugly Mug did not need another ghost that night.

I thought it time to do a little research into Danny's past. No one at the bar could remember just where a Mecray's Drug Store was, but it WAS nearby we determined. I called a friend in town, who keeps a small library of historical books and maps of old Cape May on hand for just such research and reference. (You can just never tell when someone dead will show up at your door and need to be identified.) I told him the story of Sawyer and the pharmacy, and although it did not ring a bell yet, he would look it up in the morning. He had a hunch the pharmacy was right across the mall from the Mug, where the clothing shop now resides.

The next evening, I got the information I was hoping for, and more. My friend was able to research an article written about Colonel Henry Sawyer's life. It shed light on what Danny had told us. Sawyer was not feeling well one day, and his doctor was out of town. He went with friends to see the pharmacist, who was also a doctor, at his drug store on Washington Street for some mint tonic for his sick stomach and chest pressure. While in the bathroom he passed out and fell to the floor. The doctor got him up and brought him to the sofa where he died from the massive heart attack... in front of Danny perhaps? Marcy and Mecray's Drug Store was RIGHT across the street from The Ugly Mug, which at the time was a haberdashery shop. The date was October 16, 1893, and now I realized that *Danny Boy* had been around for more than 100 years, hanging out with the folks at The Ugly Mug for the last 60 or so!

Both Lisa and Bob Ransom remembered Junior and Phil, but they also admitted neither had really experienced much in the way of paranormal activity in the Mug. I would imagine that since they were the proprietors, and very amiable ones at that, the ghosts simply coexist with them and respect what they are doing. Again, this is something everyone needs to know about hauntings and ghosts — they just need to be allowed to coexist in the same space. Most of the time you will not even realize they are there, unless of course you happen to sit on one of their bar stools while they are enjoying a drink!

The Mug has also had its share of electrical problems. One afternoon, while I was doing a little lunch/channeling session with Lisa Ransom, the lights in the dining room were going nuts. They would dim down, then flare up, and flicker on and off again. Lisa and Bob have told me they had electricians in to check the circuits out several times and replaced the dimmers, but nothing seems to help. By the way, when I finished channeling for Lisa, the lights returned to normal.

KAHN'S UGLY MUG—BAR — CAPE MAY, NEW JERSEY

Postcard from the early days of Sam Kahn's Ugly Mug.
Even back then — Danny was still a ghost!
(Author's Collection)

Bob told me that in more than one instance, staff has gone into the bathrooms downstairs, only to have the lights switched off on them once they are inside the stall! Danny playing more tricks on the staff? I love the atmosphere of "The Mug," as the locals affectionately call it. Ghosts and all.

I am not sure if Danny came with the place or moved in after the building was built. The land at the corner of Decatur and Washington has seen quite a few changes. The Ugly Mug sits on the site that was originally occupied by one of Cape May's earliest hotels called The American House, which was completely destroyed in the August 1869 fire. The next building on the spot was a smaller house owned by the O'Bryan sisters. Danny *might* be a relative of theirs.

Next time you stop by for a drink at The Ugly Mug on Washington Street, take a look at the ceiling. Members' personalized beer mugs line the place from front to back. When a member dies, their mug is turned out, facing the sea. It might be a good idea to raise your glass to the departed Mug patrons. You never know when you might be sitting on one.

The Whilldin-Miller House

The Whilldin-Miller House

A HISTORIC GEM WITH GHOSTS TO BOOT

Currently incarnated as Copper Fish on Broadway
416 Broadway, West Cape May

NEW NAMES, OLD GHOSTS. I first noticed the beautiful Victorian cottage on South Broadway in West Cape May when I was vacationing in the 1960s at my Aunt Ella and Uncle Bob's, who lived in North Cape May. Broadway was the route we used to get to the beach each day. I think the building may have been an antique shop during that time, as the old structure has had many incarnations.

A few years ago, passing by the property after a long absence from Cape May, I noticed the beautiful old house was now a restaurant called Daniel's. One night my partner Willy and I decided to give the place a try and thus began a long love affair with what became my favorite dining spot in town, which is really saying something given the quality we have here.

It was a beautiful late summer night when we invited a group of friends to join us at Daniel's for dinner. We were seated in the upstairs dining room of the house. I immediately sensed the presence of the ghost of a middle-aged woman roaming about. At the time, we were more in the eating and socializing mode than ghost investigation mode, so I decided to wait on the spirits until after dinner.

However, it is hard to keep a good medium down. Even at dinner, my first question before "Can we see a menu" is always, "Do you have any ghosts?"

The answer from our waiter was, "Yes, a woman is said to haunt the second-floor rear part of the house." Nothing makes me happier then to find a restaurant that has both great food AND ghosts, as is the case with Daniel's.

After dinner, I conducted an impromptu channeling session for everyone at the table. My friends Walt and Patti Melnick from the "enchanted" Sea Holly Inn had joined us, and I was in the middle of connecting with Walt and Patti's relatives on the Other Side when I felt a presence behind the wall next to us. It turns out that what is now a bathroom on the second floor (the room behind the wall) has seen some activity over the years.

Next, our server took me on a little tour of the place. As we finished the walk around, we encountered Liz, the hostess, looking VERY shaken by the front desk. It seems a "shadowy man" had walked by the front window and then past the front door. When Liz had rushed out to tell him that he had missed the entrance to the restaurant, he simply vanished! There was no one in the yard at all and no cars leaving the parking lot. The person seemed to be a phantom that simply disappeared into the ethers, somewhere on the front porch. Had my channeling stirred the dead at Daniel's? It would not be the last time this was to happen.

Historically known as the Whilldin-Miller House, the rear section of the building is one of the oldest dwellings in Cape May. Wills, deeds and physical evidence suggest that Joseph Whilldin, Jr. erected the earliest part of the house, built with heavy timber frame construction, between 1711 and 1718. His father, Joseph Whilldin, Sr. had come from Yarmouth, Plymouth Colony, Massachusetts before 1678. He, along with some of the earliest settlers in Cape May, bought land from the Native American Indians and set up whaling businesses. Many, like Whilldin, came from Long Island, New York and New England.

According to records, the Whilldin-Miller House represents the first new settlement by a Whaler Yeoman family on the "ocean side" of Cape May. It was about this time that the colony of New England Town or Townbank was eroding and washing into the Delaware Bay, and people needed to relocate.

The oldest, southwest portion of the house has a stunning, open-hearth fireplace with a warmer oven on the side (apparently the only example in Cape May). The large, odd-sized planks used for the floor were salvaged from the wrecks of ships that washed up on the beaches back then. This is the most active part of the building, and the place where I always request a table for dinner.

Jonas Miller, who is now haunting Congress Hall, expanded the house in the 1860s. Miller added a Victorian cottage addition, which became the front of the house. His daughter and her family eventually lived there.

I have been researching the ghost(s) of the Whilldin-Miller House for the past several years. One night, while trying a slightly different dining location, I was seated in the southern parlor in the newer section of the house. As we sat near one of Daniel's working fireplaces, the staff was eager to tell me of a ghostly experience that occurred just minutes after our arrival. A large, heavy base lamp on the sideboard in the old section hallway had picked itself up and fallen on to its side, smashing the bulb. I had seen the flash, but assumed, as there were many other diners, someone simply snapped a picture. Not the case.

During the course of my dinner, I had a bird's eye view of the same sideboard. There was a thud about halfway through dinner that drew my gaze in that direction.

I looked up, and there before my eyes (and Jeremy the waiter's) was a bottle of wine rolling off the marble top of the sideboard. It fell but did not break. He was nowhere near the sideboard when it happened. Minutes later, one wine glass and then a second fell over and crashed to the floor. Same sideboard, same circumstances.

No one was near it. I walked over with the staff, and we tried to move the heavy sideboard to see if maybe some vibration was dislodging things. The sideboard is solid as a rock and nothing was about to jar it. Nothing except maybe a ghost or two.

"Mr. McManus," said one of the wait staff, "this stuff only happens now when you come to dine with us!" Could the ghosts of Daniel's simply have been happy to see me? On the other hand, were they using my energy to manifest their actions? It is possible that some form of psychokinesis (PK) was in motion. PK happens when an individual or a ghost uses energy to manipulate things on our physical plane, sometimes consciously, sometimes not. In some cases, ghosts can use our energy to get things done. Classic poltergeists are not ghosts at all, but distressed people using their own PK to move objects and create sounds.

After a long dinner with friends one night, I started to do a little spontaneous channeling to see if I could make contact with the ghosts at large. First, an entity claiming to be "King Nummy" showed up. Nummy was one of the last Chiefs of the Leni-Lenape community in Cape May in the early days. Joseph Whilldin had actually bought the original larger tract of property from the local Indian tribe in the 1600s. King Nummy mentioned people were buried all around the area. I knew this for a fact as several homeowners in the West Cape May vicinity had found ancient skeletal remains in their yards over the years. Most of the entities I channeled that night were spirits, not ghosts, who had passed over and had come back to give me guidance and information.

Others soon followed. A Mrs. Leaming came through, who I think may have been much more current an individual than I realized at the time. She started to tell me all about the history of the place, and that Leamings were involved with the house. A few weeks later, when Daniel's owner and chef Harry Gleason lent me the historical documents for the house, I was able to confirm that the Leamings were involved with the property for a time.

Many of Cape May's old-timers seemed to be buzzing around the ethers that night. Names like Hand, Cox and I do believe Whilldin, all came through in my channeling session. Finally, a much stronger, or should I say more localized, energy appeared to me by the back stairs. It was a woman with long flowing dark blond hair. She gave me a name like Catherine. She also mentioned the Leaming family. She did not say her name was Leaming but that she was from that line.

Catherine told me she just wanted to be part of the crowd, recognized and not left out. Just like Julia, the ghost of Cabanas, she wanted the people who now own and work at Daniel's to acknowledge her existence. She stayed a while and then moved back up the stairs to the attic in the old part of the house. I guess it is less busy up there.

The booklet that Harry Gleason gave me, which was actually the nomination for the building to the *State and National Registers of Historic Places*, painstakingly prepared by Joan Berkey in 2002, has been an indispensable guide to Daniel's "past lives." All of the former owners of the building are mentioned, but not their family members.

There was not one mention of a Catherine anywhere in the booklet. Was she someone's daughter, or a servant perhaps of a family who owned the place? To date I have not been able to identify Catherine, though I've asked her to tell me about herself many times.

Catherine started up again on a later visit. We were a large group of 10 that night, so we had the entire back room to ourselves. I don't think we even finished our appetizers, when Jeremy our waiter rushed in to tell us that Beth, another server, had just been walking toward the back hall when she saw the same lamp (with the heavy, weighted base) toss itself off the sideboard and crash and blow out the light bulb.

This time I decided to take a few folks from our party and examine the sideboard.

We all tried to shake the lamp and make it fall over, but could not. We all determined the sideboard simply does NOT vibrate! So what or who knocked over the lamp? Was I ignoring Catherine again?

As half of our group went out to smoke before dessert, my friend Vicki Miller, who was dining with us that evening, expressed her frustration about never being able to see an actual haunting in action, even though they own the haunted Windward House on Jackson Street! "I just wanna see some s*** happen!" she called out. No sooner did another friend and I tell her NOT to ask for things to "happen," when a SWISH of air was heard and a blur of light was seen behind us, followed by a metallic sounding clanking noise by the fireplace.

We all jumped from our seats and found a fork had fallen off a table in the corner of the room. Not anything unusual, except the fork was bent in half! Sure enough, on the table, far out of everyone's reach, a dessert fork was missing. Did Catherine want dessert? Or was she just answering Vicki's request?

Catherine did not say, and Vicki said little else that night! You know the old saying, "Call upon a stone... and it will answer." It did.

Ghosts, or apparitions as paranormal investigators call them, usually manifest themselves in some way. Most of the time it is only in the form of audible footsteps, or doors opening or closing. Sometimes, like at Daniel's, there is physical manifestation. There have been no reported sightings of the ghosts of The Whilldin-Miller House. They find other ways to manifest and they certainly can interact with the living. I see Catherine in my mind's eye — she does not physically appear to me. Can she use my energy to move objects? Perhaps. It does seem like the place has been active recently, only when I have been there, but not every time I have been there either.

Catherine has also apparently been haunting the place for many, many years. At the time I was first writing about the house, I had called Cape May's "most knowledgeable person" Bob Elwell on other ghostly matters. Mentioning I was currently working on the Daniel's piece, he said I had to speak to his wife Jane, who had spent many summers at the house when she was growing up. It seemed Jane had a few ghost stories of her own to tell about the place.

"My mother, Jean Kirby, knew Olivia and Colonel Henry Regar who owned the house from the 1930s until the 1960s," Jane told me. "I called them Aunt Olivia and Uncle Henry, even though they were only good friends of the family. We stayed on the second floor and Aunt Olivia and Uncle Henry ran an antique shop on the first floor. One morning, as my mother came downstairs and sat in a rocker to have coffee, she heard the sound of metal clanking, like coins being dropped into a tin can. She thought it was only noise from outside and did not bother to tell anyone. The next day she heard the noise again, but this time she also heard a woman counting along with it... like 'One hundred one, one hundred two'... We had been told that old Mrs. Fow (the previous owner) still haunted the place."

Jane Elwell told me it was in the 1950s when this occurred. Could it be Mrs. Fow? Researching the name, I found Oscar Fow and his wife Jennie (not Catherine, unfortunately) had lived in Philadelphia. He was a butcher and distiller, and they summered, as did the Regars, at the house. Either Jennie Fow is using an alias, or Catherine is sharing the haunting duties with her. Whoever the ghost(s) are at the Whilldin-Miller House, they have been active for a long time.

Now, about the phantom man spotted in the front and backyard over the years. Several times upon leaving the restaurant, I sensed the ghost of a man in the back parking lot. A ghost of a man would try to lead me towards an image of a hole in the ground and then disappear. I assumed there must have been a well on the property that had since been filled in. Did he fall and die in the well? Those I asked knew nothing of a well on the property, and I simply forgot about the issue, until recently. While reading the booklet Harry Gleason gave me, I happened to notice a little excerpt of an article from 1954 about the house.

According to the *Cape May Star and Wave's* 100th anniversary brochure, published in 1954, the owners of the "Fow House," as it was then called, had unearthed a stone marker bearing the date 1713 while digging in the garden. They apparently also unearthed the body of a French soldier. King Nummy was right! But what was a French soldier doing in Cape May in 1713? Shipwrecked perhaps?

There is another story that the old house was used as a refuge for ailing and injured Revolutionary War soldiers, but this has never been substantiated. Is the phantom man a French soldier or perhaps an American soldier from the revolution who died at the house or in the area?

The ghosts of the Whilldin-Miller House are used to change. Any ghost that has resided between here and the Other Side for any amount of time must eventually come to grips with the fact that the only thing that is static in their environment are ghosts. With a house this rich in local history, there are bound to be a few ghosts hanging around. We are lucky enough at this time to have that place be a public venue. And a great public venue at that!

As I mentioned in the chapter on the Windward House, I met the late historian and Cape May native, Walt Campbell after I published the first

The Whilldin-Miller House in the 1930s when it was called The Fow House,
named for Oscar and Jennie Fow, owners of the old home until 1930.
What is left of the oldest 1711-1718 section of the building is seen to the left with
large chimney and the porch facing west. (Walt Campbell Collection)

edition of this book and was working on *Book 2*. Walt had one of the most impressive collections of postcards and historic pertaining to historic Cape May. Walt was kind enough to lend me pieces from his collection for *Book 2*, so I returned to his doorstep to ask for his help to add some pictorial history to this second edition of *Book 1*. Walt's Grandmother, Edith Stites Homan, was born in the house on the corner of Sunset Avenue and Broadway, where the 7-11 now stands. Walt told me that she remembered, from her childhood, that the Cape Island Creek used to come right past the old Whilldin-Miller house, and people would row their boats from Schellinger's Landing all the way to Broadway and right up to the garden in back of the house! Walt also related some fond childhood memories of the house when it was boarded up and abandoned in the 1930s and 1940s.

"When I was a teenager, now living back in Cape May we would quite often go by the Fow House on Broadway which had been vacant for years, but we were always afraid to go on the porch and look in the window, as the place always had an aura about it. Perhaps it was because of stories of someone being buried in the backyard many many years ago, but regardless we never had the courage to go any closer than the sidewalk. Was it haunted — who knows?" - *Walt Campbell*

Harry Gleason closed Daniel's after the 2005 season to concentrate on his other restaurant in town, the Island Grill. Fortunately, the building did *not* become condos as rumored, and another restaurant opened under the name, The Moonfish Grill. The decor has changed and the menu is lighter with more seafood and sushi now being featured. Many of the staff members have remained from the Daniel's era. The ghosts have also decided to remain behind and keep the staff company!

Willy and I paid a visit to The Moonfish Grill during their first week of operation in the summer of 2006. Chita, one of our favorite waiters, was now the Manager of the restaurant. He and the other staff members are always delighted to see me, because something always happens when I am there. The famous rocking lamp was gone and most of the familiar Daniel's props had been replaced. As we waited for our food to arrive, I sat at the table and asked the ghosts to let me know if they were around. Our waiter stood waiting by our table with anticipation. Nothing happened. I told the ghosts, with Willy listening, "Flicker the lights if you are here." Nothing happened.

About half an hour later, as we were eating our steaks and talking with some patrons at the next table, the light suddenly began to flicker violently, this went on for about 45 seconds. The lights dimmed to almost nothing and then returned to normal. One of the waiters rushed into the dining room to congratulate me for "doing it again." I felt pretty impressed until I later learned that the lights had gone out all the way up to Stone Harbor! Hmm... Maybe I don't know the power of my own transmitter! Of course, it could just be a wild coincidence.

As of this writing, the restaurant is now called Copper Fish on Broadway. I have yet to get back and test the menu at the latest incarnation of a restaurant in the old Whilldin-Miller home. It has been a few years now since my last visit. I wonder if the ghosts will still recognize me?

Next time you visit here, close your eyes and take in the view, the paranormal view that is, for this spot has layers of old Cape May history—and old Cape May ghosts.

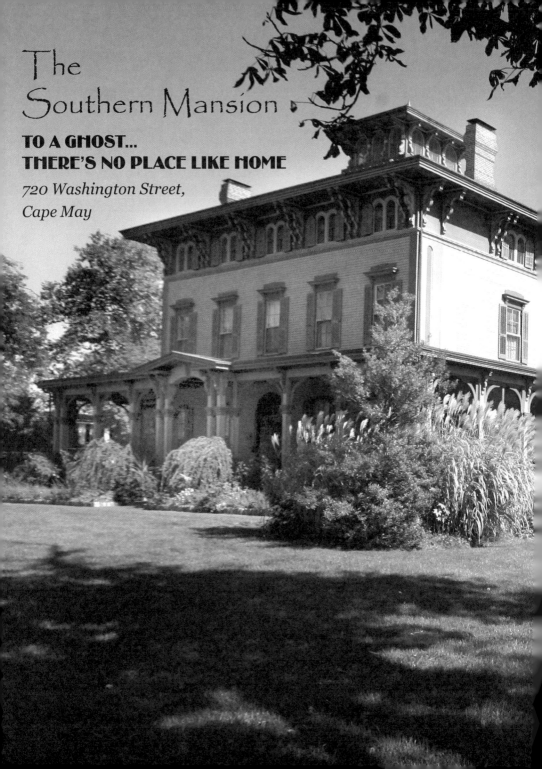

The Southern Mansion

TO A GHOST...
THERE'S NO PLACE LIKE HOME

720 Washington Street,
Cape May

"THIS HOUSE IS OURS...this house is ours..." repeats Nicole Kidman's character in the final scene of the great paranormal thriller *The Others*. Kidman's character is the ghost of a mother who, along with her two children, refuses to leave her home. This is quite a common phenomenon in the paranormal world. Many ghosts remain stuck by their own doing, holding on to some material thing through life and death. This is truly the case in several places in Cape May, especially the beautiful and stately Southern Mansion, located in one of Cape May's oldest neighborhoods, on the corner of Washington and Franklin Streets.

In 1850 William Corgie was about to divide a large part of his plantation into 10 individual lots. Philadelphia merchant George Allen purchased the entire parcel from Corgie and built a grand summer residence for his family. The design is credited to architect William Sloan and was built between 1863 and 1864 by local contractor, Henry Phillippi. The current name of the building is an homage to Sloan, being derived from the architect's "Design for a Southern Mansion" plans (which looked a lot like the current Southern Mansion) that were published in *The Model Architect* in 1868. This beautiful American bracket, post and beam villa is now run as a first-class Bed and Breakfast/Hotel. It is truly one of the most beautiful places in town.

I had heard stories of ghosts roaming the three floors of the Southern Mansion. There was also a defunct ghost tour that used to operate on Hughes and Washington Streets, which featured the Southern Mansion as one of its main attractions. The stories revolved around George Allen's niece, Esther Mercur, who inherited the estate from her uncle. It was said that Esther roams the halls and especially frequents her old bedroom on the third floor of the house. I had little to go on except folklore, but at least now I knew where to start, Room 9.

Willy and I checked in to The Southern Mansion on a stormy Sunday afternoon in March. Per my request, we took the adjoining Room 9 and Room 10 on the third floor. I also decided to bring some equipment along for backup, namely a digital camera and a cassette tape recorder in hopes of capturing a few EVPs. I did pick up faint conversations, but nothing yet discernible. I also photographed a few orbs in Room 9. However, there was a mirror on the wall, and these may have simply been refractions of light on my camera lens. My paranormal investigating gets to a point that I simply need to put down the meters, gauges and recorders, and just do it myself.

The wind was howling that night, and I had to secure a banging window before I could settle down into a light trance channeling. I could feel the cold penetrating the upstairs walls. The room was large and vast with high ceilings and wonderful period furniture. The setting and the weather were textbook haunted house material!

I put out some psychic feelers to try to find the ghost(s) of the house. They were being deliberately elusive. I could sense three of them, but they were moving around too quickly to identify psychically. Room 9 was only a passing venue for them en route around the house. Ghosts have to be willing to make contact for me to get a good connection with them. That night, they were not ready to talk, and I was tired. I turned in for the night, but just as a precaution in case anything decided to act up, I ran a digital tape recorder with a hanging microphone suspended over my bed. If they did show up in the middle of the night, they might be heard on the tape.

The next day I began to conduct my interviews with the staff. A few of the ladies who work the front desk and handle reception told me that guests had experienced the smell of roses, breezes blowing past them in rooms with windows shut and doors closing that were left open. None of these reports was anything I wanted to write about — then I met one of the servers at breakfast who gave me the inside scoop on the glass shattering ghost of the dining room!

There is a ghost in the Southern Mansion who has a thing for glassware. Wine and champagne glasses in particular have exploded into powder on trays being carried during parties! Glasses have also exploded on tables and racks with no one near them. The current owner, Barbara Bray, reported that the glasses do not just break. She told me they seem to turn to powder. (There have been no reports of anyone being injured by glass, fortunately.)

"You have to talk to the chef," implored Cathy, at the front desk. "He has all kinds of stuff happening in the kitchen." It certainly seems that is the case. I had the pleasure of meeting Brian, the chef of the Southern Mansion, the following afternoon.

He told me about a time when he was mixing a large quantity of batter for a wedding cake, and all of a sudden green dye started bubbling up in the middle of the batter. He told me there was no green dye anywhere in the kitchen! It seems that someone was partial to the color green and practical jokes. Brian has heard and felt things many times in the new addition's sub-level kitchen. "The ghost in that part of the house is also fond of throwing around gravy boats," Barbara added later. Was this also Esther? When I psychically "called out" to Esther to come forward and speak to me or speak on the tape, there was the same silence as before. Had the ghosts checked out prior to my arrival?

That evening, I sensed a new energy on the second floor in the hallway. She mentioned a name like Curley and a woman named Mary. "Curley is the plumber," Barbara joked, "and still alive." Was Mary a housekeeper for the Allens? Searching through the historical handout the Southern Mansion gave me, I found no such name, but I did find a gap in the property's history. There was very little mentioned about the history of the place between Ester Mecur's death in the 1940s and the years before Barbara Bray and Ric Wilde bought and restored the place to its current splendor. In fact, pictures of the Allen family were everywhere, but none of any other families.

"Crilly," said the new woman I spoke with at the front desk, "she was the previous owner who turned the place into a boarding house with her husband. She died here in 1994." Now we were getting closer. That evening I visited with friends in North Cape May. As fate would have it the couple was thinking about buying The Southern Mansion in 1994 when it was up for sale. At that time, however, it was known as The *Crilly* Estate! They then produced an old newspaper article from the *Gazette-Leader* entitled, "THE BATTLE OF THE CRILLY ESTATE" It was an eye-opening and sad account of what had become of the previous owners.

According to the story, Daniel Crilly purchased the property in 1946 as a belated wedding present for his wife Mary. Esther Mercur had died of alcoholism, and her husband Ulysses sold the property "as is with all furnishings." The deal was that the furniture would always stay with the house. The Crillys agreed and lived happily at the estate for many years with their two children, Daniel, Jr. and Maryanne.

Daniel Crilly died in 1964, followed by his young daughter Maryanne of cancer in 1967. Mary lived with her son in the house until his death in 1991. Unlike the Allens, who were old Philadelphia money, the Crillys were not wealthy by any standards.

In the end, all Mary Crilly had was the house and furnishings. She eventually was forced to turn the place into a boarding house to maintain some sort of income. Unfortunately, it seems her tenants took advantage of her in many ways.

According to sources quoted in the *Gazette-Leader* article, her personal possessions were being stolen from the house by borders. Finally, the time had come to sell the house. Mary was now 92 years old and bedridden. In June of 1994, she was taken away in an ambulance. Some said people she had trusted sold the house out from under her and put her in the nursing home. Neighbors even called the police to report she was being taken from her house against her will.

Mary Crilly's final wish was that she could die in her beloved home. Sadly, her health had deteriorated in her final years to the point that she needed constant care and eventually she became bedridden living in a converted bedroom on the first floor. Those were her final days at the old mansion. She was never to see her home at 720 Washington Street again.

Mary managed to survive until January of 1996, when she died in Victorian Manor, the local senior care facility. I spoke with several friends of hers who visited her in her last days at the nursing home. They said she remained sharp until near the end, always asking about her old home.

The agent in charge of Mary Crilly's estate sold the house and contents to Dr. J. Beyer Bray, who purchased the home for his daughter Barbara Bray and Ric Wilde. They began a magnificent effort to restore the house to its original grandeur during the Allen heyday.

After I read the *Gazette-Leader* article, I realized just why Mary had come back. I imagine that, when she finally died, her ghost made a beeline for the old house, instead of crossing over to the Other Side. Usually when we die, our friends and family members are there to meet us and help us make the transition. It was only when I went back and read the long article that night at The Southern Mansion, that I saw the last paragraph sub-titled *"The Ghosts of Crilly Estate."*

According to the story in the paper, a former tenant named Kathy Dubin had told Mary, when she was alive, that she had seen spectral figures in the house, that of a man and a younger woman. When she described them, Mary pulled out an old photograph and Dubin identified the two people pictured as the figures she saw in the halls. The picture was of Mary's husband Daniel and daughter Maryanne. Mary asked Dubin not to mention anything about the ghosts, for she did not want to frighten the other tenants. It seems the ghosts were staying on to look after Mary.

This is a great twist to a ghost investigation to find actual documentation about earlier hauntings at the same venue, ghosts that currently had been forgotten. I only wish people had passed down some of the great ghost stories that must have been told in Victorian times about Cape May.

I wonder if Mary got to Heaven, and when she saw her family missing, decided to go and find them, or possibly the only place Mary ever intended to cross over was to cross town and return home.

This psychic medium's feelings on the matter—with Daniel and Mary-anne Crilly still looming around the Southern Mansion, it is no wonder, then, that Mary wanted to be reunited with them. If she could not die in her home as she wished, she would almost certainly live there in spirit after death.

The second night I spent in the Southern Mansion, I was *finally* visited by a ghost. I was in the middle of a long dream when something nudged me awake. I turned and looked around the room. Upon waking I heard a sweet, older voice say, "I'm here—it's me." It was 3:05 AM. Prime time for ghosts to come a calling!

It was about the same time of night that Barbara Bray had told me most of the guests had experienced haunting activity. I fell back asleep after the activity faded, finally relieved to have made contact. The dream I had following the experience was chock full of imagery, all revolving around Mary Crilly and her family.

The breaking wine glasses mystery was also solved for me. At first, I thought it was surely Esther Mercur. She was mentioned in an interview with Mary Crilly as being an alcoholic and a wild party girl. However, I was not sensing her in the house. The same article mentioned that Daniel Crilly had a neurological disorder which eventually caused him to lose feeling in his legs and gain weight.

According to reports of people who knew the family, he may have started drinking. For whatever reason, he removed hundreds of wine bottles from the cellar, stored there since Esther Mercur's time. He promptly brought all of the remaining wine bottles out to the backyard and smashed them! Mr. Crilly may have a thing for wine bottles and glasses, especially when a wedding or other big event is happening in his old house. Could he be the one playing the tricks on the wait staff? Is the mysterious green food coloring, that keeps appearing in the kitchen, a hint at the Crilly's love of all things Irish? They were Irish themselves, and Mary often spoke of people as being "fine Irish." My wager is that it is the Crillys, and not Esther Mercur, haunting the Southern Mansion.

When I finally announced to Barbara and her receptionists the true identities of their paranormal boarders, and that it was not Esther, or any of the Allens, that it was in fact the Crillys, a sense of happiness seemed to come over the entire house. The ghosts were glad to hear the truth finally be told.

I liked this house, the minute I walked into it. Barbara and her staff have done an amazing job with restoration. It is truly one of the showplaces of Cape May.

The story has been told correctly at last, and the ghosts of the Southern Mansion can finally get the recognition they deserve. I think things may be quieting down a bit. As in life, I feel that Mary Crilly only wants to stay in her home. She is not the type to scare anyone. She would be more likely to bake you cookies!

Her daughter Maryanne also seems to be around, but I did not sense her that strongly when I last was in the house. Art, the carpenter told me a young woman kept call-

Dan and Mary Crilly
(Courtesy of Lisa Adams)

ing his name one night. He turned his radio off and answered several times, but no one would respond. He turned the radio up louder when he realized no one else was in the house. The louder the radio played, the stronger she called to him! Now, he says, he is used to the ghosts of the house. When I met Art, I assured him they were looking after the place, and that they were concerned about a "chimney area and water." Art told me they were already addressing the problem. A section of the attic, unseen by my eyes, near the chimney was leaking and starting to sag from water damage.

It seems things are well in order at the Southern Mansion. I hope that the Crillys will also be included in the official history and the picture gallery on the walls. I think they would appreciate that very much. Barbara told me she has been reading Mary's diaries. One touching entry from many years ago shows Mary hoping she will never get too old to enjoy life, dance and be active in the house. I think she has gotten her wish, if a few years late.

The Belvidere

A HOUSE THAT SPEAKS — FOR ITSELF

26 Gurney Street, Cape May

IT is always great to get a lead on a house or houses that has never before been written about. This is the case with a row of houses called Stockton Place. Today, these eight almost identical "cottages" line the west side of Gurney Street leading up to The Abbey B&B. The Stockton Cottages are some of the most beautiful and decorative examples of Victorian architecture in town. Several of them are also haunted.

Over the years, people with ghost stories have just seemed to find me. Even before I started to write about them, I would be speaking to someone on the subject or lecturing for the Mid-Atlantic Center for the Arts, and inevitably, someone would approach me with a story of his or her own. Sometimes these hauntings would be a garden variety ghost, the kind that did nothing remarkable, except to produce a few bumps in the night. Sadly, many of the stories were just that, stories. Every now and then, however, a true tale of a haunting would surface. This is the case with 26 Gurney Street.

For many years, this Stockton Cottage was called The Belvidere. The Mullen family bought the house in 2003 from Carolyn Mueller, whose mother had bought the property in the 1930s. Today, this quaint Gothic Revival cottage is a summer rental. As with many of Cape May's old real estate sentinels, when the last door is locked for the season and the lights are turned off, the summer tenants leave, and the winter tenants (read: ghosts) could not be happier!

I had heard from several people who had stayed with Mrs. Mueller about the place being haunted, but had never had the opportunity to get into the house itself. One afternoon, I got a call from Jenny Mullen, the Belvidere's new owner. She asked if I would be interested in visiting her Gurney Street home and conducting a psychic investigation, and in exchange I would be allowed to write the story of my findings.

It was a beautiful fall weekend in Cape May when I arrived at the cottage. Jenny and her husband Bob met me at the door. As I entered the parlor of the home, I could sense two distinct spirits.

When I psychically search a venue, I set my mind to look or *feel* around for energies that represent spirits or ghosts. Remember, in this book I differentiate a ghost, who is a soul that is stuck between here and the Other Side, or heaven, from a spirit, who is a soul that has returned from the Heaven to help in some way, or sometimes simply to visit with loved ones.

Can spirits be hanging around a house when I investigate it? Absolutely they can. All of us have spirit guides who work with us. These spirit guides seem to be there to help us with day-to-day problems and life traumas that we need to work through, in order to move forward in life. They do not solve the problems; that is our job, but they do guide us to solutions. Therefore, the big difference between ghosts and spirits is that spirits are around for a purpose, to help someone on this plane, while ghosts are usually hanging around for their own specific needs. Ghost energy feels heavier and more grounded to me, while spirit energy comes from a higher, stronger source. Sometimes ghosts, and their thoughts, are like an open book, other times ghosts are closed balls of energy, almost impossible to penetrate with psychic ability. Luckily the Belvidere ghosts were more open and willing to talk.

Resting quietly in the living room of The Belvidere, I could sense a woman sitting by the window, watching passers-by on the street. I sensed she had been around for a long time. How long I could not say for sure, perhaps from the early days of the house. The Stockton Row Cottages had been built, according to the *The Cape May Ocean Wave*, between 1871 and 1872, across the street from the mammoth Stockton Hotel. They were originally summer rentals that came with a great ocean view and three servants! The ten houses have been almost completely restored to their mirror images of each other. Other than paint colors, a few cosmetic architectural changes and ghosts, they are all pretty much the same in style.

The woman I first encountered at The Belvidere was wearing a long dress with colors of blue, red and purple. I am not an expert in vintage clothing styles, but I would guess she was from the late 1800s, maybe even as late as the Edwardian era. The woman ghost was sewing something rather intently, and would glance up occasionally to look out to the street. Perhaps she was watching guests come and go at the phantom Stockton Hotel, which was demolished in 1911, but still gives off lots of residual energy.

I tried to read psychically the woman's thoughts. At my lectures, I have been asked just how, if ghosts do not possess any kind of physical brain, I can *read their minds*. I subscribe to the idea that brains are merely receiv-

Stockton Hotel   CAPE MAY, N. J.
Demolished in 1911

View from Beach Avenue looking up Gurney Street at the mammoth Stockton Hotel (right) and the Stockton Row Cottages (left) with the John B. McCreary House (now The Abbey) tower behind the cottages.
(Author's Collection)

ers and transmitters for a greater electrical energy. Here on the Earth Plane, I think our human brains allow our souls to stay connected to our physical bodies. We still do not know a lot about the human brain or the human soul for that matter! As with many areas of the paranormal and new age thinking, we barely know who *we* are!

When I lock on to the thoughts of a particular ghost, it is like putting a DVD in to watch a movie. It is really quite incredible to experience. I have to be careful when operating in the psychic realm, not to get too far into a ghost's mind energy. I need to get in, find the information I am looking for (if possible) and pull my mind back to me. In my early days of conducting psychic ghost investigations and attempting ghost communication, I did not yet know how to *ground* myself. On more than one occasion, I came home depressed and anxious. At first, I felt a sense of embarrassment about what I was doing. At least that's what I thought I was feeling. I was drained and depressed by the work, but I kept going back for more!

What was happening to me, and has happened to more than a few novice psychics and mediums, was that I was becoming engulfed in the ghost's

The beautiful Stockton Row Cottages on Gurney Street.

energy. This is a type of energy which I can best describe as ethereal mood swings! Suddenly, my senses and feelings became overwhelmed with moods that were not my own. I was slowly being mentally poisoned by others' moods. The fault was all mine, as the ghosts did not intend to try to ruin my day. I had eavesdropped in a way that was unsafe. I have since learned how to ground myself and read, yet not absorb, the energy, good or bad. If only I could learn to block *human* negative energy!

Sending out a *psychic line*, I discovered some bits and pieces of information about the woman by the window. She seemed to be content with just sitting and sewing, but at the same time could not stop reminiscing about all the friends and family who were now long gone. It seemed as though she was not sure which direction to go anymore. Should she stay put as a ghost, or should she cross over to the Other Side?

One thing we must remember about Cape May is that many of these houses were summer homes. It would seem logical that if I encounter a ghost in one of these places, the person must have died during the summer months. With The Belvidere, it is still only a summer home, having no heating at all. This woman seemed a bit too dressed up to be a servant, so I am going to assume she had rented the place — and died there.

The ghost started to sniff the air, I sensed she smelled natural gas in the house — maybe there was a leak once, as the house did have evidence of old gas fixtures. I could hear her calling out the name, "Al." I am not sure there was an answer — at least I was not at the time.

When I reviewed the audio tape I had made of the investigation, in order to refresh my memory to write this story, I noticed a few things that were definitely not heard during the recording. There were *other voices* on the tape. EVPs to be exact. Whispering sounds in the form of words and short sentences. At one point, whoever was doing the speaking seemed to be responding to me, which is wonderful.

I mentioned to Jenny and Bob at some point early in the visit that I sensed, "two distinct entities in the house."

The response on the tape was, "No, no... more."

Again, to refresh, this phenomenon is known in the trade as *EVP* or *electronic voice phenomenon*. Ghosts can apparently project their voices in the form of energy onto a magnetic tape surface. The EVPs that I picked up on my cassette recorder occurred mainly in the living room. When I reviewed my cassette tape later that day, I found the EVPs began about the same time that I mentioned to everyone that I was sensing the ghost of a young man in the room.

We made our way up to the second floor. I had seen an image of a man pacing back and forth in the upstairs hallway and wanted to get a closer look. I traced the hallway from the back of the house to the front bedroom. At one point in time, a doorway existed allowing one to exit the hallway onto the front balcony. The door has since been walled over and a bathroom installed. I felt that this person was pacing from the back bedroom of the house to the front porch.

As I entered the second floor front bedroom, I again sensed a woman's voice. This was a different energy from the first floor ghost. This woman was much more contemporary. She complained about a toilet backing up and having to plunge it all the time! The ghosts seemed to have a thing for plumbing. The young man kept mentioning about a leaky sink that needed to be fixed for years. A new modern bathroom was being installed at the time and I think the ghosts were overjoyed. These ghosts were much more in tune with the house and its current state than was the sewing ghost in the parlor.

Ghosts that are concerned this much with a house are usually ghosts of past owners or proprietors. Sometimes this material love can keep a ghost *stuck*. The Mullens told me that they had been having trouble with a leaky sink in the front bathroom before the renovation. The ghosts knew the house, but now the trick was to know the ghosts!

The woman ghost on the second floor was having trouble walking, as if she had arthritis in life. I know it sounds odd that a ghost would have medical problems, but they are a *reflection* of what they were in life, health problems and all.

As we enjoyed the view from the second-floor front porch, the Mullen's delightful neighbor, Eleanor DeCurtis, peered up at us from the street.

"Oh, you're the ghost man!" she yelled out. I *was* getting a reputation in town! The Mullens invited Eleanor up to join us. Am I glad they did. Eleanor has also owned one of the Stockton Row Cottages for over 20 years — and she had her own ghost stories to tell, but one story at a time!

Eleanor told us a story about guests staying with the previous owner, when The Belvidere was a B&B. Apparently, a couple had checked in and was staying in an upstairs bedroom when, suddenly in the middle of the night, they saw a wispy, transparent figure of a woman drifting across their room! The husband raced downstairs and knocked on the door of Carolyn Mueller, the owner at the time. Upon hearing the story, Mrs. Mueller told them to "go back to bed," thinking they were simply dreaming. The couple packed up and rushed out of the house into the darkness of the night, never to be heard from again.

We talked about the footsteps in the hallway as I moved back into the second floor of the house. Jenny and Bob confirmed that they had been hearing footsteps on stairs for sometime, and that several guests in the house have also heard them. We moved into the rear bedroom that had lots of energy. It seemed like the ghost of the elderly woman might have been following us down the hallway, and then sat on the bed in the room to converse with us.

She was thankful about the Mullens fixing up the house. The word "thankful" kept repeating. The woman seemed to stay in the back bedroom to keep out of the way of the *living* in the house. This is a common occurrence in the spirit world. Ghosts will move to the highest floor, the basement or unused rooms in a house. The ghosts at 26 Gurney must love the fact that the people leave in the winter!

Eleanor mentioned another thing that hit home. A woman who owned the cottage before Mrs. Mueller had problems with her legs from arthritis and had trouble walking and using the stairs! It is great when we can make a direct historical correlation like this. Could the ghost of one of the previous owners still be watching over the place? It has happened before in old Cape May.

As we listened to Eleanor tell stories of Gurney Street and her experiences over the years, I realized that Stockton Row was a hopping place — paranormally speaking! In one house (which I had heard about) the owner tried four times to put up a Christmas tree, going as far as wiring it to the walls. Each

Phantom footsteps on the stairs are often a sign of a ghost about the house.

time, she would reenter the house to find it knocked to the ground — an Ebenezer Scrooge-like ghost at work no doubt!

In another cottage, there is a cat ghost and another ghost walking the upstairs corridors. Eleanor reported having a few friendly ghosts on her third floor also! With the Stockton Row Cottages, it is not about which houses are haunted — the question is which houses are *not* haunted!

As we passed the middle bedroom on the second floor, Jenny asked if I felt any energy. "Some," I told her, "but not much at this moment." She told me that several times people have experienced a blonde haired, younger woman in the room. Perhaps she was a guardian spirit, they thought. When the voice on my tape said, "No, no... more," it was not kidding!

As we stood near the staircase going to the third floor, I watched (psychically) as a young man waltzed up the stairs, dragging his hand along the rungs under the banister, creating a *rapping* noise.

"That's the noise we hear, like a child on the stairs!" exclaimed the Mullen's daughter Kim, who arrived at the scene just in time.

"We all thought it was a child walking up and down the stairs, but that could explain it." Jenny told me.

I felt the young man had lived in the house for some time. He told me his life ended suddenly, before it should have. He knew the house quite well.

"Problem with the chimney, cracked flue, broken bricks," I heard in my mind. "Is the flue cracked?" I asked Bob Mullen. "The ghost of the young man is telling me something was wrong with your chimney."

Indeed, there *had been* something wrong. Bob related the story of how, one day, he was removing the chimney from the top of the house. The chimney had become unstable and needed to be taken down.

"I was up on the third floor and started to pull some of the loose bricks out when, suddenly, the whole chimney came crashing down and just missed me!" Bob recalled of the startling experience.

Was the ghost watching out for him? Did he save Bob's life? Maybe that is what he meant by mentioning the chimney. It was hard to tell, but at least one of them was still alive! This ghost also liked to keep pulling the doors in the house closed. He really seemed to be obsessed with the idea of closed doors. He did not say why.

Opening and closing doors is something very common in a haunting. Most of the time the door does not actually move. Only the sound of the door moving is heard. Possibly this is a *memory* of a sound, suspended in the ethers of a place — part of some residual energy.

The spirit of the young man, whom I shall call Al, since it is the name I was given several times, was a very good energy. He was concerned with the safety and well-being of all who are in the house.

An icy cold spot moved through our space as I continued sensing the young man. Cold spots usually are calling cards for ghosts. Some paranormal researchers feel ghosts are energy fields with a negative ion charge. A negative charge, similar to what room air purifiers give off, can create a cool and moist feeling in the air. Negative ions will also cause the hair on one's arms and necks to stand up. This would account for the old saying, "the hair on the back of my neck is standing up," when someone was scared by what they thought was a ghost. Had one of the ghosts decided to walk right through us?

As we moved downstairs, I asked Eleanor if her husband, who had passed away years earlier, was a handyman — as I had sensed a man wearing a tool belt and carrying a hammer, moving from her front porch to the Mullens' from porch. The man entered the living room of The Belvidere with his tools. Had someone called a repairghost?

"No, he was an accountant. He wore one of those little pocket savers, not a tool belt," Eleanor replied. Why was a ghost repairman heading into the Mullens' living room? We would soon get our answer.

At this point in the day, I could sense some real spirits coming through. The first and strongest was Bob Mullen's grandfather, who had a great sense of humor and could have been a one-man show! He gave Bob a few very specific messages to let us know it was really him. I began doing what I do on a regular basis. I began to channel.

The ghosts seemed to step back and let the stronger spirits from the Other Side move in. As I spoke, Kim sat on a beautiful Victorian *chaise longue* that came with the house. Eleanor made a point to say that the previous owner's son, who had planned to turn the place into a guesthouse for his clients, purchased that particular piece. She told me that the man had his life end tragically in an automobile accident, and his plans never materialized. No sooner did she get the words out — when the entire side section of the piece popped out and crashed to the floor!

On examination, the large side of the piece had about 20 nails and screws holding it in place. There was really no way the entire thing could have just popped off, but it did. It was a good thing that someone in the house called the ghost repairman ahead of time!

After my initial investigation, I returned to the front porch of The Belvidere a few days later and tried to sort through the ghosts. I began to sense the ghost of a young girl in the living room who, upon sensing my psychic probing, took off up the stairs. Ghosts can hide from my view if they want to. Maybe this child is part of the racket people hear on the stairs at night.

The Mullens have great energy and are very open and welcoming to living people, as well as the ghosts. I sense the ghosts like them also. This cottage is a weekly rental in the summer, and I highly recommend it for the easy access to both the beach and downtown Cape May. If you want to step back to a calmer, quieter time and disconnect from the stress of everyday life, a week in Cape May is the way to go.

Remember, not everyone will sense a ghost and not all ghosts will let you know they are present. Most people can stay in a haunted place without ever having an experience. It is those who *want* to find a ghost and go looking for a haunting who will usually have the experience.

I love this story because it demonstrates that you can coexist peacefully with a ghost or ghosts in your own home. Just make sure the ghosts pay their own way — should they happen to break any of the furniture!

The Inn of Cape May

FROM "THE COLONIAL" TIMES TO THE PRESENT
A FAVORITE HAUNT IN CAPE MAY

Beach Avenue & Ocean Street, Cape May

SOMETIMES being a ghost has its rewards. Let us take, for example, an extended stay at a favorite haunt. Unless someone is about to start offering 100-year rates, ghosts will continue to be non-paying guests in some of Cape May's oldest hotels and inns! Many years ago, I received a gift from a friend, a watercolor of an old hotel in Cape May where she had been staying. At the time, my family had long since stopped our yearly trek to the southern tip of New Jersey for summer vacation. The image was both beautiful and haunting. It showed a majestic, grand old Victorian hotel by the ocean, all in white with blue and green trim, complete with a wrap-around porch and not one, but two witches' hats on top. Then called The Colonial, it is known today as The Inn of Cape May and retains much of its haunting Victorian splendor, both outside, and in.

Built in 1895 by William H. Church and his carpenter brother Charles, The Colonial was originally half of its current size and faced out to Ocean Street. The southern wing facing the ocean was added in 1905 to accommodate more guests with modern indoor bathrooms, electricity and an elevator! Charles Church went on to build The Star Villa across the street, now on Beach Avenue next to The Peter Shields Inn.

I was always surprised that none of the existing ghost tours in town talked about The Inn of Cape May. Each time I would walk through the vast parlor past the grand staircase, I would sense "people" around me, coming and going about their daily business. Were these the ghosts of former staff members? Guests that had decided not to check out? I would surely find out.

Opportunity knocked on my door later that year. I had been working with MAC, lecturing about ghosts and spiritualism in Victorian times. MAC was able to persuade Beth Eastman, whose family bought the hotel about 14 years earlier, to allow me to do my lecture and ghost hunt.

When I am scheduled to do a tour or lecture I like to do a preliminary walkthrough to see what energy I pick up. Earlier that year, in April, a group of us had decided to do just that and check the place out. We felt April would be much quieter in the hotel, and I could get some psychic detective work going.

The hotel was much busier than we expected (with live guests,) but I was able to move around the structure in the evening and pick up a sense of what was going on. The second and third floors seemed relatively quiet, at least on a paranormal level. As I ascended the staircase to the fourth floor, however, I began to get a sense that whatever was haunting the Inn of Cape May maintained a presence on that floor.

At this point, no one would really discuss anything about ghosts. Beth brushed aside my questions, merely stating, "There have been stories about the place." One of the stories, actually the only one that I had heard, was of a woman who watches people as they shower. She seems to show up in their bathroom and just stare blankly through them. When they realize someone is standing watching them, she vanishes.

As I moved through the hallway in the "old" section of the building toward the Ocean Street front side, I sensed a psychic image of a woman wearing a vivid blue dress, something almost too blue and extravagant for every-

The Colonial.   CAPE MAY, N. J.

The Inn of Cape May circa 1907 as The Colonial Hotel
(Author's Collection)

day wear. She moved in and out of the doorways, as if looking for something she had lost. I sensed she might be checking the rooms. She would look at the room numbers on the doors and then look around at the other rooms. It was at this point I realized that the room numbers on the doors made little sense. Many of them were completely out of order!

"In the old days, people would always want the same room they had the previous summer," Beth told me. "The original owners did not want to lose business, so they would move the doors around to a room that was available... that is why the doors are out of numerical order." Could the ghost be lost? Even I would be confused if the doors kept switching, creating an effect of moving rooms! Think of what the ghosts must have felt. They are confused about who they are and where they are to begin with. This must have just added to their confusion!

I followed the "lady in the blue dress" until she vanished into a wall. This is NOT what a ghost will usually do, unless the wall was added after the person had died. Ghosts, like living people, usually have common sense; there are exceptions in both cases. They simply do not try to break the laws of physics, even though their mere existence does just that.

Examining the walls more closely, I noticed a faint outline of a door that had been walled up. As my enthusiasm for the fantastic raced, thinking I had possibly discovered some secret walled up room, my ego quickly deflated when I noticed that doors were walled up every twenty feet or so. It turns out, so a chambermaid later informed me, that once the bathrooms were added to each room in the 1920s, shared baths became a thing of the past. Half of each guest room was now converted to a private bath. Ah! A mystery solved! Our lady in the blue dress was NOT a peeping (Tom?) She was only standing in a bedroom that probably was hers, which is now a bath. Some ghosts apparently always see their surrounding the way it was in their lifetime. There are also different levels of consciousness in ghosts; some are with it, some are very removed from the here and now.

Moving up the narrow and winding maid's staircase, I made my way to the fifth floor. Today these rooms offer the most spectacular view the hotel has to offer. No wonder I found the room with the best ocean view, number 92, to be the most "active."

Whoever was staying long term in the hotel was checked in here and why not? Room 92 is a wonderful airy and bright room with a GREAT ocean view... I may just come back here myself in the afterlife, or maybe I will try it out in this lifetime.

Room 92 had the energy of the woman in the blue dress again. This time I sensed that she was possibly a member of the original staff. I had thought she may have been a member of the Church family, but recently found out the family did not live in the hotel. Nevertheless, I had my ghost.

"The Lady in Blue," Beth stated very matter-of-factly, glancing around the room almost seeming to be looking for her. I often confused Beth's early reactions with those of disbelief. It was only later, when I knew her better, that she would tell me to stop telling her "stuff," because she had to close the hotel alone some nights, and I was scaring her! Beth recounted a story about a couple staying in a room on the third floor with their son. The boy came into the room one day and saw an old woman in blue, rocking in the chair. She suddenly vanished.

You do not have to ascend the great staircase in order to experience the paranormal happenings at The Inn of Cape May. Much of the reported activity has taken place in the lobby and in some of the rooms used for banquets. I have done several lectures here and can attest to the fact that I have sensed a few ghosts buzzing around me! I spoke with Carol Menz, Beth Eastman's sister-in-law. After she first took over the hotel, Carol had some first-hand experience with the ghost of an old woman while she and her two young children were preparing tables for a banquet.

"My son Tai (he was almost four), and my daughter Ami (18 months who was in her carrier asleep), saw the ghost. It was before the restaurant and antique shop were split up. The restaurant was one whole room. The hotel was closed. It was early evening when the sun is just starting to go down. I remember the time of day because we were just beginning to get the hotel ready to open for the season, and the electric was off in the dining room. Tai and I were filling salt and pepper shakers to get ready for the season, when I felt the dining room get very cold. I believed at that time that it was getting cold because the sun was just starting to go down. Tai tapped on my arm, and I looked up to see an old woman floating through the air, waggling her fingers and looking at Tai. She ignored me and floated up and out the ceiling by the window in the restaurant. I remember seeing the dust floating in the light coming through the window. We collected our stuff and left. We were not panicked, or threatened, but we were alone in the hotel since it was not yet open. I did not believe in ghosts, but knew that this was a ghost, no doubt about it, since my four-year-old spotted her first." - Carol Menz

Could this have been the Lady in Blue, or was it yet another ghost haunting the old Colonial? I myself have had some first hand experience with the woman ghost in the ballroom of the Inn, though I didn't know it at the time. During my lecture in March of 2003 for MAC, my assistant snapped some shots of me speaking about ghosts in the hotel. When we had the pictures developed, there were orbs, or blobs of light, in several of them, appearing all around me.

As I said earlier, orbs are controversial with modern ghost investigators. Some feel they are nothing more than light reflections bouncing off something shiny and refracting on to the lens. Most orbs do seem to be just this. However, some do not seem to be explainable. I have orbs in pictures taken with both film cameras and digital cameras. When I have tried intentionally to create orbs with my cameras, by photographing shiny surfaces or windows, the effect has never been the same. I feel some orbs do represent a form of energy. Whether that energy is of a spirit or ghost, I still do not know for sure. We need science to catch up and help us out with that one!

In one shot of me lecturing to the crowd, there appeared a large green-blue blob of light right over my shoulder facing the crowd. It was not the perfectly round, whitish green or blue orbs I usually see in pictures. This misty glow had a definite outline and irregular shape. When I magnified the orb, it took on the distinct shape of an older woman's head, floating in the air next to my shoulder! This is the closest thing to a ghost picture I have ever obtained, and I am sure she is the genuine article.

In this third edition of *The Ghosts of Cape May Book 1*, I have decided to include that very picture of my "ghost." In a day when anything or anyone can be added to a picture, I had, in the first edition, hesitated to include this picture for fear of sending the skeptics screaming. So many readers have asked to see the picture, I have relented and included it in this edition (See next page.)

In my opinion this picture certainly does seem to be the real McCoy. I have had light refractions bouncing off glass, rain, snow flakes, dust and shiny paint, create myriads of orbs in pictures. I have never had one of these orbs look so much like a human face as this one. I cannot explain it, you may come to your own conclusions about it.

I have included it because it is one of the few pieces of tangible and physical, paranormal evidence I have ever come across. EVPs are wonderful, but I would trade them all in for more great photos like this one! Can a ghost's energy actually be captured by a camera?

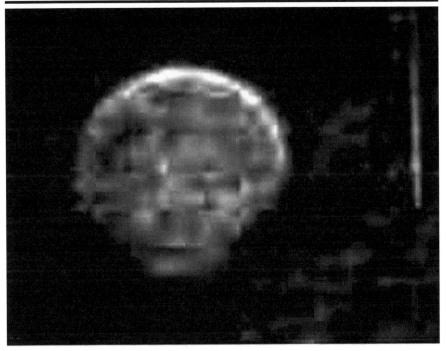

Could this strange orb of light captured on film during one of Craig's ghost lectures at the Inn of Cape May actually be the apparition of the "Lady in Blue," the hotel's head ghost? (© *2012 Craig McManus)*

It was dark in the room while I was speaking with the exception of some perimeter lighting. The white blotches to the right of the "face" are my face and plaid shirt. The ghostly face appeared in the photo as larger than my own head, yet hanging right next to me as if it were a cohost for the event! A few years after this lecture I ran into a woman at a book signing who had also attended the event. She told me she was somewhat psychic and sensed a woman standing next to me as I was speaking. Apparently, she also got some kind of light distortion in a few pictures she had snapped at the same time my picture above was taken. I have yet to see that picture.

It seems the Lady in Blue is not haunting alone at The Inn of Cape May. One night, as I searched the upstairs with my two assistants, a young boy joined us, about seven years old, who seemed to love the fact that we were looking for ghosts. He watched us intently and then pulled himself along the fourth floor banister going on his way to play some imaginary game. He said nothing. I also noticed he was wearing unusual clothes, old black and white shoes and a sweater that looked like it was out of the 1940s or 1950s. He vanished out of my sight. I commented on the occurrence to my two assistants, who had also seen him. My assistant Pierre had noticed his odd clothing, too, and the total absence of sound coming from him. We had all seen him, in full color, not ghost-like at all, so we all assumed he was just a kid dressed up for some event in town—or was he?

Carol Menz told me that, when they bought the hotel, one of the "old timers" who had stayed at the Inn for years told her about a couple who came every summer with their two children.

"I was told by an old-timer who used to stay at the Inn that a young rich couple would stay there years ago, and that the husband's mother would watch the children (one boy and one girl.) One day the little boy drowned in the ocean, and the grandmother was devastated. And after she passed away, now haunts the Inn." Carol prefaced this recount with, "I do not know if this is true or not."

True or not, it would make sense: a boy in period dress who makes no sound, then vanishes, and an old woman who seems to move throughout the Inn in search of something, very caring and fond of young children. Could this be his grandmother?

What about the Lady in Blue? Is this the ghost of a former maid or hostess? Or am I simply seeing the grandmother at different phases of her life, sometimes a young woman, then as she looks in old age? She certainly seems to watch over the place to make sure everyone has a good stay.

Is the Inn of Cape May paranormally active? Just ask Katie, the night manager at the front desk. Katie told me she has heard her share of phantom footsteps walking down the stairs and across the lobby... only to look up and see... nothing. One night it seems "someone" wanted her yardstick, which is kept behind the front desk. "I put it back twice and it kept getting pulled back out, and I was the only one here that night," she told me recently. When I mentioned Room 92 to Katie, she found it more than interesting. "Recently, we had a couple staying in that room who told us the wallpaper above the door just started peeling off in front of their eyes!" The Inn just underwent a major renovation last year, which tends to stir up ghosts and hauntings in a place... so it seems the ghost in Room 92 might not like the wallpaper!

During the renovation, Beth was kind enough to let me venture with my assistants through the hotel, which was dark and empty at the time. I spent about a half hour in Room 92 and, unfortunately, did not pick up any activity. As we sat in chairs in the center of the hall, one spot of activity popped up on the fourth floor. I sensed a presence coming down from the fifth floor where there were NO stairs now... then I sensed two more ghosts following the first. They passed by and THROUGH us so that each of us experienced cold sensations THREE distinct times.

I had heard that one of the night managers of the place would occasionally take a nap on one of the Victorian couches near the fireplace in the parlor. In the quiet of winter, when the hotel was empty and he was laying quietly on the couch, he would hear footsteps coming and going on the stairs and in the lobby. After a while, I was told, he would not even bother to get up and look, for nothing was there.

In another instance, Katie told me a couple on the third floor had heard children playing ball in the hallway at about two in the morning! The husband came down first, hoping his wife had not heard the ghostly sounds, and told the desk manager. The wife, thinking only she had experienced the activity, quietly told what she had heard to the front desk, not knowing her husband had already beat her to the punch! Both husband and wife heard two girls calling to a boy by name—Alex, I think. Was this the boy we saw on the fourth floor, who may have drowned years ago? Has he found a few ghostly playmates from town or does the hotel have even more long-term guests than previously suspected?

The majority of hauntings I have investigated have been benevolent. The ghosts at the Inn of Cape May certainly fit into this category.

On a recent visit to Cape May, I had set up equipment on the fifth floor to attempt a little paranormal data collection. I was told the fifth floor was empty, and since I was staying at the hotel that week to teach an Elderhostel class, I was able to float around the hotel late in the evening, when all was quiet. After about ten minutes of meditating, I sent out a psychic line and asked the ghosts to present themselves in the large hallway on the fifth floor. This has traditionally been the paranormal hot spot of the hotel. I started my recording equipment and began to ask questions, leaving enough of a silent pause so that if any ghosts were present, they may be able to answer me on the tape. A few good EVPs makes the entire ghost investigation worth while.

I was recording for about twenty minutes in the silence of the fifth floor when suddenly I heard a man and a woman arguing in one of the rooms! A light was also now shining from under the door. Horrified that guests were occupying the room, and I was recording outside their door, I gathered my

Art imitates life—and death.
Craig finds himself in a wall hanging on the fifth floor.
Are those the ghosts with him?

equipment and snuck back to my room. I ventured down to the front desk and asked the person on duty why she had told me the fifth floor was unoccupied when, in fact, it *was* occupied!

"There is no one staying on the fifth floor," she told me giving me a rather stern look. When I told her about the light in the room and the voices, she checked again and repeated that the floor was empty.

Walking up four flights of stairs is not exactly my favorite thing to do, but I figured I would go back and check for myself, and take a picture of the light under the door. I returned to the fifth floor, this time with only a camera in tow, and found—nothing. The room was dark, quiet and presumably empty. It was midweek during a slow time of year and very few people were in the hotel, or in town for that matter. Someone was arguing in that room. If it wasn't living people, it must have been dead ones.

Ghosts arguing about what? I thought. The EVPs that I later found on the tape were even more interesting. A boy's voice is heard yelling "Help me please, let me out of here!" A male voice is heard soon after that directing someone to keep him quiet. Had I stumbled onto some form of ghost hostage?

The interesting thing about the recordings was that the arguing voices I heard with my ears, did not appear on any of the tapes. I have often assumed that hauntings happen on various levels. Maybe the audible noises/voices I heard were coming from another set of ghosts.

About a year later, I was in Cape May again to host a paranormal weekend for MAC. Willy and I were staying at the John F. Craig House, and we had brought my friend Steve along to take pictures. Steve had never been to Cape May before, so I thought I would treat him to a nice, active haunt in town. The fifth floor of the Inn at Cape May came immediately to mind.

Before we went to bed that night, I asked Steve if he wanted me to come up to his room on the fifth floor and we could run some equipment. He opted to turn in early, and we said goodnight. I turned my phone off and went to bed. About 9 AM the next morning, when I turned my phone back on, I had about ten missed calls and twenty text messages from Steve!

Shortly after going to bed, Steve had heard people coming and going in the hallway, slamming their room doors in the process. He was trying to fall asleep when suddenly he saw what looked like a long, shadowy arm reaching across the bed, right over his body. He bolted.

The next morning he told me that he spent the rest of the night, until about five in the morning when the sun came up, sleeping in the hallway. Luckily the noisy crowd on the fifth floor had also gone to bed—or so he thought. When we checked with the front desk they told me, once again, no one else was staying on the fifth floor but Steve. Excellent.

The fifth floor was added later in the hotel's history and was used for staff quarters. It offers some of the best views of the ocean in town. Even though the hotel boasts having the first elevator in Cape May (which is still in use) many people staying at the inn opt for the lower floors. Since ghosts are trying to maintain their own space, and we often invade their privacy, a less-used floor like the hotel's fifth floor would be the perfect place for ghosts to get away from the living. At least that's my theory.

If you want a great vacation getaway, with kids or without (you can borrow some from the hotel) this is the place. I can see why so many folks decide to come back here over and over again — in this life and the next — it is truly one of Cape May's Victorian gems that will delight generations *and ghosts* to come. Don't forget to get a room on the fifth floor. It's quiet and peaceful, and it's got the best view—of everything.

Lace Silhouettes Lingerie & Cotton Company

WHERE "PIERCING THE VEIL" TAKES ON A WHOLE NEW MEANING

429 Washington Street (Mall), Cape May

" I HEAR NOISES — like things moving around, the basement door opens and closes. We are in the back of the store counting out — alone — when we close the store at night... we turn all the lights off — things start to happen."

So Jessica from the Cotton Company told me one dark and lonely night, moments before she would be, once again, turning out the lights on Washington and Decatur Streets, the place where the ghosts come out to play after the lights go off.

I suppose it was bound to happen eventually. My *Ghost Writer* column in *Exit Zero* magazine set off a run of ghost sightings all over Cape May. Not that the sightings are new, as most have been happening quietly for years. It seems that people now feel it's okay to come clean with their own stories of the Other Side of Cape May. I couldn't be happier!

As I sat sipping a glass of Irish Cream liqueur at the (Ugly) Mug one summer afternoon, Colette, the Mug's manager, rushed over to tell me that the woman who managed the clothing and lingerie stores across the street had ghosts of her own and had to talk to me. It sounded urgent, and haunted.

The Washington Street pedestrian mall was for many years a main thoroughfare in town. There were shops, cars, fires, more shops, and finally pedestrians when it was enclosed as "Victorian Village" mall in 1971.

This is one part of town that has seen lots of comings and goings. It is also rife with ghosts. They seem to be around every corner and down every dark side alley. Maybe they just congregate here at night, like the living do. We still have very little idea of the types of social environments in which ghosts exist, and whether they acknowledge each other or not. Only time and research will tell.

If you recall my visit to The Ugly Mug, it was Danny, their young ghost living up on the third floor, who talked about working across the street at Marcy and Mecray's Pharmacy. Today the building is the home of the Cotton Company, a woman's clothing store, and Lace Silhouettes Lingerie, two smaller stores within one big store — with two smaller ghosts. It seems that there is more beneath the undergarments than meets the eye here.

When Colette told me about the store across the way, she mentioned the owner, Suzan McClure, had sensed the ghost of a man roaming about. Could this be Colonel Henry Sawyer, who perished at the counter of the old pharmacy?

There was one way to find out. I crossed over, so to speak, and had a quick look around the place. I am not in the habit of looking at women's lingerie.

Really, I'm not. I am sure I turned a few heads by sniffing around the racks for ghosts! I could sense two distinct presences. There is a certain feel to ghost energy, and the Cotton Company (which is how I will refer to both stores) definitely had two ghosts.

Upon returning in the morning with camera and tape recorder in hand, I met the store's cheerful, friendly manager, Suzan McClure, and her daughter Maggie. They were more than happy to see me as they had been experiencing their ghost(s) for some time, but had no one with whom to share their experiences, officially. The store had switched from its perennial pharmacy shell to a clothing store in 2001. Suzan and her staff had sensed something the first winter they occupied the place, but it was not until last fall that they knew something was sharing the space with them.

"The activity would always start in the late afternoon, in the fall and winter, when it was quieting down in the store and starting to get dark," Suzan recalled. The basement seems to harbor the ghosts of the building. The staff was afraid to go down because of experiences they had. Suzan would be the only one who would not be afraid to face the unknown in the ancient cellar beneath her store. Sometimes what she would experience would be quite unnerving.

KENNEDY'S UNITED STATES PHARMACY, E. Cor. Washington & Decatur Sts., CAPE MAY CITY.

Prior to 1869 Dr. James Kennedy was the original tenant of Lace Silhouettes/
Cotton Company Building. He later moved across the street, selling the building
to Drs Marcy & Mecray. Notice how little the look of the building has changed
compared to the preceding picture on page 148!
(Walt Campbell Collection)

"One afternoon, I went down to the basement, and on the floor was a bright, red spot of paint. The floor was dirty, and that spot was not there earlier. No one else had been down there. It was really weird," she remembered. Was the red paint some kind of message from the ghost? It seemed Suzan's ghost was more than a little active down there. "On another occasion, the fluorescent bulbs were smashed in the light on the ceiling. I asked the other staff members about it, and no one had been in the basement since the day before. We nicknamed the ghost George. So now, when I go down the base-

Stairs to the ghostly getaway — the old dark cellar beneath the store.

ment, I would talk to George, and I had sensed him following me around at times," she continued.

As I talked with Suzan, I began to get a feeling that we were not alone. It seemed George was moving in on our conversation. Besides managing the business, Suzan also lives in the apartment above the store. George has also made himself known to her on those dark winter nights when she would forget something at work and come down to retrieve it.

"In December I came down at eight o'clock in the evening to get my CDs out of the player. When I came through the Cotton Company and started through the foyer, I felt and heard someone walking behind me... I said, 'Oh George, it's just me, getting my CDs.'" George certainly does seem to keep track of Suzan's movements. But why? Only the ghost would be able to tell me.

The cellar seemed to be the hot spot of energy. Suzan pulled back some garments to reveal an old cellar door in the shop. The door creaked and groaned in true "haunted house movie" fashion. My partner Willy and I made our way down the narrow stairs into the old, brick-lined basement. As I turned the corner, three headless women standing in the center of the cellar floor startled me! Luckily, these "ethereal guardians" were nothing more than dresses shifting on a clothesline! This would have sent some running into the street. In ghost investigating, you need to keep a cool head.

I set down my cassette tape recorder on a shelf and started to meditate. The basement was quiet as a tomb, the perfect place to meditate and link up to the Other Side. There was definitely a presence in the cellar. I let the ghosts know that I had a tape recorder running, and they could speak into the tape recorder and communicate via EVP.

Electronic Voice Phenomena at a haunted location sometimes works well by running a tape recorder and asking questions. Nothing turned up on the tape this time.

I was sensing the presence of a young man; he gave me the name of Albert. I also got the name Hand, but I am not sure if the names went together. Albert was not an old man, rather a young boy, maybe 10 or 11 years old. I then sensed a ghost behind the ghost! It was an even younger, female presence that gave me the name Caroline.

I think they died at different points in time of childhood diseases. My arms started to itch; perhaps I was picking up some of the residual energy of one of their diseases. Albert showed me his ear, and I felt a painful feeling in my own ear. Albert had died of some kind of ear infection. Caroline was very pale — ghostly would be an apt description. She continued to hide behind Albert.

I know what you are thinking. How can a ghost hide behind another ghost? Are ghosts transparent — sometimes. When I see a ghost in my mind, I see a space distortion with a person's outline and maybe some personal features like facial characteristic, hairstyle and color or dress. That's it. Remember, I am investigating in the awake state, not in a trance. In a trance, I would be able to focus and get a better picture of the ghosts, but trances take time and lots of energy. I simply have to conserve sometimes.

I needed to get some information from them. It can often be difficult to get the ghosts of children to talk and answer questions. We are, after all, in death as we were in life. A child will be childlike as a ghost, evasive and playful. I asked Albert what year it was. The answer was 1872. Marcy & Mecray's Pharmacy, which later became Central Pharmacy, would have been in existence on this spot in 1872. Colonel Henry Sawyer died several years later of a massive heart attack on October 16, 1893 in the pharmacy bathroom. Prior to Marcy & Mecray, Dr. James S. Kennedy had his Pharmacy here beginning in the 1860s. It's an old building with a lot of history.

Were Albert and Caroline children of the pharmacist I wondered? What you are about to read next are the actual channeled words I received psychically from Albert. They added a touching new dimension to the case, one that brought a tear to my eye and to Suzan's.

"We came here," said Albert. "I brought her here to make her better. They had medicines here — we tried them all — nothing made us better again." I soon realized from the visual imagery that I was receiving from Albert and Caroline that they were aware that a Doctor worked in the pharmacy and had many kinds of medicine around the place. The only thing they did not realize was that their illness was death. No earthly medicine would be able to "make them better" again, but they tried and tried repeatedly.

"The soda made us better," Albert quipped. I was sensing a very sweet taste, like dumping strawberry jam in seltzer water. Yes, I am sure the soda did taste much better than all the medicines they had tried. I wonder how many unexplained broken medicine jars Dr. Marcy and Dr. Mecray had in their store back then. Albert seemed to admit to accidentally breaking a few to get the lids off. It is exceedingly difficult for ghosts to lift a physical object. Most of their activity affects electrical based objects.

Albert really got me with the next images. He told me that Caroline's mom was very upset when she got sick, and he had to help her get better so she could go back home. He said she was not his sister. He said that his sister had died earlier, and his Mom was devastated by the deaths. He was the only one left, so he thinks.

Albert told me his body "walked away from him," that he "couldn't catch up to it," and finally, "the men took it to the graveyard." He was so frightened he ran home. He found Caroline crying in an alley near his house and "adopted her." Caroline was lost and could not find her house or remember which street she lived on. She still does not.

This is a common thing with ghosts. They lose track of time. When they "sleep," days, weeks or years may go by. This is why hauntings do not occur on a regular basis. Their sleeping seems to be their energy phasing in and out of our time continuum. They have never crossed over, so what awaits them is an eternity between here and the Other Side that has no set rules and a special space/time existence. The Ghost Plane, as I like to call it, is truly in a fog.

Albert and Caroline desperately want to get well again. Albert kept referring to Suzan and giving me the warm feeling that he felt for her. Could Suzan get them to cross over to the Other Side? Albert was very much attached to her, so perhaps in time, she can convince them to go. As I finished my Q & A with the ghosts in the cellar, I passed over the red spot on the floor. The ghosts wanted me to look at the spot and the water heater next to the spot. They indicated that in past winters they would huddle up against the hot water heater to keep warm.

"Suzan... Suzan... my mother's name," Albert cried out. I am not sure what he was implying, but I think his real mother's name may have been "Suzanne." It seems that the attachment to Suzan was more maternal than I thought!

The basement was their home. They would venture up into the store, but would not stay there because, "people were afraid of them." They also

Before the mall days: Washington Street in 1869 looking west.
The Commercial House is on the left and the original Kennedy's Pharmacy, pre-
decessor of Marcy & Mecray's Drugstore, is on the right. The third
incarnation of Congress Hall is in the distance at the very end of the street.
(Walt Campbell Collection)

told me something that really shed some light on Cape May's hauntings on a larger scale. The ghosts *do* see each other and interact. They seem to act out roles in their realm and stake their claims to property and territory. Some even try to "take away" the weaker and younger ghosts. A dark side to the Other Side?

"The other kids try to fight with me," said Albert, "We are safe in here." The "people" in white who came to try to "take them away," I think, were spirits trying to rescue the stuck kids from the Ghost Plane. However, again as in life, stubbornness can be one of the soul's eternal personality traits, and Albert and Caroline have to want to cross over.

I returned to the floor of the shop above to bring the news of Suzan's ghosts to her. She was amazed to hear that she had two ghosts, and that they were both children. Albert and Caroline followed us up, and Albert, I sensed, lifted himself up to his "perch" on the sales counter.

I told Suzan that Albert and Caroline do not go up to the apartment above because a "man would chase them away," and he would "be in a bad mood" sometimes. Suzan laughed and acknowledged that she knew who the man was. He was a former boyfriend, but he was now gone.

Albert spoke sadly of how the longer he and Caroline have been "sick" the more the people in the store start to fade and become "see-through." Perhaps their energy is changing planes, and they are slowly fading from ours permanently into the shadows of the Ghost Plane. It seems to happen this way.

I told Suzan and her two daughters, Maggie and Emmy, that the ghosts like to run around the shop and play hide and seek with unsuspecting customers. They told me they get very lonely when the shop closes at night. Caroline likes to peer out through the clothes and even enjoys trying to get into the outfits on the racks! This puts a completely new spin on the term "piercing the veil!"

Maggie mentioned that many times they have heard hangers clanging at night and have often heard the basement door open and close... when there is no one else in the store! Maggie also had an experience in possibly the same bathroom in which Colonel Sawyer made his final exit. "I was in the bathroom and left to get paper towels... when I came back the sink was filled with water, but the water faucet was never turned on!" I think maybe the children were just trying to wash up, or was it just Colonel Sawyer's ghost adding to the show.

I could feel a sense of relief from everyone present. "He's become very attached to you," I told Suzan and she started getting teary-eyed at the news of her new "adopted kids."

I told the ladies that, on one occasion, they had locked up for the night while Albert and Caroline were still outside and the children got locked out. (Ghosts still respect physical boundaries from their time) They are fearful of going out now, so they stay inside.

Suzan also solved the mystery of why the children stay in the basement to stay warm. "We turn the heat off down here in the winter," she said, sadly reacting to the children huddled up in the basement.

As for Suzan's two children, Emmy is not old enough to work in the store yet and likes the ghost-free zone upstairs better at this point. Maggie, according to Albert, "talks on the phone all the time." Maggie says she is talking to customers on the store phone all the time!

Caroline *loves* the color blue, Albert told me. He also has taken to the fun practice of snapping the brassieres on the wall racks at night, I told them. Suzan gasped. It seems his slingshot game had just caused an entire wall rack of clothes to rip off it's hardware and collapse onto the ground, leaving

Suzan a pile of clothes and hangers laying on the floor the previous morning!

The most touching thing about this case came in the final moments of my interview with Suzan and her daughters. Albert asked me to ask Suzan if he could call her Mom. We all paused and got a little choked up. "Yes... Oh my God!" Suzan said, choking back tears.

Albert and Caroline may not be home yet, but they had found a loving adoptive family to stay with for a while. It must be a lonely life, being the ghost of a child. They had their lives cut short in their prime, and their ghosts did not want to give up those lives, even if it meant crossing over into heaven. A little compassion and maybe even a little love will shed a whole lot of light on the ghosts of Cape May and perhaps help them eventually cross over and live again. Suzan McClure eventually left the business and last I heard had moved back to Pennsylvania. I have been in touch with the new guard running both businesses and the activity continues on a weekly basis.

I think one of the most interesting book signing I have ever done is at Lace Silhouettes Lingerie. There I was, the Ghost Writer, sitting at a table signing books beneath a rack of brassieres! If I was uncomfortable, you should have seen the ladies coming in to purchase lingerie, including the one who upon seeing me, proceeded to spell out the word B-R-A to the sales lady! I told her not to be embarrassed, I had a mother and a sister in my house where I grew up and I knew what a bra was! It was an interesting event. The highlight however, was not the setting of the book signing.

As I spoke with Jessica and Suzan at the time, I mentioned as customers shopped around the sales floor, that they should put up signs announcing "favorite garments of the ghosts." With that a rack of *blue* nightgowns ripped off a wall far away from everyone and crashed to the ground, as if on cue. This is a very active haunt and lots of fun to boot! However, the next book signing will be in the front foyer, safely away from anything *too* private!

In the last couple of years, I have stopped by the stores for a ghost check. I even ran into Suzan one weekend when she had returned to town to do a guest stint as manager once again. While I sensed things may still be paranormally active, I have not received any recent reports. A building with this much history is bound to have a few ghosts. Hauntings do run in cycles, and perhaps the ghosts are taking a few years off. Time will tell.

This is a great place to shop when visiting Cape May in the summer. Just make sure the ghosts do not happen to be wearing something that you just purchased to take home!

The Sea Villa

WHERE THE GHOSTS CHECK IN...

Guest Suites — 5 Perry Street, Cape May

T HE sign read "Ghost Friendly," and there were only a few rooms available for the tired and dead. Now that you are a semi-expert in the field of ghosts, I would like to introduce you to a wild new frontier of the paranormal. This is a story about what I experienced at a place by the beach in Cape May. It completely changed my thinking about ghosts. I do not expect you to believe everything I believe, but I can tell you this; when you are a psychic medium who delves into the Spirit world, as I am, strange things like this are bound to happen! Just keep an open mind, and keep on reading!

You and I might not notice the ethereal signs or all the comings and go-ings at the Sea Villa on Perry Street, but the ghosts do! Their story is one of the most amazing I have encountered as a psychic medium ghost investigator in Cape May. It truly begins to shed light on an existence we are only starting to understand. Theirs is a version of life, which is certainly not "death" by any means. The Ghost Plane, as I call the realm of our spectral neighbors, is a place where the dead and the living quietly coexist, most of the time.

I seem to recall someone mentioning to me that the Sea Villa had quite a bit of ghostly activity going on at the old hotel. I decided to pay proprietress Debbie Longstreet and her family a visit and do a little psychic detective work for them. Unfortunately, at the time, I was not writing my column, and I made only mental notes on the place. Luckily, Debbie remembered almost everything of our walkthrough, and combined with my most recent visit, I think we have nicely pieced the mystery of the Sea Villa together. You see, haunting parameters are constantly changing. On a certain day I may sense lots of activity, yet on another day I may sense little or none.

During one of my recent lectures, a man, who was obviously dragged in kicking and screaming, was not the least bit impressed with anything para-normal. He sat yawning away until something must have sparked his in-terest! "How can there be more than one ghost in a place?" he asked. "I've never heard of ghosts talking with each other!" Suddenly he was the expert in all matters paranormal. The reason I recount this dull exchange is the man brought to light a fact that many people do not realize; ghosts are just like us, except they do not have bodies. Of course, there are those who close their minds to everything extraordinary in life, including one ghost.

To assume a place is limited to having one ghost is as absurd as thinking ghosts cannot see or interact with each other. We humans tend to think of ourselves as privileged and special, having characteristics that are only available to our species. The argument is similar to assuming that animals can't communicate with each other, or there are no other life forms anywhere but on earth. We are not alone, and we are certainly not the only ones talking!

When I investigate a haunted abode, I have now taken to running a tape recorder, not just to capture possible EVPs, but because I have found that my memory from years of retail punishment and channeling workouts does not always serve me well. I am always amazed by the little things that I may sense and mention on tape that occur in a split second, like a color of a ghost's outfit or a sudden smell in the air that vanishes as quickly as it arrived. The work of a parapsychologist in a haunted place is difficult and time consuming; the work of a psychic medium investigating the same place can be altogether mind-numbing. There is something about being around ghosts and the energy they give off that can really scramble one's thinking process. Sometimes images and names start coming at me so fast that I forget if someone doesn't remind me about them later. A tape recorder is just what the doctor ordered!

I let the tape recorder document what things I psychically pick up at a place, what "voices" I am hearing and repeating and what the witnesses of a haunting have to say. It works out SO much better for all of us!

Shortly after the great November 1878 fire, local architect Enos Williams built the small hotel in 1879 that is today called the Sea Villa. The new building sat on the former site of George Dougherty's Avenue House. It was first called Beirn's Cottage, then the Rudolph, the Sevilla and now, the Sea Villa. The Ghosts call it their favorite hotel in town. Yes, they actually *come* to the Sea Villa to stay for a while!

A Ghost Hotel you say. I would call it more of a hotel for us and them. Apparently, they are very respectful of us, but we are "the noisy neighbors" who drive them out each summer season. So don't go looking for lots of ghosts at The Sea Villa during peak summer months. All you will find is great rooms and probably one of the best ocean views in town.

On my first visit, I encountered Henry in Room 6. It seems Henry was a sailor, who traveled and worked around Cape May. He enjoyed all the "pretty ladies" who stayed at the hotel. He found the place restful and mentioned being thrown out of another local hotel because as he put it, "They don't allow ghosts!" Nonsense, I thought! What self-respecting place in Cape May would not want a ghost or two? People *love* ghosts and places that have good ghost stories. More tourists today specifically ask me for haunted lodging recommendations than ever before. Anyone who thinks a ghost will scare away business is out of touch with the times. This is the 21st century now—ghosts are IN!

The Sea Villa has been in continuous use as a small hotel longer than any other establishment in Cape May. It reminds me of one of those great old hotels in the *Gunsmoke* TV series from the '60s. Debbie is certainly a perfect stand-in for Miss Kitty! Her low key, charming, witty personality and love of all things new age make her the perfect proprietress for this marvelous old hotel.

One of the most beautiful rooms at The Sea Villa is the front bedroom on the second floor facing the ocean. On my first visit, I encountered the ever-slumbering Minnie. It seems she has taken over the front room, but does not get much of a chance to enjoy the beautiful view. Minnie, it seems, worked (and works) "at night." Enough said. The ghost of Henry told me that Minnie would often retire to bed early in the morning and rise in the evening with the sounds of the player piano.

Several of the ghosts mentioned and complained about the piano being removed, and Debbie acknowledge that they had indeed taken it out and replaced it with a pump organ. I can't see a pump organ belting out the *Gunsmoke* theme, can you?

I had the chance to speak with Debbie and Dave's son, Ian, who seems like an old soul. Ian was more interested in the ghosts on my last visit in 2003, however. A year older, he is more interested in his living friends outside who call to him, instead of the ghosts. But he does have a story.

When Ian was about six years old, he was climbing up to get to the top shelf of the laundry room. From another part of the house Debbie heard a crash and rushed to find Ian lying on the floor, surrounded by fallen supplies and shelving.

"She pushed me," he told Debbie. "The little girl was on the top shelf and pushed me away." Debbie reminded Ian of the story recently. Now, five years later, he only remembers falling from the shelf. The idea of a ghost doing it is now hidden away in his subconscious.

Young children can generally see ghosts and even communicate with them. Up to about five or six it seems, our suspension of disbelief is in place, which allows us to see and hear things the adults no longer will. Ian had such an experience, as have many other children in haunting investigations that I have done. "Unseen playmates" are often ghosts in a house or spirits of relatives coming back to "play" or visit. Most times, they are harmless; apparently this little girl meant business.

"I bought a small children's rocker at an antique shop and put in it one of the rooms," Debbie recalled the activity a few years back at the hotel. "As soon as we put it in the room, all sorts of crazy things started happening. Keys would levitate, doors opened and closed, light bulbs would explode. Soon it started scaring the guests, so I decided to take the rocker out of the room, and as soon as I did the activity stopped."

At that point, I sensed a woman named Mabel or simply Mae coming down the grand staircase. She seemed to be hanging up keys on the wall. "There used to be a key rack there, from years ago," said Debbie. "We took it down."

Mabel introduced herself to me as an old proprietress of the hotel, possibly even from the building that sat on the same space before the Sea Villa. Mabel heard us talking about the little girl and told me to tell Debbie that she "came with the rocker." It seems the little girl was ill with a childhood disease of the time and could breathe more comfortably rocking upright in the chair. Sadly, she eventually died in the chair and refused to move on. She felt the chair was her security blanket, and she would not loose sight of it. When Debbie bought the chair, the little girl was sitting in it. It seems that the child did not like the strangers in her new home and threw more than one tantrum. She eventually took to hiding on the top shelf of the laundry room until that fateful day young Ian discovered her.

Ian scared her as much as she did him. Mabel told us that the girl raced in fright and frustration down the stairs and out the front door and is now somewhere over on Congress Place in one of the "old houses."

As Mabel spoke, an older gentlemen ghost entered the room. His name was Arthur. He told me a few eye opening things about ghosts that I had never read or heard anywhere before. As he started, however, Mabel quipped to him not to "scare the folks on the ground floor." It seems we the living and where we exist are referred to as the "ground floor." Arthur paid her no attention and continued his story.

He was a traveling ghost. He lived and died in Philadelphia and was on his way to see his *dead* sister up north. He told me ghosts move distances by willing their energies around. They look at the lighthouse on the point and will themselves to it. Walking is reserved for short distances and for new ghosts who have yet to get their "sea legs," he told me.

"When you first drop dead," he grunted to me psychically, "you have no idea what to do—if you get stuck without help to cross over—you wind up here—in the place we roam around in." Arthur emphasized that the ghost plane is not an aberration of nature or some sort of purgatory. It is a "version" of nature, a realm different from ours and not as advanced as the Other Side. This is a wonderful explanation. However, most people want science to be able to test a theory under laboratory conditions to prove it really exists. Those people are missing out on a lot of extra knowledge that life has to offer. Open your minds. You don't have to believe everything you see and hear, but try to keep an open mind, and you just may learn something you never thought could be possible before. The paranormal is a whole new classroom situation in which to learn. Just don't fall asleep on your desk, or they will bury you!

Arthur told me the ground floor was more of a hassle, and he does not miss it much. He has freedoms now that he didn't have before, but he also misses some of the earthly pleasures. Most importantly, he told me, the ghosts LIKE it where they are. That is why most of them stay.

So now, what is a Ghost Writer to do? That little bit of information throws out a lot of previous theories about ghosts and hauntings. Am I getting closer to the truth about ghosts? I think this whole study of Cape May is in fact doing just that, moving the truth within our grasp.

I have always assumed ghosts were "stuck." It seems that some are indeed stuck, but there are many more that are willing to stay put in the ghost realm. It certainly does clear up some cases where I thought I must be dealing with a more enlightened spirit who had come back from the Other Side to help me with my work. Perhaps I am just encountering a few of the more enlightened ghosts in town. Could ghosts actually interact with each other, socialize and exist as if they were alive? I would have to give a definite "yes" to that question. Nevertheless, as always, the closer we get to the truth, the more questions arise. The skeptics have a field day with verbiage like this.

Why are some greater beings, or Angels, not coming down to gather up and bring home the ghosts? In a recent trance channeling I conducted, my spirit guides had answered this question. Higher beings will not interfere in a soul's free will and independent existence. If a ghost wants to stay in the Ghost Realm for a while, they have every right to do so. It seems that as we learn many lessons on our plane, ghosts continue their learning experience on their plane as well.

It would be funny, wouldn't it, if becoming a ghost was part of a soul's natural evolution? As I said, the more I uncover about ghosts, the more questions I have. There have certainly been many books written on ghosts and hauntings. But few of them talk at any length about a ghost's actual existence. What is for sure is that ghosts *do* exist. I am firmly convinced of that. Exploring their plane of existence may take the rest of *my* life. This book is also not out to preach and change other people's beliefs, but I need to express my feelings on the subject fully, to deliver the goods, or ghosts.

Meanwhile, back at the hotel—Mabel talked with Arthur (and us) about a woman named Irene who also stayed at the hotel. It seems Irene *loves* milk, and because she is a ghost with no need to ingest food, she craves the old sensation of cold milk. I saw an image of her grabbing at milk, but her hand passing through the glass. "I used to spill milk all the time" remembered Ian of his "youth." Perhaps Irene just wanted to get her hands on a cold drink.

After uncovering the identity of "the trunk lady" in Room 10 at the Macomber as being an old woman named Irene Wright, I began to wonder if this was just a coincidence of two ghosts with the same name or in fact was it the *same* ghost moving from hotel to hotel? Irene Wright was a new discovery that came with the second edition of this book. When I wrote about Irene at the Sea Villa in the first edition, none of us yet knew about Miss Wright. Maybe the Ghost Realm is a little more difficult to travel around than I had thought. Perhaps ghosts cannot move *that* far. Are they all confined to the boundaries of Cape May or within a certain distance of where they haunt?

It would be a fascinating exercise to engage the ghost of The Macomber's Irene in Room 10 and The Sea Villa's Irene to find out if they are one in the same. I wonder if Deb also has a "Room 10?" Pinky at the Macomber talked about the lad in Room 10 asking for fresh linens and glasses everyday. The Irene at The Sea Villa also seems to have a thing for glasses except the kind filled with cold milk. One ghost haunting two completely different places is nothing new in Cape May. If Katherine can do it at The Saltwood House and

Windward House, why can't Irene? The haunting activity in Room 10 at The Macomber is only certain times of the year. Is Irene Wright on the move?

I also started to wonder about Arthur. Could he also be the same Arthur that we encountered at the Macomber? Two Irenes and two Arthurs haunting two buildings on the same street? I think it is more than just a ghostly coincidence. I guess if you are haunting Cape May for hundreds of years, why stay in the same hotel? Cape May is turning out to be one big cocktail party for ghosts!

Speaking of drinks, there is a room, now the dining area, downstairs at the Sea Villa that *really* has the feel of an old saloon. Dave asked me to tell him what the two holes in the floor were, using my psychic abilities. "There was a bar here — a long time ago — sometimes in the open, sometimes hidden," I told him. Dave confirmed that they indeed did think there were pipes to the cellar for drainage and perhaps a feed for beer coming up into the room. Debbie recently found out that the hotel was originally the oldest gambling house in Cape May! Perry Street must have been hopping in Victorian times, when gambling was still legal, with the Blue Pig gambling house on one side of the street and The Avenue House on the other. And the many other "frills" in the neighborhood!

"Irene and her friend Stella, with their blond hair pinned up high, are wearing heavy perfume," I told Debbie, as I saw the ghosts of the two ladies glide across the porch upstairs. It seems that gambling was not the only evening activity going on in the old days at 8 Perry Street! "I smell perfume all the time," Debbie told me. This was another confirmation, which is important to a psychic investigation.

The ghosts used to wear perfume, and they think they are still wearing it. Their thoughts become so saturated in the ether that sensitive people like Debbie and I can sometimes sense it, not through our olfactory bulbs, but through our brains.

The heavy perfume was also something that Jerry Reeves mentioned about Irene Wright at The Macomber. He said she bathed in the stuff. Another tip off that my two Irenes may be one in the same, although I do not think Miss Wright was the "Lady of the evening" type! I will have to update these books on a regular basis the way new information keeps coming to light about the ghosts!

Arthur then complained about Millicent in the front bedroom, saying she "had the same room forever," and that she "never checks out." He told Debbie she needed to be evicted! Debbie mentioned that when she first bought the place 10 years ago and they would sleep in that certain bedroom. She could feel Milly sleeping all around her, as if she was moving into Milly's personal space! This can happen.

I have heard more than once of people having direct hits with a ghost. When a "sensitive person" moves through the exact space a ghost is occupying, should the ghost not step out of the way, our energy seems to mix quickly with the ghost's. A resulting dizzy or giddy feeling may overcome the living member of the encounter. One person described it as feeling like laughing gas that a dentist gives you. The effect is instantaneous and usually gone before we can realize what just happened. So next time you think you just had a mini-stroke or a dizzy spell, better first check to see if the place in which you are standing happens to be haunted!

The ghosts at the Sea Villa seem to respect the living guests and vacate the rooms when they are rented. Perhaps this is why they resent Milly for overstaying her welcome! From what I have been experiencing in Cape May, ghosts do socially interact. I suppose, if we are in death as we are in life, then our personalities would go with us. If the ghost plane is another plane of existence, wouldn't it be correct to assume that socialization would take place?

Here is one of the more interesting things that came from this investigation. According to one of the ghosts at The Sea Villa, most haunting activity is nothing more than an aggravated or angry ghost. Many times, one ghost barging into another's space, like a brother or sister barging into your room when you were young and wanted to be alone, causes that aggravation. Ghosts react with an outpouring of energy that seems to set all kinds of things happening. Doors swing open and close, electrical appliances can malfunction, objects move or disappear. This is certainly not to say every haunting is the result of a peeved ghost, but it seems many are. Luckily, most ghosts, like their human incarnations, get over it with time.

Most fascinating about the Sea Villa investigation was the fact that there seems to be a kind of ethereal "Ghosts Welcome" sign floating over the place. The ghosts seem to mark an area energetically that they feel is safe and comfortable for their journeys. The energy at The Sea Villa is certainly some of the best and most peaceful in all of Cape May.

The "management" at the Sea Villa also has great energy. Mabel keeps her eye on the entire house and the grounds. She is particularly annoyed that someone keeps trying to take down the sea wall on the property. Debbie told me they have been trying to preserve the 100-year-old sea wall between their hotel and George's Place Restaurant, but someone kept removing rocks from it. I recently mentioned to George's Place owner John Karapanagiotis about the ghostly gripe over breakfast one morning. This is actually how I found out about this great little dining spot. (If you have not eaten at George's yet, it is one of the *best* casual dining spots in town.) John K was amused by the ghost's reaction and told me his father-in-law, George, had originally wanted to buy the Sea Villa and tear it down to make room for a parking lot!

Glad that did not happen John — your pancakes would have been flipping themselves right out to sea!

As I mentioned earlier in the chapters on the Southern Mansion and the Craig House, ghosts will often warn a property owner of problems with the building. Henry complained about a beam under the house on my first visit. Dave had been in the process of repairing one of the porch supports. This is another example of just how "in the know" ghosts are. Not a bad type of ghost to have — conscientious, works for room and board!

The ghosts at the Sea Villa seem to be perfectly content to coexist with the living. They understand just what we are going through and see it from an even greater perspective. Arthur complained that Debbie "took away his checker board in the middle of a game." She admitted she did move the board out of the room. Arthur quipped, "it may just be a game for you, lady... but for us, a game of checkers can take a lifetime," a poignant reminder of the great idleness that can come with being a ghost. Our ethereal friends at the old Sea Villa had a lot more to say on that stormy afternoon.

The wind howled in from the west and the gray sky threatened; a great storm was on its way. The ghosts were not concerned. To them, we the living are the real storm, barging into their space and evicting them from one place to the next. They are quite content the way they are, in their quiet realm.

Just don't get them peeved. You may be in for a rude awakening at about three o'clock every morning! Remember the old saying, let sleeping ghosts lie.

The next time you want a great view, wonderful breakfasts and a very reasonable place to stay with charm — and spirit — try the Sea Villa. Tell the ghosts Craig sent you. I may get a commission from them, or at least a few more good stories!

The Emlen Physick Estate

THE DOCTOR IS NOT IN...
BUT HIS DEAD AUNTS ARE

1048 Washington Street, Cape May

ABOUT 12 YEARS AGO, I had the pleasure of conducting a group channeling session for a few of the ladies who worked for the Mid-Atlantic Center for the Arts (MAC). After a long evening of reconnecting everyone with their deceased friends and relatives on the Other Side, we got to talking about their jobs, what they do and the old mansion on Washington Street, where their offices were located. At the time, I had no idea I would be writing a column about ghosts, or books for that matter. Channeling was my vocation, writing was still just a hobby, but ghosts were always a passion!

Known as *Cape May's original haunted house* by the locals, the stately estate of the late Dr. Emlen Physick was then, as now, an imposing structure. Built in the avant-garde, stick style of the time, by the famous and eccentric architect Frank Furness (1839-1912), the Physick Estate has been restored to its former grandeur, thanks to MAC.

No longer does it resemble the ramshackle abode into which it had deteriorated when MAC rescued the property from the wrecker's ball in the early 1970s.

It is no wonder then that MAC has wanted to shed the haunted house image that the locals grew to know so well over the years. The house does not look haunted anymore! It is now a beautiful Victorian home-turned-museum open for all to experience, and you all should.

My first unofficial trip to the Physick Estate was a few years ago, during one of those hot Cape May July days. We were vacationing for the week, and I was anxious to get to the beach. My friend Kathy DeLuccia, who was traveling with us, had other ideas. Kathy LOVES museums, art, and frankly, anything ancient. The Physick Estate must have been calling her name because she kept bringing it up each morning. Finally, I relented to give up my day at the beach and hit the antiquities circuit with her.

As we gathered on the lawn by the house, I instinctively looked up at the tall gables and noticed the chimneys were turned upside-down! Our guide told us that the architect did many unique and odd things like this. I gazed up to the second floor, and thought I saw an older woman walking past one of the windows. She was in period dress, but this could be easily explained, I thought, as even our tour guide was wearing an old-fashioned dress.

The Physick House was built in 1879 after Dr. Emlen Physick decided to retire to Cape May at age 21! He had just completed his medical degree, but had decided it was gentleman farming, not medicine, he would rather pursue as a career. The property was purchased from his mother, Mrs. Frances Ralston, and her house was moved across the street, where it still stands as the Ralston Physick House. Dr. Physick came from a very prestigious line of medical men. His grandfather was Dr. Philip Syng Physick, known as "the father of American surgery." Dr. Physick decided to use some of his inheritance from the Physick wealth to build the huge stick style mansion and out buildings on the 22 acre estate. When completed, he moved his mother and her sister, his Aunt Emilie Parmentier into the house. It seems Aunt Emilie just can't get enough of the place.

As we entered the mansion's incredible entrance hall, with its beautiful wall treatments and heavily carved woodwork, I had to stop myself and refocus for a minute. I had just seen FIVE dogs run up the staircase! I realized in a few moments that what I had seen was a "psychic image" received telepathically from the dogs. You see, these dogs had their day, about 100 years ago! The Physick Estate, it seemed, had gone to the dogs, but the dogs had never gone to their maker... WHY?

The first thing I usually ask any tour guide at an old estate is, "Are there any ghosts?" Most guides will give me an honest answer. Some will try to make light of it. I had sensed the presence of two women in the house, dead ones, and they were moving back and forth on the second floor. I could sense them almost running around. When I think back to that day now, I realize they were obviously trying to get the dogs out of the house! I wonder if ghost dogs track mud or ectoplasm on the rugs.

"How many ghosts do you have?" I asked our guide. "Just one, Aunt Emilie, and she's my friend." "No," I muttered to Kathy, "she has two... and a whole lot of stray dogs!" I was annoyed at the blatant attempt to keep the ghosts under wraps, but we were there for a historical tour, so I behaved.

As we made our way to the second floor, I could see Aunt Emilie. She had great energy and a vibrant smile. She was very cognizant of what we were doing there. This is a ghost who *knows* everything that is going on in her home!

But what about the dogs? I posed the question to our stoic tour guide who kept dodging my questions about the ghosts! She told us that Dr. Physick loved dogs and had many of them during his tenure on the property. I refrained from telling her about the dog sighting or the other woman, who seemed to be in poor health.

When I try to solve a haunting, I first check the place out psychically. Next, I ask questions. Many times people will talk about the people who lived at a particular haunted site until they find out I am researching ghosts. It does get frustrating sometimes.

As I parted ways with the Physick Estate that hot summer afternoon, I knew I had to get back. Luckily, for me, the women from the group channeling obliged my request to have a "private tour" after hours when the house was empty and quiet.

It was another humid day. I decided to walk over to the Estate from where I was staying. The huge, voracious mosquitoes that day could have carried away small children, but I made it to the Physick Estate with SOME blood left in my arms and legs!

The empty house had a completely different feel. I could imagine how Dr. Physick must have enjoyed the old place when it was in its full entertaining heyday. One of the ladies decided to video tape my walkthrough. All seemed

Aunt Emilie Parmentier with her young
nephew Emlen Physick.
(Courtesy of MAC)

quiet until we made our way into the music room, and I sensed yet another dog — this time a shaggy black version!

A woman suddenly appeared on my psychic radar and swooped in and around us. Everyone present could feel the cold breeze — and there is no AC in the building.

It would seem our lady friend was after the errant pup. She must have got him, because they both vanished. The ladies at MAC told me that while Dr. Physick did have many dogs, they were never allowed in the house. So who was letting them in? As we made our way to the second floor, I could not sense Emilie. I did feel a woman in Mrs. Ralston's bedroom, however. She seemed like she was ill and bedridden. Mrs. Ralston was in her eighties when she died, so I assumed it was her.

Over the next few years, I had begun an annual lecture series on ghosts, hauntings and Victorian séances for MAC. I had returned to the Physick Estate many times, but still could not solve the mystery of the phantom dogs, or for that matter, who the invalid woman ghost was.

On one visit to the Physick Estate, I saw Mary Stewart, MAC's Deputy Director I noticed out of the corner of my eye the ghost of some type of spaniel running around as we sat in the tearoom on the Estate. I heard the name Eddie, Neddie or Teddy. Mary told me that the original dog run was right behind us, and she would check to see if there was such a dog listed. We wandered around the property a while, so that I could take a few photos of the grounds and get a better feel for my *Exit Zero* article. Up upon a small hill behind the main house stands a modest building called Hill House.

Hill House now serves as administrative offices for MAC, but at one time acted as a private workshop for Dr. Physick. I had heard a few stories from the locals that Hill House had its own ghost. The people I spoke with said they encountered a strong feeling around the house, when the larger house was being refurbished in the early 1970s. Mary took me inside and offered me a tour of the cellar under the house. I must admit, if there were any ghosts at Hill House, they were out at the beach for I sensed nothing. Could the ghost of Aunt Emilie and friends have taken up refuge in Hill House while the main house was being renovated? Hill House was considered haunted by the neighbors many years ago.

Ghosts do not seem to like noisy or loud people in their space. Renovation can send them, literally, up the walls. Usually they wind up on a third floor or in the attic simply to get away from us! I truly believe that most of the third-floor hauntings in Cape May are not ghosts of servants. They are simply ghosts on the run. Quiet a paradox — ghosts scare us, but we annoy them!

The ghosts were back in the main house that day, for sure. As I parted Mary's company, I again sensed a woman watching me from the upstairs window of the main house. It was not the ghost of Emilie. It was a different female ghost energy, with some kind of illness or medical condition. I asked if it were Mrs. Ralston haunting the place along with Emilie. "No," was my answer. "Bella" was the name I saw. Was this a friend of Emilie's or maybe a servant? There was no mention of a Bella on the tour, or in the MAC booklet on the house, so she was a mystery.

When I ran this story in *Exit Zero*, I asked my readers if anyone could help to solve this mystery. Several months went by when I received an e-mail

Dr. Emlen Physick with one of his many furry friends at the Physick Estate
(Courtesy of MAC)

with a copy of an old census from the late 1800s. On the list, living at the Physick Estate with Dr. Emlen, Aunt Em, Mrs. R. and the servants was a sister named *Isabella!* The mystery had been solved. Next to Bella's name on the census was a listing that she was crippled!

Mary Stewart's son had been working at Cold Spring Cemetery that summer, and Mary had asked him to dig up, uh, I mean, look up the Physick plot. Isabelle Parmentier is listed on the tombstone. It is amazing that no one, including everyone working at MAC, had known of Isabelle's existence. Now they do.

During another visit to the estate, there was something trying not to catch my attention, quickly letting the dogs in through a back entrance! It was Aunt Emilie. I finally figured out just who was letting the dogs in the house... it was Emilie all this time! Mary recently told me that Emilie took care of the dogs. She not only fed them, she *cooked* their food in the kitchen each day! Her strict sister Frances would have nothing of dogs in the house, but obviously Emilie feels differently.

This is a question I am often asked as a psychic medium: do our pets cross over with us, and can I channel them? The answer is yes to both, and they can get stuck on the ghost plane for a while, just like human beings. Had the dogs loved Emilie so much they decided, one by one, to stay with her after they died? A man who took one of my Halloween tours made a good point. When I mentioned how many cat ghosts were in Cape May, but how few dog ghosts there were, he responded that cats are usually attached to places, while dogs are attached to people. It does make sense.

People are usually surprised to hear of an animal ghost. Ghosts of pets, however, are more common than you may think.

Mary Stewart emailed me the next morning after my visit to tell me they found a picture of Dr. Physick with his cocker spaniel, Neddie. It seems that Neddie was fonder of Aunt Emilie's cooking than of Dr. Physick's companionship!

But why does Emilie stay? I asked her the other day. She very matter-of-factly told me that when she died and her neighbor sold the property, it had begun to decline. When the property really went down hill in the 1960s, local youths would hang out in the basement. This concerned her terribly. She decided to stay and watch over the place. After she died, she realized many of the beloved dogs had gotten "stuck" as ghosts on the property. Instead of abandoning them, she has decided to stay behind to take care of them until the day that they finally go home to meet their master, who is probably waiting for both them and his beloved Aunt Emilie.

There are other yet undiscovered ghosts on the property. A few of the ladies who work in the offices in the carriage house had once called me to tell me they saw a man, in the dead of winter, walk up to the carriage house entrance and into the building. When they went to check, there was no one anywhere and the door was locked! It would make sense for an estate this size to have a ghost staff!

Since we started the *Historic Haunts Combination Ghost Tour* in 2006, fearless ghost enthusiasts have been able to enter the dark and shadowy Physick mansion — at night. On the very first tour, as the guide was telling the group about the ghosts in the house, three different tour-goers experienced an "older woman" moving in next to them, almost "pushing them aside" and "touching their arm." It was only when these unwilling guests of the house turned to look or checked in an opposing mirror on the wall, that they realized the woman had vanished!

A few years ago, I started hosting one of our most popular events at the Physick Estate, ever. It is called *Midnight at the Physick Estate*, and it is just that. 25 lucky people get to follow me around the rooms of the old Physick Mansion, late at night. The tour begins with a séance in the parlor, where I will try to contact the dead of the house, and ask them to participate in our event. The house, and the ghosts, never seem to disappoint.

What most people expect of a haunted house is usually the complete opposite of what really happens. During our *Midnight* event, the hauntings are usually very subtle. While phantom footsteps parading around the upstairs and disembodied voices have been heard, they are not the norm. What most people experience are intense feelings in various rooms. Everyone perceives ghosts differently, some of us do not sense them at all. My goal with the *Midnight* tours is to demonstrate to people what actually happenings in a haunting. It is a lot different than what happens on TV or in the movies, where hauntings are often staged or "enhanced" to look more frightening than they really are.

People at the *Midnight* events have felt their hair pulled, arms or hands touched, and have even experienced strong emotions like sadness or happiness in various rooms. It can be quite an eye opening experience, one all of you should try to experience.

The great thing about this mansion is it is open to the public, ghosts and all. If you want to get up close and personal with a haunted house, run, don't walk, to the Physick Estate!

The Peter Shields Inn

CHILD'S PLAY

Bed & Breakfast and Restaurant
1301 Beach Avenue, Cape May

FOR people visiting Cape May for the first time, an ocean front drive past the beautiful collection of old homes on Beach Avenue is a must. One of the most impressive and stately of all of the homes facing the sea is The Peter Shields Inn. With its imposing large white columns rising three stories high, this is a place that visually commands respect. Peter Shields' large sweeping hallways and grand staircases are truly eye-catching. So possibly is the ghost of the young man who walks these corridors at night, restlessly existing for almost a hundred years at the large home in what was once known as East Cape May.

The eastern end of Cape May is somewhat bittersweet in energy for me. It seems miles from the main section of town, but really isn't that far at all. It has an isolated and lonely feeling that I just cannot describe. Maybe it is a past life experience there? Surely some of the best places I have stayed in Cape May are on this end of town, Peter Shields, Angel of the Sea, Rhythm of the Sea to name a few. So what is it with the energy down here that makes me feel like time has stopped?

I think somewhere back in time, things happened down at this end of town that were not pretty. While staying at a beachfront B&B in East Cape May one summer, I can remember picking up some troubling past images near the surf. Some people pick up other people on the beach; I pick up dead people on the beach. It's wonderful being a psychic medium sometimes.

The images I saw in my mind happened a long time ago, maybe the mid 1700s. I saw a small ship, damaged and taking on water. It was on its way to Philadelphia, I think, from New York. For some reason it had to make an emergency docking in the surf, and the Captain evacuated the wealthy couple who had chartered it, along with their children. He put the family into a small boat and sent them ashore.

As I was receiving this image, it was as though time itself had shifted me back three hundred years, and I was seeing it first hand and feeling the terrible anxiety that the young couple must have experienced as they landed on to the deserted section of Cape May's long beach. At this point in history all the activity and civilization in Cape May was much further west, near Jackson Street and Perry Street, so this end of Cape May would have been isolated and filled with marshland and brush.

It seems the isolated character of much of Cape May's shoreline in those days brought out those who would take advantage of such innocent victims. At that time, Cape May, like other parts of the eastern seacoast, had its very own pirates and privateers. From what I saw, the pirates, who were camped out near the beach, wasted no time in "helping" the young couple and the Captain to the shore. I sensed there were gunshots, and the Captain and another crew member were shot and killed. I saw blood washing up in the frothy surf and staining the white sand. I heard screams of the helpless family and a plea for mercy from the husband. He offered his wallet and gold watch, but these fiends wanted more.

The couple, fleeing onto the beach with their young children, watched helplessly as the men sailed to the ship and pilfered what they could. I saw that the pirates were drinking heavily, and it was getting dark. The young couple probably did not know that civilization was nearby. The image ended in a horrible manner. The couple's children watched their parents die at the hands of the pirates, and then they too were shot running away down the beach, like a sick game of target practice. I think the images of this event were given to me by these three young children, who are now ghosts roaming the beaches.

That was almost three hundred years ago, however, and I am just picking up on the anxiety from one small piece of time. Tragedy happens everywhere, but does not always leave a psychic mark or a stain. There has to be a certain energy created at the time or maybe it is simply the place.

Many have had the idea to develop the eastern end of Cape May over the centuries. At the end of the nineteenth century, Cape May was beginning to feel the pinch from its new flashy competitor to the north, Atlantic City. Turning the eastern, marshy section of Cape May City into New Jersey's Newport was a top priority for many. Millionaire oil and coal real estate investors were brought in from Pennsylvania to reclaim the land, dredge the harbor and return Cape May to its former glorious position as Queen of the

Seaside resorts. The land may have been reclaimed from the sea, but the residual energies and ghosts were not about to leave.

In 1905, the Cape May Real Estate Company, under the direction of its new President, Peter Shields, began construction on the massive New Cape May Hotel, later to be called the Hotel Cape May, Admiral and finally, the Christian Admiral. When the hotel finally opened in 1908, it closed for repairs six months later and was plagued by problems, bankruptcy proceedings and strange happenings.

The large and imposing brick and steel structure never really caught its breath and struggled for years, until finally being torn down in 1996. Peter Shields was also never to recover fully from the events of the time.

When I look at some of the old postcards of the Hotel Cape May, it gives me the same isolated and lonely feeling that I get today in east Cape May. There are certainly plenty of houses, some magnificent mansions, plenty of summer vacationers and year-round residents, but something is just different about the place.

I can remember, a few years ago, getting a call from a woman staying at the Peter Shields Inn. She had asked if I would do a channeling session with her, which I agreed to do. It would be held in her room on the third floor of the house. It was my first time traveling to that end of town in a long time, and I was amazed to see so many large and beautiful buildings hiding "around the corner" in east Cape May.

As I walked into the house and mounted the grand staircase, I could sense the ghost of a young man. The woman working there at the time told me it was the ghost of Peter Shields. I would later research him to learn what I have just told you in the above paragraphs. He was indeed a torn and defeated man, finally resigning his post as President and leaving town in 1912.

As I conducted the channeling for my client, the large bedroom door, which was closed, kept opening, slowly, very slowly. The windows were closed and there was no noticeable draft, yet something was opening the door, three times in a row! Finally, I invited whoever wanted to come in, in, as long as they did not interrupt my channeling session. You see it is simply rude to tell a ghost to "get out." Ghosts are souls with feelings just like the rest of us. Nature sets up many varied life forms on different levels. My feeling is one must respect all other things that coexist with us here on the Earth Plane, including ghosts. Something at the Inn wanted to see what I was doing and could feel that I could sense his presence.

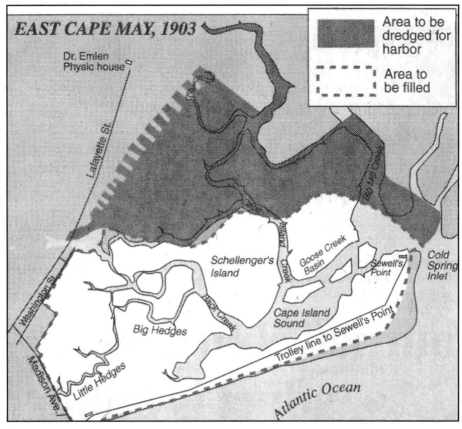

Walking on water *— The 1903 Map showing what would be filled in and what would be dredged to create the new harbor in East Cape May.*

(Walt Campbell Collection)

I have always felt that the area known originally as East Cape May is paranormally charged because most of the land here was either marsh or actual tidal creeks at one time. Water conducts energy and filling in the old waterways to create new real estate did not weaken the energy in the area. Driving down Beach Avenue, turning the bend and heading east, one can sense he has driven into a completely different place. The energy feels detached from the main section of town — creating the sensation of boating out to some far away island.

I was not to return to the Peter Shields Inn until the next spring. A client had told me about a ghostly encounter on the stairs with a young man, and the story sparked my interest in the old estate again. This time I decided to try out Peter Shield's restaurant for dinner, while doing a little surface ghost investigation for dessert!

It was a delightful dinner with friends and great food at the beach. Questioning our host, I found out that they did indeed have a ghost named "Ernest." The previous owners and staff had seen him, but no one recently had any experience. Lori Whissell, who now owns the Peter Shields with her family, has had more than her share of ghost experience at their sister property, Angel of the Sea (see next chapter).

After dinner, one of our party made a trip to the restroom, which is located on the lower level in what used to be the home's cellar, and later, an after-hours bar for many years. The old bar must still be serving drinks, and the folks from the afterlife must have been packing the place. My friend returned upstairs, shaken, not stirred, for we had come to find a ghost, and it was obvious we had. My friend reported a terrible feeling of someone watching her in the cellar, someone who had died tragically.

My turn to go and investigate. The cellar was quiet and quite large. As I moved down the long hallway towards the restrooms, I felt the air temperature start to drop and get very clammy and cold. As I moved past a large bust of Shakespeare standing in the corner of the basement, I was overwhelmed with a dreadful feeling of remorse. It was not a feeling of panic or anxiety, just sadness and despair. I had just walked into something or someone that I was not about to take lightly. It was not a malevolent energy at all, just a strong one. Had I found Ernest, or did Ernest find me?

When I quickly returned upstairs, I needed to shake the negative energy. This will happen sometimes when I channel, even with the best grounding methods in this world, I still absorb strong emotional energy like this. "Someone either died down there, or was murdered," I said.

Next, my friend Owen Miller, who was with us that night, insisted on meeting the ghost. I really do think Owen is quite psychic. It is just his "thrill-seeking gene" that keeps him too busy sailing to explore his other talents! "Somebody drowned down there," he said with a nervous edge to his voice. We all took a walk around the place and went up to the second floor after dinner. Who was this ghost called Ernest? Sandy Miller, who was also dining with us at the restaurant that evening, had been visiting Cape May since her youth, but did not know the answer.

I checked with Bob Fite, who has lived in town his whole life. I was interviewing him about his family's reign at The Colonial, now The Inn of Cape May, for one of my earlier articles. Had someone drowned in the Peter Shields basement? I had heard that, during the 1944 hurricane, the basements along the beachfront did indeed flood.

"No," Bob Fite told me calmly. "There were no casualties, not there." A dead end, so to speak?

Owen's words of sensing a death in water kept echoing in my head. I then telephoned my friend Harry Bellangy, who has also spent his entire life in Cape May. He said he knew of other deaths at that end of town, but not at Peter Shields. The next day Harry emailed me to tell me he had recalled a story his grandmother told him as a child. It was about Peter Shields' son, who died in front of the house in the water while his parents watched. Bingo! I was thinking now, more than ever, that Ernest was a Shields!

Soon after reading Harry's email, I was telling *Exit Zero's* publisher, Jack Wright about what I had learned. "Did you not read my book?" he growled at me with his thick Scottish accent. I must admit I am a lousy reader — ADD runs in my family, and I have it a hundred percent when it comes to reading. I was the last one in school to finish reading a chapter in class, and it takes me weeks to get through any book I buy! Jack's book, *Tommy's Folly*, is chock full of great historical stuff, and I had never seen the page about Peter Shields and his son *Earle*, who died in a *hunting accident* in 1907! I am always the last to find out anything in Cape May.

Now it was confirmed. Ernest was simply a corruption over the years of Earle. I imagine the owners of the property passed down the stories and had their own ghost experiences over the years. Like a game of "telephone," the names were scrambled with each retelling.

Historical accounts could later be found at Cape May Court House in old newspaper articles from both the *Herald* and *The Star and Wave* had written accounts of the tragedy (see next page.)

According to the reports, Peter Shield's 15-year-old son Earle had decided, against his father's orders, to go out to the sounds, hunting for marsh hens. He and his friend, Frank Edwards, Jr., hired a yacht and a smaller boat. It seems they were unlucky in their endeavor and decided to return home empty handed.

At 6:30 PM, as young Earle Shields stepped from the smaller boat back up to the yacht, using his loaded gun as a crutch, the gun suddenly went off, shooting him in the face, fracturing his lower and upper jaw, blowing out his eyes and lodging the bullets in the base of his brain. This is the severe trauma energy I sensed in the basement of the Peter Shield's Inn when I first encountered Earle. He is not in pain anymore, but the imprint of that trauma stays with him.

Earle's friend Frank Edwards quickly returned him to the Cape May Yacht Club, the newspaper report stated, and every doctor in town was called in. His family was summoned at 9 PM when all hope of saving him was lost. His father, away on business, and Earle's mother managed to return just in time to see their unconscious son pass at 10:30 PM the same night. His body was taken back to the family's home in Bryn Mawr, Pennsylvania. His ghost, it seems, stayed behind.

Earle had died. Instead of crossing over to Heaven, he decided, as any kid would probably do, to follow his weeping parents back to the house by the sea that he loved. Some ghosts haunt where they died, but most return to where they lived. In Cape May, the case is usually where they summered.

Armed with this new information, I returned to The Peter Shields for dinner. Earle was nowhere to be found when we checked the basement.

A TERRIBLE ACCIDENT

Earle A. Shellds Accidently Shoots Himself While Gunning

The community was sadly shocked last Thursday evening when it heard of the awful accident which had occured to Master Earle A. Shellus, son of Mr. and Mrs. Peter Shellds. The young lad who was only fifteen years of age, was out gunning with Frank G. Edwards, Jr, son of Capt. F. G. Edwards, for marsh hens. About half past six o'clock in the evening, while it is said he was attempting to get from one boat into another in order to return home, the gun was placed in such a position that it went off and shot him in the face and so wounded him that he died about half past ten that evening.

As soon as the lad was discovered he was brought to the club house of the Cape May Yacht Club and there all of the attention which could be given him was given by doctors F. J. Haerer, Walter H. Phillips, Richard Norris, Frank R. Hughes and Thomas Neilson. His father, who returned from Philadelphia that evening, and his mother were at his side when he passed away. He was unconsiou from the time that he was brought into the house.

The body was taken in charge by Undertaker William H. Thompson and on Friday afternoon was removed to the winter home of the Shields' at Bryn Mawr, from which place the funeral occurred at ten o'clock on Monday morning.

Master Shellds was a bright young man and had a host of friends, not only with the younger people but also with the older ones about Cape May. He was prominent in the younger social set and was esteemed by every one. He was manly in his bearing, and his death is a great loss to the community who greatly sympathize with t e bereaved parents.

Had he left and gone somewhere? It was during dinner, after our waiter had spilled my *entire* glass of red wine all over the front of my white shirt (it was OK because the great food made up for it) that I realized Earle was hiding on us. I could psychically hear his young laughter coming from all over the house. It reminded me of the old *Ghost and Mrs. Muir* television series where Captain Gregg's roaring laughter echoed through his seacoast home. Since, I now resembled an accident victim, covered with red stains, Earle was amused. Soaked and stained, I was still happy to see, or should I say, "hear" him.

I was able to let Earle know that the truth would now be told. He seemed relieved and began to open up to me. This does not mean he pulled up a chair and shared some wine; what I mean is the ghost of Earle Shields, any ghost for that matter, communicates psychically. One thing that a ghost can do is read people's thoughts. It comes with the territory. This is the way they hear us, using mind-to-mind energy, not verbal sounds. Earle told us that he lives up in the attic, on the third floor. "It's mine," he responded, giving me the feeling that everywhere else in the place was used for guests or the restaurant.

Earle let me understand that he stays out of guilt, because he made his mother very sad, went against her and his father's wishes, and went hunting. As he was well liked, he caused widespread sadness in the community, and he regretted it very much. He misses his friends, his family and just being alive.

He also told me something else that helped to change the way I now think of ghosts as a community. Some paranormal investigators and psychic mediums believe ghosts cannot see or interact with each other. I do not subscribe to that particular theory. I think that they can see and interact with each other and do exactly that in Cape May. What I did not realize, until investigating hauntings in greater depth in Cape May, is that ghosts seem to form a community. Sometimes it seems to be a state of anarchy that reminds me of the novel, *Lord of the Flies*, where ghosts do as they please and have their own places to stay, while a few try to dominate.

Earle told me that a man who died in an elevator nearby chases him home some nights. The man is angry and does not like children bothering him. Later, Harry Bellangy confirmed part of this story, revealing that two people had died in elevator accidents at the Christian Admiral in the 1950s.

On my next trip to Cape May, I contacted Peter Shields' newest owner, Lori Whissell. Lori walked me through the property and mentioned that most of what she has experienced is at her older property next door, The Angel of the Sea, which adjoins the Peter Shields property. While some of the housekeepers who currently work at Peter Shields have reported experiencing minor things upstairs on the third floor, it seems that the former owners and staff members experienced much more of the haunting activity, especially mentioning the area in the basement where I first met Earle.

As I entered a beautiful old cedar lined room on the third floor, I realized that this must be where young Earle calls home. A small, old, wooden ladder leads up to an even larger attic that I imagine any young boy of 15 (or 115 in his case!) would love to explore and hang around. This room has magical energy to it. I told Lori it would make a great library! I think Earle has put a hundred years of "kid energy" into it, and the room is buzzing with a wonderful feeling of fun.

The one thing that amazed me with this story, and many others I have researched in Cape May, is how the facts got so darned mixed up. All of the previous stories and articles on the Peter Shields Inn seem to say that it is Peter himself haunting the place. Not so. Earle's name and the accident itself are remembered incorrectly. Local historian and postcard man Don Pocher recently said to me, "Cape May's history will never be completely right, because a lot of it was never written down."

One of my goals with this book was to bring the ghosts to light. Another goal was to get the facts straight, both personal and historical! I hope this book will act as a little "booster shot" for future historians seeking facts or ghosts in old Cape May.

So many children are stuck on the ghost plane in Cape May. At least they have company. I am not sure why they do not all cross over to Heaven and move on with their soul lives. Unfortunately, unless we someday become ghosts, we will never really know for sure what the reasoning is behind staying behind. At least Earle has a great house to haunt!

Recently I returned for dinner at the Peter Shields. I walked up to the third floor between courses and could sense Earle's presence once again. Later, as we finished our dessert, I asked Earle if he had followed me back to the table. There was something ghostly about the room now. We finished dining and paid the check. Within a few moments, we heard an alarm outside. We all went out to look. It was the fire alarm for the Peter Shields itself! Not a trace of smoke was in the air, but something had set off the alarm. As the rest of the diners were escorted, plates in hand, to the front lawn, we left in our car, and I bid Earle *adieu*. He had indeed arrived—with bells on.

Angel of the Sea

HAVE GHOSTS — WILL TRAVEL

Bed & Breakfast

5-7 Trenton Avenue, Cape May

ONE of Cape May's most beautiful and elaborate B&Bs just happens also to be one of its most haunted. A house divided cannot stand, so goes the old adage. Don't tell it to Angel of the Sea, though. It has been divided and still standing for over 150 years, and just not standing still. In the last chapter, I told you the story of the ghost of the Peter Shield's Inn. Not too much of a ghost racket is going on there, besides one lonely young chap, who has been quietly roaming about the stately old Colonial Revival house for about a hundred years. Even the staff doesn't seem to notice anything special in the haunting department at Peter Shields. Then there is the Angel of the Sea, Peter Shield's extravagant next-door neighbor. The activity is so varied, and has been going on for so long at such a constant frequency, it's hard to tell exactly how many ghosts reside in the two old buildings. What a difference a hundred feet makes!

Investigating ghosts is not an easy thing to do. Many people ask me if it is "fun" or exciting. It is exhausting, especially when there are too many humans running around getting in my psychic way! To research the stories for this book, I sometimes had to choose times that were not exactly optimal for a thorough and quiet investigation.

Since I live two hundred miles north of Cape May, my investigation window closed even tighter. Then, of course, there is the fact that Cape May is a summer vacation spot, and Angel of the Sea is one of the hottest B&Bs in town.

So why is the Angel so haunted? I think it has to do with the fact that the building itself has been cut apart and moved twice. One thing is for sure; most of the ghosts at the Angel of the Sea came with the buildings when they moved to Trenton Avenue in the mid 1960s.

This is a great example of how ghosts will generally move with a building, if it is relocated. Ghosts can anchor themselves just like a piece of furniture

When Ocean View Hotel owner Victor Denizot had his new Hotel Lafayette built on Beach Avenue in the summer of 1881, William Weightman's son had his father's cottage (right of the hotel) moved next door for a better ocean view! The cottage's two halves could not be joined back together once they arrived at their new beachfront home. (Author's Collection)

in a house. The way ghosts see it, a house belongs to them. Move it and you move the ghosts.

The two buildings, known today as The Angel of the Sea, began life in another venue in Cape May. Built as The Weightman Cottage in 1850, for one of America's richest men, William Weightman, the original building was one large home and was located at Franklin and Washington Streets, near where the post office stands today.

William Weightman made his fortune in the chemical business. He was President of Powers and Weightman Chemical Company in Philadelphia, until his death at age 91 in 1904. Weightman is credited for introducing quinine (tonic) water into the United States. His business made him one of the richest men in America. He was also very practical.

In 1881, he decided his family would rather have their "summer cottage" with an ocean view. He purchased land on the corner of Ocean and Beach, from developer John C. Bullitt, on the site of the lawn of the old Columbia Hotel, destroyed in the 1878 fire.

Instead of building a grand new mansion, as the town's people had hoped he would do, Weightman decided to be frugal and have his cottage moved to the new site. Local farmers were hired in the off-season and instructed what to do. Labor in those days, was cheaper than wood, so many houses in Cape May were moved and relocated instead of being torn down. The ghosts were free and went along with the houses.

The local farmers planned to move the great house in the typical fashion of the time. They would prop the house up on long logs and pull it along the streets with mules and horses. The first problem they encountered was the size of the place. No matter what they did, they could not get the entire house off the ground. Therefore, they came up with a novel idea; they would cut the house in two, move each piece separately to the new site and put the two pieces back together again! Mr. Weightman would never be any the wiser.

When the house(s) finally were placed on the site, it was time to put them back together again. Unfortunately, for the farmers, horses and mules pull much better than they push. No matter what they tried, they could not re-join the two halves. Summer was approaching and the Weightmans would soon be returning to Cape May for the season. With some quick thinking, the farmers enclosed the sides of the houses, creating two unique buildings in close proximity to each other.

The good news for Mr. Weightman was his home was moved and ready for summer; the bad news was he now had two smaller homes instead of one large one! History does not record his reaction. When William Weightman died in 1904, he had outlived his wife Louisa and their two sons, John Farr and William, Jr. Only his daughter, Ann Marie, was left as the sole heir to the Weightman fortune.

According to Henry Needles, whose family owned the Lafayette Hotel for many years, the cottages were sold to a man by the name of James Nichols who opened them as The Ocean View Hotel. Denizot had already sold the La-fayette to a man named Colonel Tracey who in turn sold the hotel to Henry Needles, Sr. in 1921. Needles purchased the cottages next door in the late 1950s and added them to his holdings, calling them the Lafayette Cottages.

Henry Needles, Jr. told me they eventually sold the cottages to Carl Ma-cIntire for $1.00, instead of knocking them down to make room for a new hotel in 1963. Luckily, Reverend MacIntire, grandfather of Cape May's Cur-tis Bashaw, had the foresight to save the old buildings and move them to their present home in East Cape May on Trenton Avenue. MacIntire needed extra buildings for lodging his students at his new Shelton College in town, and the Weightman cottages would be just perfect. This time, the two large buildings were moved with great spectacle down Beach Avenue on a flatbed truck!

From 1963 until 1981, the Weightman Cottage was used to board students and then employees of other Inns. After MacIntire's college was moved to Florida, his buildings in East Cape May were left standing empty. From 1981 until about 1988, the Weightman Cottages, once again standing side by side, were simply left in disrepair to decay slowly.

Around 1988, a builder and developer named John Girton and his wife, Barbara, had crawled through the broken windows of the old buildings to look around. Even though the place was in shambles, and the ceiling and walls were caving in, John and Barbara decided the old place could be saved and restored to its former beauty. Today, under the ownership of their daughter, Lori Whissell, the old Weightman cottage exists as the new and beautiful Angel of the Sea, Bed and Breakfast.

The ghosts of the Angel of the Sea seem to stay in their own buildings. Each building has activity of a completely different sort. In the main building, a woman with a personality of someone who oversaw operations in the past looms large in the psychic spectrum. She seems to have come to a mutual understanding with Lori and wants to help her "run" the place.

I slowly made my way around the labyrinth of hallways, moving room to room, armed with tape recorders and cameras. I must admit, it was difficult to investigate a place so active with tourists, living ones at least. After my psychic walk-through of both buildings, I sat down with the Angel's longtime manager Sharon Falkowski and compared notes with her.

"Most people who report haunting things happening say it's in the second building," Sharon started. "It seems like we always get a lot of people reporting things. Pants that were folded over a chair would be moved to another chair. Chambermaids always reported that they had just cleaned a whole room, only to come right back in and find the bed turned down, or the drawer was pulled out, or the TV back on or the light relit. This happens in the whole second building, on the second and third floor."

Indeed, on my walk-through, I felt multiple presences in the second building. Some rooms had a lived-in feeling; others felt like we had walked in on someone, yet no one was there. I began to wonder if I was experiencing some kind of a warp in time. There were overlapping energies everywhere in the rooms on the higher floors.

The Weightman Cottages on Beach Avenue — reincarnated as James Nichols' Ocean View Hotel in the 1930s. (Author's Collection)

Lori was soon able to rejoin us for the interview with Sharon. Sharon told me that one of the other managers, Bridget, used to tell the story about the ghosts on her tours of the Inn. Today they refrain from mixing in ghost lore, as they feel it might scare some of the patrons away. I disagree, but it is their Inn!

In the second building, there is a feeling on the third floor of a distressed young woman. I could not tell exactly how she died. Had she been abused or murdered? I was not sure what to make of her. She gave me the feeling that she was afraid of some man and that he was threatening to her. Sharon related a story of just what that ghost might be implying.

"In the beginning, Bridget used to tell the ghost stories on her tour, and someone called her up and told her about a death that happened here. This was years and years ago. It happened sometime when the building was being used as a dormitory. Supposedly, this is the way the story goes. There was a girl who used to work at the Christian Admiral (hotel,) and she was running very late after breakfast, and was coming back here to change because all of the kids who worked there were required to go to the services that the

Reverend MacIntire had. If they did not go, they would be in big trouble. If they did not dress appropriately, they would be in bigger trouble. So she had to come back and change." It was the next turn of events that would add another ghost to the lineup at the Weightman Cottage.

"When she got back here, she discovered that she left her key to her room back at the Christian Admiral. So, rather than be even later for the service than she already was, she climbed up the fire escape of the second building, up to the third floor. She went out on the ledge and tried to go through this screen window. When she pushed the screen up, it popped out, and she fell to her death." The unfortunate young girl never made it to the prayer service that day. She fell to her death between the two buildings sometime in the early 1970s.

Rooms 26 and 27 had a good deal of energy in them. It seems the girl's room was number 26. "That's why we thought she was the ghost, because the things that were happening were things a chambermaid might do, and she was a chambermaid here," said Sharon.

Indeed, the chambermaids at the Angel of the Sea are quite unnerved by their ghostly fellow staff member. "The chambermaids are very religious and do not even like to talk about these things." Lori told me. "If we can keep a few good chambermaids who will do the nighttime turn downs, we are very happy!"

There is another interesting twist to the East Cape May zone. The old Christian Admiral, it seems, also played a role in the ghost energy of surrounding properties.

This is something I have heard more than once. "The interesting thing was, for years, we would get at least once or twice a week somebody making a mention, or even sometimes every night somebody would even say something... but once they tore down the Christian Admiral, we don't get that many reports anymore." Sharon noted to me.

Could the old Christian Admiral have had some kind of negative energy? As I said in my column about The Peter Shields Inn, it seemed everyone involved with the building, from its beginnings as The Hotel Cape May until its demolition a few years ago, had problems keeping the place alive. If this was the ghost of a girl named Mary Brown, who had worked for MacIntire in the '70s, could she have been relieved when the old Christian Admiral was finally torn down? It has not stopped her from continuing her regimen as Chambermaid at the Angel, that's for sure.

Let's get back to the ghosts. It seems that people have two distinctly different experiences between the main building and the one next door. In the second building, with all of the reports of beds being turned down by ghostly hands, lights coming on and off and footsteps being heard, no one has actually reported seeing a ghost. The activity makes up for the loss of visual effects, however!

One night, a taller guest had a first hand experience with the specters of building two. "We had some guests who checked in. It was in the springtime — he was booked in a room with a footboard, and he was like six-foot-seven. When he checked in, I told him I had another room available without a footboard," Sharon remembered. "I told him he may be more comfortable in this other room, so I took them up to the room. Now, generally as a rule, we keep doors unlocked in a room if there is no one in it, but we got upstairs, and the room was locked. We all heard someone walking around inside the room. I was a little embarrassed, because I thought the room was unoccupied."

Sharon left the couple standing in front of the doorway in the hall of the third floor guest rooms in the second building and went to retrieve a key from the front desk and to double check if the room had been rented. It had not.

"When I went back upstairs to unlock the door, it was unlocked. Now I had left the couple up there, and the funny thing was their first reaction was, 'We heard somebody in there. We absolutely heard somebody walking around in their while you were gone.'" Sharon, in an effort not to frighten the new guests, simply dismissed it as 'the wind' and opened the door to reveal a clean and empty room! It was Room 27, next door to Mary Brown's Room 26. Could Mary be sharing both rooms? Or does she also have a ghostly neighbor? I was beginning to wonder if the feelings of distress I felt from Mary might have been her feeling about another ghost in the place. Perhaps she is impinging on someone else's turf, or vice versa. No one has ever seen a ghost in the second building, so it is hard to say just who is haunting the place.

Not so in the main building.

The woman I sensed watching us from above in the dining room has been seen by both guests and staff members at the Angel. She is always well dressed and wears a large hat. As I interviewed Lori in the dining room, I could feel this older woman's glare looking me over and listening carefully to every word I spoke. She was listening intently as I spoke of my feeling about her and the other ghosts. She had the feeling that she was the matriarch of the place. Was she a past guest or a past owner?

"Years ago, one of our girls came in early to serve breakfast. Her name was Denise. She came in one morning to cook and found a woman looking out of the kitchen door — she thought it was actually a guest and walked into the kitchen to find her, and nobody was there. All the doors were locked, and this building was closed—all the guests were in the second building." Sharon recalled of the ghostly early morning visitor.

Sharon also told me a situation that happened about two years ago, when she was standing in the doorway of the dining room. She saw a reflection in the glass of the breakfront in the dining room of a woman wearing a large hat move up behind her. She even felt the person's presence. All the guests were eating in the dining room, and it was full. She turned around to tell the woman the dining room was full, and there was no one present.

This is a very typical ghost experience. When we sense a ghost in a place, we sense them as just a presence or "someone near us." Seeing a ghost is much more uncommon. You will rarely see a ghost. Remember that the next time you hide under your covers at night!

Sharon feels that the presence of the woman in the main building is more "aggressive." Lori disagrees. "I don't think she's aggressive. I just think she wants acknowledgment." I did not psychically sense any aggression from the ghost of the woman in the main building, just a sense of proprietorship or of someone guarding the place, at least guarding the place from any of the living that may cause trouble.

Room 13 has also had its share of wild experiences at night, when it's dark and empty. "So we're going back when we first opened—when I got pregnant with my daughter. When I got pregnant and stopped talking about the ghost, it was like she got pissed off." Lori remembered. I think the ghost may have become jealous of the new addition to the family, which was now stealing away Lori's attention.

"I was living at the Inn, and I would try to take a nap in the afternoon. She would pull up the shades and turn on the lights—a lot!" One night, as Lori and Greg and some friends watched a Civil War documentary on the television downstairs, they began to hear bizarre scraping noises up in Room 13. Lori, who was still pregnant at the time, wondered if the woman of the house was in a jealous rage once again.

Lori and Greg's friends were talking to Lori about being pregnant when the noises began. "There was nobody else in the house—when I went to check the next day, all of the furniture in Room 13 was moved six inches back! It wasn't like a truck went by and everything rattled—the bed was moved—everything was moved six inches in the same direction."

On another night, trying to find rest in an adjoining room, Lori and her husband began to experience even stranger phenomena. "One night when Greg and I slept in Room 12, it was like a hurricane was going by! Things in the other rooms were banging and clanging. We only had two other rooms at the time and they weren't up."

It seems all of the rooms on the third floor have had activity. Room 15 has sent people downstairs to spend the rest of the night sleeping on the couch! Another couple staying in Room 15 during Lori's pregnancy was so upset about their experience, they would not tell Lori because they thought she would begin to be affected by the energy, and her baby would be possessed! Luckily, everyone is fine and in good health today!

It seems that the frantic poltergeist-like energy surrounding Lori's pregnancy died down after her daughter, Emily, was born. Can a pregnancy set off haunting activity? I would imagine any introduction of new soul energy to a place that is active might "upset the applecart." Luckily, it seems in this case, it was only a temporary upset.

In parapsychology, the term *poltergeist* comes from the German, *poltern*, to knock and *geist*, ghost or spirit. Most cases involving poltergeist activity (knocking noises, objects moving by themselves and apports, objects dropping in from nowhere) are usually attributed to a living person, not to a ghost. It is found that certain people possess the ability to manifest psychokinesis (PK.) It is this person, in a distressed state, who radiates PK energy and causes "ghostly" effects in a place.

In the case of Angel of the Sea, the haunting activity is genuine. I just have to get the ghosts to want to talk!

During my interview with Lori and Sharon, I kept trying to cut through the "human interference" of the place and talk to the "lady of the house." It was hard to pick out her energy. There seemed to be a strong message coming from the "head" ghost at Angel of the Sea: "Leave us alone. We have work to do!" I took the hint.

Angel of the Sea will require several more visits to work with the ethereal staff members and get to the bottom of the ghostly goings on there. As I left the Angel that day, I ran one more psychic scan of the place. I felt like I was walking through a funhouse, with all the rooms turning and mirrors changing the real look of everything.

My psychic impressions of the place were constantly changing and refocusing, as if the house was trying deliberately to confuse me. I realized that the house has moved so many times, it is still moving, not physically, but energetically.

In a way, I am glad I could not learn more about the ghosts that day. It presented me with a challenge. The Angel of the Sea had its ghostly secrets that were hidden in time eternal, but I only have the remainder of my lifetime to solve them!

The Red Cottage

THE HESTER HILDRETH CHRONICLES — PART 1

Guest Suites — 22 Jackson Street, Cape May

THE FORMER INN at 22 Jackson Street is one of the most talked about and written about houses in Cape May. It is featured on tours, in books, and is known to be one of Cape May's more interesting haunted spots. It is now called the Red Cottage.

The story goes like this: A nanny or maid named Esmeralda, who once lived and died in the turret apartment of the house, still haunts the place and loves to play with children. She is a kind, gentle ghost who uses a secret doorway behind the bed to access an old servant's staircase to come and go from her third floor lair. A man who visited a previous owner had told him about Esmeralda and how the children loved her. The stranger then asked the owner if she still haunted the place. Thus, the mystery of Esmeralda was solved, or the stories began, depending upon which way you looked at it.

This is the kind of haunting gossip that really annoys me! If any one of the people who claimed to investigate 22 Jackson Street, historically, psychically or with equipment over the years, had bothered to take the time to research the property correctly and thoroughly, this story would have been put to rest years ago! Let us now get out the Wite-Out® and finish the job!

As it turns out, there never was a woman named Esmeralda. There is no secret staircase. The whole story, as I later found out, was "maid" up! This story proves just how convoluted and distorted a ghost story can become. One of the reasons I set out to write this book was to get the facts and the ghosts straight.

The story of Esmeralda always sounded like a playful and somewhat embellished tale that I assumed became whitewashed over the years. I decided to spend a few nights in the turret suite on the third floor of the Inn at 22 Jackson after Labor Day, when the crowds were finally gone.

Today the house is part of the Virginia Hotel-Congress Hall Cape Resorts group. The house at 22 Jackson Street, with its high turret and elaborate gingerbread, is one of the most photographed homes in Cape May. A man named

Aaron Roseman built this beautiful old Victorian in Queen Anne style in 1899. Roseman also built, and possibly lived in, the "twin" house to this one, the one that stands at 132 Decatur Street.

Upon entering the beautiful old home turned B&B, I set my psychic senses looking for Esmeralda. I could sense a few ghosts, but none seemed to have the energy associated with the name. Let me explain the feeling as a comparison for you. Imagine going into the home of a childhood friend. Someone asks you about "Mark" who lived there, but there was no Mark. Your response would be to think of all who used to live there, and say, "There was no Mark." During this thought process, you are remembering every person you knew who lived there. You begin picturing their faces and maybe a familiar scene or two from the past.

When I work psychically in a setting, I also see people and get names through past images. The only difference is I have never seen the original. These "memories" are simply energies stored in the ether of a place, like a photo album stored in the mind of the house. As a psychic, I am able to access this past information. As a psychic detective or researcher, I can use the stored information to compare current stories with past facts. It is not a perfect science; after all, I am only human! It does work for me in most cases, however, like a quick reference guide.

In this case, the energy of the house stored no image of an Esmeralda.

After arriving at the Inn, I was greeted by Maria McFadden, who manages the property and also works across the street at the haunted Virginia Hotel. Maria led us up the turning staircase to the third floor, which is now called the Turret Suite. It is a beautiful and spacious suite with two bedrooms, a private bath and a living room with a back and front deck. This is one of the best accommodations in Cape May, and I would highly recommend the house, especially the Turret Suite.

Maria showed my partner and me the bed where people have said to have been visited by Esmeralda. I mentioned to her, even at this early point, that I just do not know about this name. After Maria left us, the first thing I did was pull the bed out to reveal a small door hidden behind the pillows. Was the maid's stairway hidden behind this tiny door? If it was, either Esmeralda crawled back and forth or she was about two feet tall! The door was no bigger than a large kitchen cabinet door.

I opened the door and found my answer. It was simply a storage space under the eaves of the house. No dead maids or ghosts to be found.

Examining the layout of the third floor, I also realized that what many people had been saying about a bed in the turret itself was also a bunch of stories. The turret has always been a small room that is accessible to the whole house, simply an observation tower and a great place to do a séance. (More about that later.)

Later that day, I met the Inn's other resident innkeeper, Janina, who has worked at the place for eight years through three different owners. Janina is a lovely and warm individual who was more than willing to talk about her experiences with the ghost. Now don't get me wrong. There IS a ghost or two, just not one called Esmeralda.

As we talked about this pseudo ghost, Janina agreed that she too felt the name was wrong. She told me about a couple staying at the inn with their two children in the place. The young girl, about three or four years old, told Janina and her parents that she had been visited late that night by Rosie, a woman with long black hair.

The woman was very friendly and smiled to the young girl, sat on her bed and then vanished. Another girl, about thirteen years old, encountered the same long haired woman. The two girls, on their separate planes of existence, apparently played ball late one night on the stairs!

Janina and Maria have both felt the presence of a ghost or something in the kitchen in the back of the house. I, too, felt the strongest energy in the kitchen, not on the third floor. As I psychically explored the kitchen, I was drawn to a closet that Janina opened for me, revealing an old winding maid's staircase. It had been sealed up when the house was turned into apartments in the 1950s. However, this staircase was not connected with the third floor closet! It was not even in the same spot.

If the kitchen had most of the activity and "feeling" of being haunted, usually, I would assume the ghost worked or lived in the area. Ghosts haunt where they lived, not where they died. Could this ghost be that of a servant from the past?

I met Leo the next morning. Leo has worked for Congress Hall since moving to the United States from Latvia in 2002. He also lives in the house at night in a room on the first floor. "In the beginning," he told me, "I used to hear things in the house when I was alone, upstairs. Now I sleep too well. I don't hear anything anymore." Nevertheless, Leo was more than interested in what I had sensed in the old place!

The night before, high up in the turret of the house, Willy and I had decided to hold a séance or a channeling session. This is what happens. I relax, get myself into a trance state and try to send out a signal to get the ghost(s) to talk with me. Some psychics reserve the term channeling for communicating with spirit guides or angelic energies. They refer to one who talks with the dead as a medium. I interchange both words to mean a communication with another plane of existence.

We had just enjoyed a GREAT dinner across the street at the Ebbitt Room in the Virginia Hotel with friends, and all decided to finish off the night with a good old-fashioned Cape May séance.

This time we ran two tape recorders, one digital and one cassette. This would both record the voices and words coming out of my mouth, and possibly pick up some other EVPs.

As we stood in the turret room and gazed down upon "haunted" Jackson Street below, I could feel, psychically, a stream of energy running through me. It was almost like standing in a wind tunnel or being knocked around by the surf. There was some kind of energy vortex up there, which just happened to converge near the turret room of the house. It was a strong, but positive energy, the type of energy in which I was able to channel really well.

I could feel myself just melting into the ethers of the place, as if I was becoming not only part of the house's energy, but the street's. (No, I had not been drinking heavily.)

Is Jackson Street so haunted because of some unknown energy vortex? There are well-known energy spots around the world, some thought to be very beneficial to one's health, like the vortices in Sedona, Arizona. Maybe the Inn at 22 Jackson should become a health club!

Before I knew it, I had slipped into a trance. The next thing I remembered was waking up in the living room section of the suite hours later! It seems that I had been channeling up a storm of various different entities. The only problem was most of them did not belong to the house. I had my transmitter turned up too high I guess!

After talking with all present and reviewing the tapes, it seemed that the dominant voice on the tape was that of Hester Hildreth, who is supposed to be haunting Winterwood Gift Shop in RIO GRANDE! It turns out Hester, who talked for hours about old Cape May, has moved in with her cousin George Hildreth, who lived across the street. She had left Winterwood in a boycott, but more about Hester in the next chapter. We stopped by Winterwood on the way home to alert the women in Rio Grande about their disgruntled ghost, and they admitted she had disappeared and had even told customers, "Hester is on vacation!" More about Hester in the next chapter!

In between Hester Hildreth's rambling tirades on the tape, an eerie, breathy voice is heard telling us to go downstairs. The voice kept repeating the name Parker and Harry Parker. Another man came through who identified himself as working at the New Columbia — as I mentioned in the Windward/Saltwood House Chapter, this was a large hotel built on the site where The Inn at 22, Windward and Saltwood Houses now sit. The hotel only lasted about 10 years before it burned to the ground. In that time period, it does seem to have left a few residual imprints in the space.

If a building goes, the ghosts usually do not. They will keep on existing in their own plane and maybe even still seeing the original site from their time. Several ghosts on Jackson Street belong to earlier, buildings that no longer exist. I guess it is like someone taking your chair, and you eventually find another one, and pull it over into the same spot. Ghosts seem not only to be stuck in the Ghost Plane. They seem to be stuck in a physical location on this plane as well. Except Hester Hildreth, but that's another story.

The next night, I tried again to contact the ghosts, sans Hester Hildreth. I specifically asked the woman in the house with the long, dark hair to come forward and clarify who she was. I felt a presence of a young woman, perhaps a teenage girl, who gave me the name Anne. She was asking for my help, but would not tell me what it was she wanted of me. On reviewing the tape a few hours later, an EVP in a high pitched young girl's voice says "Anne, Anne!" about a minute before I got it psychically, and repeated it to document the name on the tape. This type of phenomenon is really exciting, because it shows how a ghost sends its energy out, and that the tape got it before I did.

Willy and I then decided to take a break and get some food. We started down stairs and the house was very quiet. We needed to take some pictures of the place as Maciek Nabrdalik, *Exit Zero's* photographer at the time, was not feeling well, and might not be able to make it. As I snapped a few shots of the living room, I felt something hit my foot and heard a rolling noise. A Baci ball had fallen out of the dish on the sideboard and rolled across the room. I assumed I had bumped into the sideboard and dislodged it, so I put the ball back into the bowl.

As we started to exit the house through the front door, there was a thud and the sound of footsteps coming down the stairs. We turned to see what the noise was and witnessed another ball bouncing down the stairs from the second floor! Was someone playing ball on the stairs and had forgotten to put the ball away? Maybe we accidentally kicked it while walking down the stairs. No, I don't think so. Someone wanted to play ball, and it wasn't the two of us. We left quickly and went to eat. Yes, even a ghost investigating psychic medium can get spooked, and I did!

I told Janina the next morning about the evening's events. I also reassured Leo that the energy in the house was a 100 percent friendly, and he could continue to sleep tight at night! It is true, the energy at the Inn at 22 Jackson is great. In fact, I slept peacefully each night — well, except for the dream I had in which I was arguing with a ghost across the street at the Virginia. You see people have seen doors open and close there and felt presences in the lobby, but I have yet to track down the ghost itself. In the dream, I was standing on the balcony of the turret and yelling across the street at the ghost, demanding it reveal itself. It gave me the psychic equivalent of the finger. There was lightning in the sky and then an explosion — which woke me up. It seems a transformer exploded nearby and blacked out the entire neighborhood! The last time I was down in Cape May, I had not even made it into the Macomber to check in when a transformer exploded above us! That's the problem with energy, you just never know which direction it will go!

As I sit here typing these pages for the final draft of *The Ghosts of Cape May*, the two ceiling lights above me decided to go off and stay off. The switch is on, the bulbs are good, and the breaker has not tripped. Energy is as unpredictable as human nature.

I digress. After breakfast, I spoke with Janina and told her the ghost's name was Anne. I was not sure what the gentlemen ghosts had to do with the Inn, if anything. They may have simply been drawn, like a moth to a flame, to my channeling energy. It happens.

Janina wondered if the "Anne" perhaps was "Roseanne," like the child got. I know I just got Anne, so for now I will leave it at that.

I wondered if there was an Anne in the house's history. Ah, I thought, Barbara Masemore is the one to ask! After all, she had owned the Inn from 1991 until she sold it three years ago. After finally hooking up with Barbara by phone, I could barely get the words "I don't think there is an Esmeralda" out of my mouth when Barbara adamantly told me, "Lies, it's all made up. It never happened. It's all made up!" Wow. There's a strong opinion, and I hadn't even asked the question yet!

I remembered one night, on one of the ghost tours, someone yelling from the Inn at 22 Jackson about the stories being made up. It puzzled me why an innkeeper would do this. I am not sure who was yelling that day, but Barbara's story reminded me of the event.

Barbara told me the real story. Roll the video please! Aaron Roseman built the house for a Harry and Dorothy Parker in the year 1899. The Parkers lived in the house until the 1940s when a woman lawyer bought it. During the war, the Navy took over the house and put in central heating, as there was none. After the Navy left, the woman who owned the house was so annoyed that she tore the heating out, and it was not until 1991, when Barbara and Chip Masemore bought the place, that they put heating back in.

In the 1950s, a family by the name of Wolfe became the new owners and changed it into the Cape Colony apartments. The Wolfes split up the rooms and added extra bathrooms, sealing up the maid's stairway to create a bathroom on the second floor. Some of the Wolfe children who later visited Barbara and Chip made up an imaginary playmate called "Esmeralda" and used to sing her name to the tune of the old *Davy Crockett* television theme song.

"It was a nice song," Barbara told me, "but that was all there was to Esmeralda. They made it up."

So how did Esmeralda become a living (dying?) legend at the Inn? Barbara recalled that when the building changed hands in the 1970s, they had a relative or friend who wrote for the Philadelphia Inquirer Magazine. The friend needed a ghost story for the Halloween edition and the Inn would be a perfect setting. Weaving a tale from the Wolfe kids' stories of Esmeralda, the writer wrote some three thousand words about the ghostly story of a nanny named Esmeralda, who loved children and lived in the turret apartment, and died there. The secret doorway was also embellished to make the story even more fantastic and spooky.

So there you have it. A ghost by any other name is not an Esmeralda. The story should now be put to rest or at least, retold. I have done my part.

As for Anne, the real ghost of 22 Jackson, she is a kind and gentle soul. Maybe, it is she who loves children and likes to play ball. Possibly, she was a daughter of a previous owner or a servant. I will not commit to any theory just yet, as I do not want to get the stories rolling again!

In the meantime, book the Turret Suite for that special occasion you want to celebrate. The Red Cottage is a fabulous B&B. The breakfasts are great, the staff is wonderful and the house... speaks for itself.

Winterwood Gift Shop

THE HESTER HILDRETH CHRONICLES — PART 2

Route 9 South, Rio Grande

I N THE paranormal world, anything is possible. That anything was named Hester Hildreth. Hester Hildreth? She was supposed to be haunting the Winterwood Gift Shop on Route 9 in Rio Grande. I knew ghosts could move from place to place, but this gabby ghost seemed to be peeved about something back at home.

There we were, at The Inn at 22, to find just who was haunting the B&B. I began to channel and, as I moved into a deeper trance and started to contact the ghosts in the house, a moaning, whispery voice started telling us something about the place. The tone of the ghostly voice was very quiet, like an eerie wind blowing through an old house at night. All three "living" members of the audience had hovered close to me on the couch, with tape recorders in hand. Suddenly, a crackling, highly charged voice of an older woman burst onto the scene, sending everyone present jumping back several feet to their seats!

Once the rambling voice started, there was no stopping it! On and off for almost an hour and a half, the group listened intently as a woman who claimed to be Hester Hildreth rambled on about anything and everything to do with old Cape May. For hours she dished the dirt on housewives she hated, husbands who cheated and old Cape May family secrets that have been lost in time. Gossip eternal was this ghost! I cannot say for sure if this was the ghost of Hester Hildreth, but she certainly seemed to be the genuine article to all present. The story is just too good not to retell in its entirety.

Hester Hildreth's ghost complained about minute details like her name misspelled on the Winterwood sign, "Hestor," instead of "Hester." She also helped us find lost facts for some of the other stories I had worked on in Cape May. Many of these facts have since been validated.

Now my curiosity was piqued. Since I started recording these channeling sessions, I am now able to hear everything that comes through, the voice changes, the anecdotes, the bits of history and sometimes, the sage advice.

The old Hildreth Homestead now the Winterwood Gift Shop in Rio Grande.

I have to admit Hester Hildreth could have her own one-woman show, if she weren't dead. During the channeling, Hester told the group we should write a story about her entitled," An evening with Hester Hildreth." I had not planned to do a story on the Winterwood Christmas Shop, since it has been done to death. Hester has changed my mind on the subject, however, and I have discovered there is a lot more to the Hildreths and their ghosts than meets the eye.

During the channeling session, the ghost claiming to be Hester Hildreth was quite upset about her old homestead in Rio Grande. It seemed she had walked out, left home so to speak, because "the ladies who run the place loaded a bunch of furniture and crap in front of my stairway," and she could not get up or down from the second floor of her former house anymore. Therefore, on our way back from Cape May, after the channeling session, we stopped by Winterwood to deliver the message from their ghost.

It was a typically busy day at the Winterwood Christmas and Gift Shop. The old house, which belonged to the Hildreth family since it was built by Joshua Hildreth in 1722, is now home to one of the state's busiest holiday decorating businesses. There is also a Winterwood Shop in Cape May's

Following page: The Rio Grande Cemetery on Route 9.
Hester Hildreth's final resting place — or is it?

Washington Street Mall with a ghost of its own. This story is about the Winterwood in Rio Grande, to keep our ghost stories straight!

The day I visited Winterwood I was not exactly sure how the owners and staff would react to another ghost investigator come a-knocking. As I revealed just who I was and what the message was from Hester, the women all gasped and talked among themselves for a moment. It seems things at Winterwood had been quiet for the past year and a half! One of the women who works at the front counter has been telling enquiring customers, "Hester is on vacation."

"Hester is *not* on vacation," I replied. She is in self-imposed exile. According to Hester, she has been staying with her cousin George on Jackson Street in Cape May. Great, I thought. This is just what Jackson Street needs — another ghost.

After meeting one of Winterwood's owners, Tom Alvarado, I agreed to come back another day and bring the tape of the channeling session and interview them about the haunted happenings in the place. I also toured the inside of the store to search for Hester's stairway that had been blocked. It took me a few passes, but I finally found the staircase. It was an old, narrow, spiral staircase next to the fireplace. It was covered up by tons of stuff, furniture, Christmas trees and Christmas ornaments, piled high in front of the entrance! The staff admitted they had blocked the entrance for the last couple of years!

After reviewing the "Hester Hildreth tapes," I decided that, yes, there was a story here. So I set up an interview with Tom and his wife, Cindi, and we talked for a few hours about everything that goes bump in the night and day at Winterwood. We sat in Winterwood's office, located in the upstairs section of the old house.

The home was in the Hildreth family from 1722 until the 1950s, when Hester's last sibling, Lucille, or "Lu" as the family called her, passed away. Hester had died a few years earlier at the ripe old age of 90 in 1940. Hester and Lu lived in the home, never marrying for their entire lives. Even in Hester's day, the house seemed to have "unseen occupants." According to Dottie, one of Winterwood's long-time employees, the grandson of the Hildreth's caretaker came to visit one day. He told Dottie about times when he was young, and his grandfather would sit with him in the living room of the house, looking out the window.

"They would sit downstairs and hear footsteps walking back and forth on the second floor, but no one else would be home," Dottie remembered.

"The young man would ask his grandfather about the noises, and the grandfather would simply state, 'they are just folks from another time. Don't worry about them.'"

It seems even before Hester there was activity in the house. I told Tom and Cindi I detected ghosts of children in the upper level. They told me that in the 1970s a well-known New York parapsychologist brought a team of researchers into the house. Several psychics on the investigation that day also detected the ghosts of children in the house.

"When my parents first opened the store, there was so much activity," exclaimed Cindi. "There were voices, footsteps, the vacuum cleaner would turn off and back on — the music would turn off and back on," she explained.

Were those children Hester's brothers and sisters? It was possible. She was one of ten children born to Alexander and Sarah Hildreth on their large farm in Rio Grande, which, by the way, was originally called Hildreth.

There was also the presence of a man with a pipe and a cane. He was smoking cherry pipe tobacco, which Cindi confirmed is a smell they have detected for many years in the shop. The man gave me the name "William," which I would later find to be a brother of George Hildreth, Hester's cousin. The Hildreths were a large, old family in Cape May.

The Hildreth sisters in life, circa 1880,
Hester (R) and Lucille (L)
(Courtesy Jeri Hoffman McDaniel)

The idea of turning the private, old Colonial house into a gift shop was the work of Cindi's parents, aunt and uncle in the late 1970s. It had been a private residence until that time. One night, when Cindi's mother, aunt and uncle were gathered on the first floor of the house, they started hearing footsteps upstairs. Thinking it was Cindi's father playing a joke on them, the uncle snuck up on the other set of stairs to surprise him. It was the uncle who was surprised, however, to find no one in the upstairs section of the house! The father had gone out. "Things always happen when there would be no one around," Cindi added.

Who *does* walk the floors upstairs at the Hildreth house? One theory involved a British soldier who had defected and was taken in by the family during the revolution. David Hildreth was a patriot during the Revolutionary war and must have been happy to see a defector taking the side of the Americans. The soldier was apparently so happy to be given safe haven, that he carved the mantelpiece that still graces the fireplace today.

When Cindi Alvarado's parents owned the shop, before she and Tom took over in 1991, people would hear steps going up and down the spiral wooden staircase. Occasionally, heavy footsteps and a few thuds would be heard. It was thought the ghost of the soldier was walking upstairs to go to sleep and taking off his boots. However, according to a few notes related by Hester before she died, the soldier was housed (or hidden) in a rear building of the property. I sincerely doubt they would have hidden anyone in the upstairs bedroom of a house on the main road in those days, so the footsteps must come from some other source.

The original site of the house was about two hundred yards south of its present location. The house was rolled to its current location sometime in the mid 1800s. The chimney was the only part of the house that did not make the move well. It is rather crooked and whimsical looking today, slanting its way up through the old attic to meet the roof of the house.

As I made a psychic walk-through of the upstairs of the house, I sensed the spirits of a girl and her little brother, sitting on a lumpy old mattress in what might have been the children's bedroom on the second floor of the addition to the original house. The children gave me the sense that they loved to play with all the great stuff that was stored in the upstairs storage room. Being a Christmas shop, the storeroom is filled to the ceiling with all kinds of fun toys and decorations. It looks like a well-stocked playroom of a very wealthy and lucky kid!

The interesting thing about the hauntings at Winterwood is most of the activity is not in the original part of the house, but in the section of the house that was added on in the 1900s as a two car garage and storage area. The ghosts can see that this is also part of the store today. Possibly, the children feel that it is safe to play with things, as long as they are not in the main house. Staff members have found teddy bears and dolls lined up or in circles on the floor in the newer part of the building. Someone is having a lot of fun at Winterwood — after hours, when the lights go out!

Cheryl, who works in the shop, reported a box of votive candles exploding into the air one day and scattering around the floor. Several people saw it happen.

Cindi told me they would constantly be missing things like car keys, only to find them hidden behind a box on the shelf. This type of activity is not the work of an adult ghost, but that of a child. Again, I will stress, we are in death as we were in life. Children do things they should not do, like hiding our keys or playing with our computers. Usually, once you ask them to stop, they listen. Unfortunately, in the case of a child's ghost (of which Cape May has an abundance), most people do not think to say, "Stop it, please." Ghosts of children, like living children, will usually respond to a request to cease and desist. The only problem is they are better at ceasing the activity than starting it back up again!

The activity in Winterwood, according to the Alvarados, has subsided in the past year. I asked myself why? If these same ghosts have been haunting the place for all this time, why leave now? Cindi asked me why the children do not just cross over. Every ghost has a reason to want to stay. Perhaps after they died they would not leave their living family. It seems that many ghosts wait for family members to come and get them, but sometimes, sadly and for unknown reasons, they never come back to get their lost kin. I do not have the answer. I can only speculate that eventually the next-of-kin may reincarnate and are no longer spirits on the Other Side.

As souls, we have the choice of free will. If we choose to stay "stuck" in the ghost plane, we cannot expect other souls to wait for us forever. They, too, eventually have to continue their karmic journeys. Have these children's parents come back to this side? Are they living somewhere else in the world this time around? It is rather sad to think that these children could move on, but choose not to.

Was the soldier who was taken in by the Hildreths named William? Could he be smoking the pipe? It is thought that even Hester smoked a pipe in her day! I would now have to trace the Hildreth family history myself.

Jim Campbell had tipped me off that, while George Hildreth and his family are buried in Cold Spring cemetery, Hester's branch of the Hildreths were buried right down the road, next to the site of the new Lowes Home Center. Off to the cemetery I went, camera in hand.

The Rio Grande Cemetery is not a large place by any means. It is odd to see a giant Lowes Home Center overshadowing this once quiet, country graveyard. Most of Hester's family is buried there, including the old gadabout herself.

I snapped shots of all the Hildreth graves and brought them back to my office in northern New Jersey. I concluded that the Hildreths were a healthy bunch. Most had lived to a ripe old age. Only a few babies had died in the generation after Hester.

I was no closer to an answer. One name that came to me in the house was Sarah. Sarah was both Hester's mother's name and her sister's name. Her mother was 60 when she died.

Cindi told me about an experience she had one night while she was in the shop with one of her sales representatives. "I was working for my parents. It was an afternoon, we were alone with another sales person, and we heard the women talking. I went 'Oh, I didn't know there was anyone here.' I felt bad because there was someone else in the store and I didn't know where they were — the girl was completely freaked out who was working with me. I said, 'I'll walk through the store and find out where they are.' I went through the store, and she checked the parking lot, and there was no one there. I heard them talking, but couldn't understand what they were saying." Hester and her sister Lu?

The Hildreth house is such a great old house with wonderful energy. It is no wonder the ghosts may stay behind. I could picture the place in its heyday as a cattle farm with Joshua Hildreth watching over it. I was never a big fan of things Colonial, but after spending a few hours in Winterwood, I may be redecorating my own home.

Doing some further research, I have stumbled upon a reference to "George Hildreth's cottage" on Jackson Street! George Hildreth, born in Rio Grande in 1822 built, among other things, The Columbia House, The West End House, The Wyoming Cottage and The Carroll Villa, all in Cape May.

The Carroll Villa (above the Mad Batter) is the only building surviving today. Hester's cousin, George (I think their fathers were brothers) also built a summer cottage, next to The Carroll Villa, for his family to be near the beach in the summer. Today the cottage is called Poor Richard's Inn.

After my original story on Winterwood ran in *Exit Zero*, I received an email from Jeri Hoffman McDaniel. Jeri, as it turns out is Hester's great grandniece! She was only a few years old when her "Aunt Hess" died, but knew a lot about the house and her family!

Jeri spends her winters in Arkansas near her daughter and returns to Rio Grande each spring. We had been emailing each other for several months trying to catch up with each other's research.

I asked Jeri if she had heard any of ghost stories that had been passed down from her family about the old homestead. While she did not have any particular stories to tell, she mentioned her daughter had a strange encounter at Winterwood. She also reminded me of the old family burial plot located at the rear of the Winterwood property where the earliest Hildreths are buried, along with the Hands and Cresses that married into the family. It is from this old plot, that I feel the ghosts of Winterwood walk each night, returning to the house where they once lived, and died. There are also several young children buried in the family plot, which may be the source of our two younger ghosts!

"The stones are interesting as they have some history carved into them; one grave marker of a 15-year-old girl has a poem written on it by her sister that goes something like this:

In thee I lost a sister dear,
A kind and loving friend sincere,
She left this world of care and pain,
And only died to live again.

That's not an exact quote, but it is close," Jeri told me. Has young Mary returned from the dead, as her tombstone reads? Perhaps instead of crossing over she strayed to the side of her family that was still living in the house when she died. Jeri added, "David and Jane (Edwards) Hildreth were the parents of Ephraim Hildreth, Esq., and Mary, the 15-year-old with the poem on her stone. I had always assumed it was written by a sister, but perhaps it was written by Ephraim. I am not sure how many were in that family."

"David" had been a name that also came to me in Winterwood. Could young Mary and her father, David Hildreth, be haunting Winterwood to this day? After Jeri and I had exchanged emails several times, I realized that a further investigation of Winterwood would be in order in the spring!

The house does have a special energy about it. It also seems that once a Hildreth, always a Hildreth. Jeri has also had her own special connection to the house in the past.

"I used to go out to the fence around the graveyard before it was so overgrown as it is now. The 'old aunts' lived in the Winterwood place. Several years after graduating and moving to Florida, I started having dreams about the family graveyard behind Winterwood. Because this happened several times, I telephoned my mother in North Wildwood and asked her if anything was going on at the old place. She had ridden past there on the senior citizen's bus and told me that they were working behind the building. Apparently, this is when they were working on the rear parking lot. The parking lot was finished before it reached the old graveyard and my dreams ceased."

Were the ghosts sending out a psychic line to Jeri? Sometimes, when one grows up in a place that is haunted, he or she develops an unconscious psychic bond with the ghosts that continues through life. It is not a bad thing. It just seems like something that naturally happens to a person who is around a ghost or ghosts for a long time. Were the ghosts upset with the urbanization of their old backyard?

Unlike most of the buildings in the city of Cape May, which were built in the mid to late 1800s, Winterwood was built 100 years earlier. The older the dwelling and the more people who have dwelled in it, the bigger the possibility for a ghost or two! The old Hildreth homestead has many possibilities and lots of great energy. No wonder the Christmas shop that presently occupies the building is so busy. With all of their ghosts, they could make the claim of being open 24 hours a day!

In 2006, Tom and Cindi Alvarado decided to move their Cape May location of Winterwood down a few doors to a larger venue. What was originally a bank on the corner of Ocean Street and Washington Street, and was later an art gallery, is now the grandiose home of Winterwood in Cape May. When I was first visited the store to deliver cases of books, I started to notice someone or *something* following me around. It was a strong male presence and

The Winterwood Store on the Washington Street Mall in Cape May

I do not believe it is the former ghost of Dr. Loomis, who had previously haunted the old location up the mall. This was a different personality.

My experiences were usually strongest on the upper level balcony. My psychic mind would get a flash of a man in uniform. The man was staring coldly down at the sales floor below. My first thought, and my feeling today, is that this is the ghost of a former bank guard. If he died while on duty, or returned to his former place of employment after death is unknown.

Some ghosts want to communicate and make it easy for a medium to understand their thoughts and feelings. Other ghosts are in a world of their own, literally, as if they exist on a plane of consciousness that blinds them to the living. As a medium, I have experienced both types of ghosts. This ghost does seem to see the store, or perhaps it is the former bank that fills his ghostly view. Something is making him stay tethered to the building, and that reason is being hidden from psychic minds like my own. Another mystery waiting to be solved in haunted Cape May.

Now off to Jackson Street we go, knocking on the door of the beautiful Poor Richard's Inn in search of Hester Hildreth.

Poor Richard's Inn

THE HESTER HILDRETH CHRONICLES — PART 3

Bed & Breakfast
17 Jackson Street, Cape May

IN the previous chapters, I told you about encountering the ghost of Rio Grande's Hester Hildreth, the resident haunt of The Winterwood Gift Shop on Route 9. It seems Miss Hildreth (she never married) was quite upset at her former family homestead being "cluttered with Christmas stuff." I think what she did not realize, in her ghostly existence, is that the old Hildreth homestead, built in 1722 by her ancestor Joshua, is now a Christmas shop! The historic building is now filled with everything holiday, everything except Hester, who has "left town" and gone to stay with her cousin George in Cape May.

What are shopkeepers to do when their ghosts move out in a huff? What about their reputation as an *authentically haunted business?* What will the customers think? How disappointed will the kids be, when they find the ghosts have gone? WHAT do they do?

Well, first, no one knew the head ghost was "officially gone" at Winterwood. There was a "feeling" by the staff that the ghost might be missing. One staff member was even telling customers that their ghost, Hester was on vacation, which is really somewhat correct. She is spending her time by the ocean on Jackson Street, and she has *lots* of paranormal company!

Cape May keeps me busy enough finding ghosts, without them finding me first! However, this one did find me, and I brought her message to Winterwood's owners, Tom and Cindi Alvarado. Their response: "We've got to get her back!"

I returned to Jackson Street to The Inn at
, but there was no sign of Hester at all. I had never assumed her ghost was hanging out there. She just found me. Trailing Hester Hildreth became an adventure into the history of Cape May itself. The Hildreths were Puritans from New England. David Hildreth first arrived in Cape May in the late 1600s. His son Joshua built the house that is now part of Winterwood

on Route 9 in Rio Grande (formerly Hildreth). Both George and Hester are descendents of these two founding Hildreths. I believe George's father, Ephraim, and Hester's father, Alexander, were brothers. Unlike Hester Hildreth, who seems to have spent her later years living on her farm with her sister Lucille and working for the county in Cape May Courthouse as a clerk, George Hildreth is well documented to have been quite the entrepreneur throughout much of Cape May.

Captain George Hildreth was also a well-known man of the sea. His seafaring skills were legendary in Cape May. He was also a savvy businessman, building and running many of Cape May's hotels and private lodgings at the time.

In 1847, he built the original Columbia House Hotel on "the meadow" between Ocean and Decatur from Washington Street to the beach. In 1850, he married Sarah Worrell. Then, in 1851, sold the Columbia house, and built a home, which still stands near Cold Spring Village.

George Hildreth built several other homes and hotels in Cape May in his time. The West End Hotel (which burned with the Windsor,) the Knickerbocker Hotel (which burned in the Great fire of 1878) and the Carroll Villa, which still stands today, are a few of his noted properties.

Hildreth operated Cape May's Life Saving Station #39, which would rescue passengers from stranded ships off the coast. He also operated a feed and grain business in town in his spare time!

The fire of 1878 took out many of George Hildreth's current and former properties including Columbia House and The Knickerbocker Hotel. He wasted no time in rebuilding his properties on Jackson Street, replacing the Knickerbocker with the Carroll Villa. On the lot next door, he built Hildreth House, his new private residence by the ocean in 1882. Today, the house located at 17 Jackson Street is known as Poor Richard's Inn. This would be my first stop on the trail of Hester Hildreth.

After spending some time talking with a few Cape May historians, I found that eventually George Hildreth's first wife Sarah died in 1880 of a massive stroke. He remarried a woman named Beaty (short for Beatrice) in 1885 and is documented to have "brought his new bride to his Jackson Street home" after their honeymoon.

In some of the haunting investigations I have done in other parts of the country, I have felt some ghosts were indeed trapped either in their own internal drama or in some intense emotional or traumatic energy. Many ghosts seem to be unable to move on to the Other Side; however, many of the ghosts on Jackson Street simply do not want to move on. There is a big difference. The ghosts on Jackson Street are of a quieter and amicable nature, whereas, in other parts of Cape May, some of the ghosts really have an attitude.

Poor Richard's Inn is a wonderful old home, now a B&B run by artist Harriett Sosson. I recalled standing in front of the house a few times and sensing spirits in the place. I vividly recall psychically seeing a few ghosts sitting around a table in the side parlor playing cards and gambling, something not unfamiliar in old Cape May!

It was a beautiful autumn Sunday, and we decided to make a day trip to Cape May's Jackson Street. My goal would be to try to see just where Hester was hanging out and to see if I could contact her again and get her to rethink her hasty exit from Winterwood. Now, I know this is sounding less like a ghost story and more like a family quarrel, but you have to remember one thing; ghosts are spirits of people. They were people in their previous lifetimes, and they still act like people in their ghostly form.

When I spoke to Harriett on the phone the night before, she had told me that "yes," there was activity at Poor Richard's, but she was not sure just how much she wanted to talk about. As I mentioned in the introduction of this book, this is a common fear of B&B owners. There are always a few potential customers who will not stay in a haunted place. Alternately, a lot more customers *will* patronize a place because they hear it is haunted. I think in the future Cape May will realize that one of its best attributes as a destination for vacationers and day-trippers is its ghosts.

As I entered Poor Richard's Inn, I was struck by how charming and inviting the inside of the house was. I really felt welcomed. Was it just my psychic sense noticing friendly energy? Maybe.

At first Harriett seemed a little closed down to my interview, guarded if you will. However, as time went on she really opened up, and I was able to see what a lovely and interesting person she was.

Poor Richard's Inn is definitely radiating "Harriett" energy. Since buying the place with her husband Richard in 1977, she has almost single-handedly renovated the entire house, including cutting and replacing 1600 pieces of decorative slate for the roof! Now that is impressive! Actually, the entire place is impressive. I would buy it, if I had the money and it ever came up for sale! In the meantime, I would just highly recommend staying there! I digress.

What about the ghosts at Poor Richard's? Were Hester and George Hildreth watching me from the eaves? As I listened to Harriett tell me the story of how the house went from a private residence to being divided up into rentals, I started to sense a Spirit of a woman. She was moving side-to-side back in the kitchen, almost as if she were cleaning up or fixing a meal. Harriett noticed my distracted glances and finally starting talking ghost! "He must be seeing someone — can you sense her?" she asked my partner Willy, who also joined us in the old dining room of the house.

"Yes," I replied, "Do you know who she is?" I asked. Harriett told me that she did not know for sure, only had a "few theories." The ghost of the woman was not Hester, unfortunately. This ghost was more like that of a servant. Perhaps she had worked for the Hildreths. On the other hand, was it the ghost of Beaty, George's second wife? I saw her dash to the back room and move upward in direction. After ascension to Heaven was ruled out, I assumed there was a maid's staircase in back.

"The back stairs up to the maid's room are back there, and we did have an experience up in that room," Harriett noted. That would validate my servant theory. The woman of the house would use the main staircase to get around, I assumed.

"When Richard Boyd, who sold us the house in 1977 left town, his girl-friend Ellen stayed behind and rented some rooms. She said to us, 'Listen the house is haunted, but don't be scared... there is a (ghost of a) woman on the third floor who likes to flush the toilet.'"

As I said, ghosts are people too. They laugh, they play, and they flush. What they do not do is try to scare people, usually.

So was this a former servant? Jackson Street seems to have a plethora of dead help on its hands, all cleaning faithfully for the last century or so.

"I had two women renting the maid's quarters. One was asleep and the other woke up in the middle of the night. She saw a wispy figure of a woman moving across the bedroom and adjusting her hat by a mirror." Harriett said the woman also appeared transparent, and then completely disappeared. Could this have been the ghost of a servant of the house? I would bet it was the case. Why else would anyone be getting dressed in a former maid's quarters and wearing a large, old-fashioned looking hat?

It seems you also have to be careful of what reading material you choose to peruse at Poor Richard's. A few years ago, Harriett had three women guests who were sharing a room with three separate beds. As one of the women thumbed through a magazine, she claimed it was yanked out of her hands and tossed into the closet! The other two women also witnessed this experience. Perhaps the maid was just cleaning up a little too soon?

Harriett is a trained artist who resided in New York City before coming to Cape May. Her theory is that perhaps it is her energy, which people have sensed in the house. "At the time the woman saw the 'ghost,' we had innkeepers running the place. We would come from our house on the point on Friday, clean like crazy and go back home on Sunday." Harriett thought it was her image, which people may have been experiencing, in the form of an imprint. Nice try.

No, I think there definitely is a ghost. It is a friendly presence, which seems to move quietly around us, not wanting to disturb anyone, but a ghost none-the-less.

I thanked Harriett, and we went on our way. I took a step back and looked at the grand old house, built for George Hildreth in 1882 by local builder Charles Shaw. I could sense ghosts in the John McConnell House to the right (featured in *The Ghosts of Cape May Book 2*) and even a presence in The Carroll Villa to the left, but no Hester. Not a Boo...

Then a few weeks later, two hundred miles away, Hester paid me an unexpected visit. I had just retired to my big leather chair in the living room after a wonderful home-cooked fall dinner. I thought I had fallen asleep, but when I awoke several hours later, my partner Willy was sitting next to me with his ears perked up — I had been channeling in my sleep again!

The main star of the show, once again, was Hester. OK, I know what you are thinking. How can a ghost get from Cape May to North Jersey? Well, I suppose a ghost can move to wherever he or she wants to move. If Hester found her way to her cousin George's place in Cape May, why couldn't she travel up to me? I have always stated that the four walls around us are merely an illusion. There is a much bigger picture than our simple view of reality. Maybe ghosts can see the bigger picture just a little more clearly than we can.

Hester explained many things that night. Luckily, Willy started the tape recorder. Reviewing the tape, I found Hester presented some rather interesting, and, I am sure, controversial things about ghosts.

It seems that ghosts, most of the time, choose to remain stuck in their plane of existence. Hester called her place of existence the Ghost Realm, which I since have used to refer to the place where ghosts exist. They *do* have a chance to cross over to the Other Side. They are even asked to come by higher Spirits. Most choose not to go. Hester felt that souls should be able to do whatever they want and stay put in the Ghost Realm if they wish. I guess she is right about that, for it has always been indicated to me that a soul, or spirit, has free will to do as he or she pleases.

Hester told us that Cape May has a large population of ghosts because they like to go there. It is a gathering spot. Cape May Chamber of Commerce, take notice! Ghosts, I have found, do act in sociable fashions with each other. Forget the theory that ghosts cannot see each other. They can and do. As you have been reading in this book, they also interact.

According to Hester, when people die, their friends and loved ones come from the Other Side through an energy gate to greet them. Sometimes, we are not in the best mindset at our demise. Sometimes we simply do not want to go with them or do not want to give up our emotional or material ties to this world.

If souls stay in the ghost realm, says Hester, they eventually are able to move away from their places of death and back to where they lived. They may even be able to move to other locations they knew in their lifetimes. They can travel. Many ghosts eventually get bored being alone, and they seek out the company of other ghosts. They quickly realize there are other beings that they can communicate with on a regular basis, not just psychics and mediums, but other ghosts.

Cape May seems to be one of the destinations for our ethereal friends and Jackson Street seems to be prime real estate!

So where does this leave Hester and Winterwood? On the tape, she did not once mention her old haunt. Has she become a free spirit? Luckily, Winterwood has a few more ghosts hanging around the rafters to take her place, and Poor Richard's is calmer and quieter without her!

It is possible for a ghost to follow a person home. With Hester, it seemed to be much more than that. I now realize that ghosts and spirits are basically the same thing, disembodied souls. We are all spirits actually, just existing in our own specific plane of existence. Some ghosts stay in one room of a house, forever performing the same activities repeatedly. Others visit many different haunts and carry on a life of their own.

Hester Hildreth's spirit has come through in channeling sessions several times since I wrote the first edition of this book. She is an enlightened soul who knows how to move around. I would not classify her as much a ghost as I would a free spirit, always looking to socialize with people that can hear her. Was the living Hester Hildreth as much of a gadabout? I think we are who we are and that goes deep down to our soul level. Out of our bodies, we might be more free with our emotions, thoughts and opinions. When I channel, people's loved ones come through larger than life. Their personalities seem to be amplified. This, I feel, is pure soul energy. On the Other Side spirits are not concerned with what others think. They just speak the truth.

Maybe there is some kind of magic in the ghost realm. Maybe ghosts can connect with all of their higher energy and are using the time for self examination and to see what they still need to accomplish on a soul level. Who knows? Ghosts' lives could be like writing their own autobiography—posthumously of course—of their accomplishments and perceived failures in life. Maybe we all become ghosts eventually for a short time before we move on to Heaven. We will all find out eventually, won't we?

In the meantime, there's always Cape May, America's oldest—and most haunted seaside resort.

WEST CAPE MAY 3

5 MYRTLE 4

2

BROADWAY

PATTERSON

BEACH DRIVE

1

NORTH

S. LAFAYETTE

CONGRESS PL.

6

18

WEST PER

GRANT

WINDSOR

CONGRESS

PROMENADE

7

WASHINGTON ST 22

17

CARPENTER'S LANE

12

PERRY

JACKSON

8

11

10

9

13

14

15

16

28

DECATUR

OCEAN

26

27

1

Atlantic Ocea

Where
To
Find
The
Ghosts

5. Wilbraham Park
6. The Seahorse
7. Congress Hall Hotel
8. The Sea Villa

9. The Inn at 22 Jackson
10. Windward House
11. Saltwood House
12. The Merry Widow

13. The Virginia Hotel
14. The Carroll Villa
15. Poor Richards Inn
16. John McConnell House

17. Fralinger's
18. Wildberries
19. Richardson's
20. WaWa area
21. Cotton Company
22. The Ugly Mug
23. capemay.com
24. Fairthorne Cottage
25. House of Royals
26. Columbia House
27. Inn of Cape May
28. Martini Beach
29. John Craig House
30. The Mason Cottage
31. Brendan's Ghost
32. The Belvidere
33. (Former) Atlantic Books
34. The Macomber
35. The Sea Holly
36. The Chalfonte Hotel
37. Memucan Hughes
38. Southern Mansion
39. The Physick Estate
40. Hadrava House
41. John Hand House
42. Angel of the Sea
43. Peter Shields Inn
44. Cresse/Hand House
    (Lower Township)
45. Cold Spring Church

Epilogue

NEW INFORMATION on ghosts and hauntings continues to be discovered and new theories are written all the time. I have learned more about ghosts than I ever could have imagined and in Cape May alone! This book certainly doesn't contain everything there is to know about ghosts and hauntings. It is what I know and believe to be truthful. Every person will experience a haunting differently. What you have just read has been my personal journey through the paranormal via Cape May.

In *The Ghosts of Cape May Book 2*, I discuss ghosts and hauntings in greater detail. If you think you have a ghost of your own, use what I have told you as a general guide when dealing with ghosts and hauntings. You should not be afraid of ghosts, they are more concerned with themselves than they are with the living.

When you are done with *Book 2*, *The Ghosts of Cape May Book 3* will be waiting for you! In *Book 3* you will find many wonderful haunts in the often overlooked section of the Cape called, West Cape May. I know I said in *Book 2* that I was taking a breather before *Book 3*, but there have just been too many great ghosts popping up in my path not to mention them! I have moved the chapter on The Albert Stevens Inn that originally appeared in *Book 1* to *Book 3* so that I could group all of the new West Cape May haunts together in one book. (One should always have his ghosts in a row.) In *Book 3*, I return to Cape May to investigate new haunts that have been sitting right under all of our noses! The lighthouse and its ghosts are also discussed in detail. Did I mention *400 Years of the Ghosts of Cape May*?

Should you choose to stay at one of Cape May's wonderful abodes that has a ghost, please treat both the ghost and the property with respect. I heard a horror story of guests staying in a haunted B&B, and in an attempt to "summon up the spirits," lighting a dozen votive candles on the bed and setting the mattress on fire! Thankfully, the B&B was not set ablaze by this reckless behavior. That B&B, with a wonderful ghost story of its own, has now chosen to be removed from any writings or ghost tours. We have all lost a valuable view into the paranormal because of a few over zealous individuals who took personal ghost investigations a little too far. Please do not attempt something like this in someone else's home. Running a tape recorder to capture

EVPs and taking photographs is a much safer way to ghost hunt when staying at a B&B, guest house or historic hotel in Cape May.

You may or may not experience the paranormal while staying in Cape May. Remember, not everyone is open to the energy. However, if you have chosen to read this book from cover to cover, you are heading in the right direction! The most important thing you can do to further paranormal investigations in Cape May is to give positive feedback in the form of your patronage to the many innkeepers and store owners listed in this book, who have graciously given their time and energy to allow me to conduct my investigations.

If you stay at one of the places listed in this book, let them know that you want to stay there because they have a ghost! If inn owners start to realize that ghosts are good for business, we will be able to get more of them to open up with their own ghostly tales. I can tell you there are many more haunted places on the Cape. I am just not permitted to write about all of them—yet. With your help, that can change.

Since the first edition of this book was published in the spring of 2005, I have developed three **Ghost Trolley Tours** in collaboration with MAC, that run year-around in Cape May.

The first haunted tour, **The Ghosts of Cape May Trolley Tour**, will take riders throughout the dark and winding streets of Cape May at night, passed many of the houses and buildings that I have investigated and written about in my books. Riders will hear details of my investigation, as related by one of MAC's knowledgeable guides on the trolley. The trolley leaves from near the intersection of Ocean Street and Washington Street.

The second tour is called, **The Historic Haunts Combination Tour**. For the first time, the old Physick Estate Mansion is open at night! Tourgoers will disembark from the trolley at The Physick Estate and get a first hand look, and feel, of what it is like to be in a real haunted mansion—at night! Inside the Physick Estate you will hear about the Victorians and their love for ghosts and especially séances, while you gather around an authentic séance table in the parlor. I have heard numerous reports of people seeing a mysterious woman standing next to them in the mirror in the room, only to turn and discover no one is beside them! Some have even reported having their arms and shirts tugged by the ghosts.

My latest ghost tour is called **Ghosts of the Lighthouse.** I have long wanted to include West Cape May and the lighthouse in my ghost tours. I

created this third tour in partnership with MAC, based on new research I have done in West Cape May and in and around the old 1859 light at Cape May Point. If you loved the other ghost tours I have created, you will really enjoy this new tour. West Cape May has some of the oldest buildings in Cape May and — ghosts abound! Tickets for all of my tours can be purchased at MAC's ticket booth at the end of the Washington Street Mall on Ocean Street. I will be hosting these tours several weekends a year.

Please visit my website at CraigMcManus.com.

On my website, you will find information about what I really do for a living, channeling as a medium. Remember, in this book I have mainly talked about ghosts. Spirits are another matter entirely, and I discuss them at length on my web site. You can also book a private or group channeling session with me through my website or by calling my office at 201-493-0772.

You can also find my fan page on Facebook, as well as a Ghosts of Cape May group, and a Ghosts of Cape May books fan page.

There will surely be more to come from this *Ghost Writer* on the subject of Cape May's "other side" in this lifetime, lifetimes to follow, and perhaps even a little in between. I would imagine if I were a ghost, I would probably be writing about the living. On second thought, I think I will skip the being a ghost part for a while!

At the time of updating this third edition of *The Ghosts of Cape May Book 1*, I am working on a book about my life growing up with psychic ability and how I learned to integrate it into my daily life. I think you will enjoy reading it as many of us have some degree of psychic or intuitive ability.

Until next time, keep an open mind, or at least an open book. Wait — don't close the book and turn out that light just yet — some ghosts are slow readers.

The A-Zs of Ghosts & Hauntings

Here is my version of the ABC's of ghosts and hauntings for those of you who need a refresher. Use this guide to help you on your own haunted journeys!

A PPARITION... I have been asked many times what the difference is between a ghost and an apparition. An apparition is the "supernormal" appearance of a person or animal, dead or alive. Some apparitions of the living are called "crisis apparitions." Example: Your friend is living in France. One night you are awakened to see your friend standing at your bedside. He then vanishes without uttering a word. One may quickly surmise the friend to have died. Not necessarily so. The friend may have simply been projecting his consciousness to you in a way that science does not yet understand, and he might not have any knowledge of the event. If an apparition keeps appearing, it may be a ghost of someone who has died. Apparitions have been studied since the 19th century by paranormal researchers all over the world. Most apparitions are of loved ones who have died and have returned either to say goodbye or forewarn us about some imminent danger.

B OO!... Ghosts *do not* say this! In fact, ghosts are not (usually) trying to scare us at all. They are just trying to coexist. Remember, we are more of a bother to ghosts than they are to us. We should consider ourselves lucky.

C HANNELING... A form of mediumship that psychic people use to communicate with the deceased (ghosts) and higher entities like spirit guides. I am a channel who channels, so to speak. What I "channel" is thoughts and ideas from these discarnate entities. Their energy sends a signal to my mind and I try to interpret it as best I can. Sometimes there are messages from a loved one. Sometimes I channel what a ghost might be thinking. Usually though, channeling deals with a higher energy being communicated with us here on the earth plane.

DEATHBED VISIONS... How many people have had a loved one dying in a hospital and had the experience of the person seeing and talking to people who are not there? I have interviewed nurses over the years, and they all say the same thing. At the end of one's life, we start to see people who have passed before us. The people seem to come to help us make the transition. I was with my best friend recently when her Mom was dying. It gave me an amazing personal experience with this subject. As I psychically sensed my friend's deceased dad coming through, her mother started talking about him and mentioning him by name. The mother was semi-conscious and had not heard me mention his name. In fact, what I had sensed psychically, my friend's Mom could now see for herself. Not scary at all, quite wonderful to know that our loved ones are still watching out for us from the Other Side!

ELECTRONIC VOICE PHENOMENON (EVP)... I receive thoughts from ghosts via telepathic energy. It is conjectured that they can also project that energy onto the surface of magnetic recording tape and leave a voice imprint. EVPs are collected by running a tape recorder in a haunted place. Sometimes questions are asked. The voices are not heard until the tape is played back. Some voices are just pieces of words; others are complete words or sentences. True EVPs are quite unnerving to listen to. The most recent EVP I picked up was at Martini Beach this summer. While giving a tour to the owners and staff, a woman is heard whispering "Julia" close to the tape recorder. It happened at the time I was talking about the ghost's name being Julia, not Gloria. No one was near the tape recorder.

FOLLOWING GHOSTS... Normally, ghosts will stay put where they haunt. There do seem to have been exceptions over the years. I have read a few cases in which people have attracted ghosts in cemeteries, after trying to make contact with them. These same people have later reported feeling as if they were followed home. Some have even gone to the extent of reporting haunting activity in their houses where none had existed before. The moral of this story—try to stay out of cemeteries when doing ghost investigations.

GHOST... Most parapsychologists prefer to use the term "apparition" when referring to alleged spirits of the dead. I like the term ghost. A ghost is the soul of a person (or animal) who has died and has not "crossed over" to the Other Side, Heaven, the next plane, etc.,. Just why a ghost sticks around is a very personal and individual choice. Some ghosts stay behind because of unfinished business, others have a strong emotional or even material tie to this plane. Whatever the reason, only one thing is going to get a ghost to cross over, and that is the ghost making the decision to do so. We can ask a ghost to leave... we can ask.

HAUNTING... As I often say in my lectures, I consider the term "haunting" to be a bum rap, a pejorative. Ghosts are not trying to scare us, as the term "haunt" denotes. They simply exist on a different plane from us. For unknown reasons, the two planes often mix in time and space. It is during this merging of energies that we may encounter sights (rare) or smells or sounds (common) associated with a ghost. It is no more spectacular than seeing your Uncle Bob walk past your front window. Maybe you didn't expect him to come and visit but after that, you are no longer surprised by his presence. It should be the same way with a ghost. They simply exist as do we. Get used to it and STOP being such a scaredy cat!

IMPOSSIBLE PEOPLE... I made this term up. It applies to all those skeptics who refuse to believe that ghosts really do exist. Someday science will catch up with parapsychology and will pierce through the veil of the unknown, penetrating into the ghost world. Of course, by that time today's skeptics will BE the ghosts! As for all of our friends who represent the "impossible people" category and who claim such things impossible and fantastic, I wonder if they believe in cell phones and space flight yet?

JAMES, WILLIAM (1842-1910)... Here's a guy who was a well-known American philosopher and well-known psychologist who made huge contributions to "psychical research." James spent many years in England and America studying mediums. He is said to have discovered one of my favorite mediums, Leonora Piper, in 1885. I mention William James for those who want to read more about parapsychology or psychical research in the late 19th century.

K NOCKING SOUNDS... You would think a ghost who knocks at your door simply wants to come in. Not the case with many of the knocking ghosts I have experienced in Cape May. I have had a recent experience in an old Bed and Breakfast with a knocking ghost that appears to be a young child. We were awakened early one morning about 4:30 AM by a rapping at the door of our room. No one was in the hallway and we assumed it was simply a noise from outside the house. Again at 6 AM, the knocking returned. As I moved near the door I realized that the repeated knocking was coming from the LOWER section of the door, indicating a young child. This knocking continued for two days at all hours of the night. I opened the door and welcomed whomever to enter, but I guess they simply enjoyed waking us up! Knocking is something ghosts do very well—we are just not sure WHAT they are saying!

L IGHTNING... There could be a good reason behind all those old haunted house movies having thunder and lightning as a prevailing background theme. Lightning is a form of plasma energy that some researchers think may actually stir up haunting activity. It is thought that ghosts "feed" on energy to exist. This could be the reason that many hauntings take place near power lines in walls or near other electrical sources like appliances. I think a lightning storm may give ghosts a good "charge" of energy that lets them manifest more strongly, or even move physical objects around. Perhaps there is a good reason to hide under the covers during a lightning storm—you never know what might be standing by your bed!

M ATERIALIZATION... It takes a tremendous amount of energy for a ghost to materialize physically. This is why one does not usually see a ghost; one experiences it in other ways, sound, tactile sensation, and smell. One visual you might get with a ghost is a gray, black or white blur of light caught in the periphery of your vision. This materialization seems to be fleeting. Those ghosts that have materialized, once recognized by a person, also seem to vanish quickly. One of the few times I have actually seen a ghost was early in the morning, when I was just coming out of a deep sleep. I imagine I was in a semi-conscious state, and my brain was receiving a signal that was terminated upon fully awakening.

NIGHTTIME... Most haunting activity takes place between midnight and five in the morning. It is thought that the dew point is higher in early morning, and ghosts can use the water vapor in the air to manifest more easily. I think it is simply a quieter time, when we humans are asleep, and the ghosts come out to play.

ORBS... are those controversial little spheres of light that we have all seen in a photograph at some point in our lives. Are they ghost or spirit energy captured on film? Some researchers believe they are. Most, however, feel it is light refracting on a shiny surface or reflecting off dust or water particles in the air. I am not quite sure what to make of them. I have had people take a series pictures of me channeling in which, in some instances, orbs are seen moving and changing position while the photographer and I are not. I think that some orb photos do have paranormal explanations... just not many.

POLTERGEIST... The term means "knocking ghost" in German. However, a poltergeist is not a ghost at all. The haunting activity is often attributed to a preadolescent child in the house who has the ability to produce telekinesis. Furniture or objects may move by themselves, footsteps or knocking noises may be heard. When the researchers identify the "agent," it is usually found that some kind of emotional trauma or need is present. The poltergeist activity usually stops after a certain amount of time.

QUIZ... Pop Quiz: "What book do you need to buy next to keep learning about ghosts and hauntings? HINT: *Book 2 & Book 3 & 400 Years of the Ghosts of Cape May.*"

RESIDUAL HAUNTING... Not all hauntings involve active ghosts. A ghost has a consciousness and can be interacted with. A residual haunting is embedded energy with pictures attached. Think of a residual haunting as a "tape loop." The energy creates a "movie" that plays repeatedly in a certain location. People who are sensitive to the energy are able to tap into it, which may cause sensitive people to think they have seen or felt a ghost. In fact they are seeing a repeat of some early trauma energy. A residual haunting ghost will do the same thing again and again, like walking up the staircase. Nothing more will happen. The ghost will not notice you. Think of it as watching a movie on TV — you can try to interact with the characters — you can try.

SPIRIT... Spirits are souls at a higher level of being. They are more advanced and enlightened than ghosts. A spirit is a soul that has crossed over to the Other Side and has come back to help or guide someone here on this plane. When I channel, I am usually talking with spirits.

TELEKINESIS... Also called psychokinesis or PK. Telekinesis is a type of directed energy from either a person or a ghost, literally a "mind over matter" condition in which the mind's energy is able to affect the physical world. Telekinesis can occur spontaneously (you get mad and a light bulb blows out) or intentionally through a projection of will. Ghosts use a form of telekinesis to move objects, open and close doors and windows and sometimes to get our attention. Usually, living people are the main sources of this "hidden weapon." I have met some people who just have a knack for crashing a computer or causing equipment to malfunction. Ghosts can also wreak havoc on investigators' equipment just by being active energetically.

UNINVITED... Remember that great old movie, *The Uninvited*, with Ray Milland? Two ghosts stay behind to haunt a house where they once lived. This is true of many hauntings. Ghosts haunt where they lived, not where they died. Would you want to hang around a hospital or a cemetery? One thing is for sure, ghosts do not need an invitation to haunt a place. Great movie, rent it.

VARIATIONS IN TEMPERATURE... A cold spot appears where there is no air conditioning or draft from an open window, and creates an unexplainable drop in temperature of more than 10 degrees. Cold spots can be a ghost's calling card! Two theories exist on why ghosts drop a room's temperature when they are present. One says that ghosts draw energy from us, the living. This loss of thermal energy makes us feel cold. The other theory suggests that ghosts are fields of negative ions, like the breeze from home air purifiers, which feels cold and refreshing. If the cold spot is only in one small area of a room, most likely you have a ghost. Remember, you must rule out all other explanations first!

Www.craigmcmanus.com... My web site. I am a psychic medium. I channel for my clients, to contact the spirits of friends and loved ones on the Other Side. My lifelong fascination with ghosts however, has led me to interesting places and given me many memorable experiences with the paranormal. Check out my site for future book signing and lecture dates and eventually, podcasts!

X MARKS THE SPOT... Cape May is a paranormal hot spot. Why are some places so much more haunted than others? In Cape May's case, I think being surrounded on three sides by water helps maintain some form of constant electrical field for the ghosts. The setting is also a factor. Many of the ghosts lived and died in Cape May and loved spending their lives here. Many are not yet ready to stop enjoying the place. The more people I hear from in town, the more I continue to believe, Cape May might just be the most haunted spot in the whole United States!

Y EARS BECOME MINUTES... This really belongs under the heading of "temporal," but we used up "T" already! Ghosts do not wear wristwatches, meaning they have lost all track of time. After all, we use time for a measurement of our lives. Ghosts have indefinite spans of time on their hands. They do not have appointments to keep or bills due at the end of the month. They simply exist in their own realm. Ghosts also seem to phase in and out. Some hauntings happen daily, some weekly, some every 100 years. There is no pattern for a ghost's existence, and there are no parameters that will define all hauntings. For a ghost, a few years may seem like a few minutes. They are indeed in a state of temporal flux, neither here, nor there.

Z ERO, EXIT... If you can't find the latest copy of this magazine in town, you can read it at www.exitzero.us. This is the place where my weekly Ghost Writer column first appeared. Cape May in print!

Happy Haunting!